Preface

Welcome to R Programming Interview Questions & Answers Book! In the rapidly evolving world of data science and analytics, R programming has established itself as a crucial tool for professionals across various industries. Its versatility, combined with powerful capabilities in statistical computing, data manipulation, and visualization, makes R an indispensable asset for anyone working with data. As demand for skilled R programmers continues to grow, so does the need for thorough preparation to excel in interviews and secure coveted roles in this competitive field. R Programming Insights: Interview Questions and Answers was conceived with the specific purpose of equipping both aspiring and seasoned professionals with the knowledge and confidence needed to succeed in R programming interviews. This book is more than just a compilation of questions and answers; it is a comprehensive resource that delves deep into the fundamental and advanced aspects of R, offering insights that go beyond rote learning and superficial understanding.

Whether you are learning the basics of data manipulation, grappling with statistical analysis, or exploring advanced programming techniques, this book provides clear, concise explanations accompanied by practical examples. These examples are drawn from real-world scenarios, ensuring that you not only learn how to answer questions but also understand the context in which these concepts are applied in professional settings.

Table of Contents

Chapter 1: Introduction to R Programming

Overview and Evolution of R

Question: What is R, and how did it originate?
Answer: R is a programming language for statistical computing and graphics, created as an open-source implementation of the S language by Ross Ihaka and Robert Gentleman in the early 1990s.

Question: Who are the key contributors to the development of R?
Answer: Ross Ihaka and Robert Gentleman developed R, with contributions from the global R community who expanded it through packages and extensions.

Question: How does R differ from its predecessor, S?
Answer: R is an open-source alternative to S, offering similar features with greater flexibility and a vast ecosystem of user-contributed packages.

Question: What are some major milestones in the evolution of R?
Answer: Key milestones include R's initial release in 1995, CRAN's establishment in 1997, and its adoption as a major tool in data science in the 2000s.

Question: What role did CRAN play in R's evolution?
Answer: CRAN provided a centralized platform for R distribution and package sharing, enabling rapid ecosystem growth.

Question: How has R's adoption in various industries influenced its development?
Answer: Industry adoption has driven the creation of specialized packages, expanding R's versatility in domains like finance, healthcare, and tech.

Question: What are some key features that have contributed to the popularity of R?
Answer: R's popularity stems from its powerful data manipulation and visualization tools, extensive package ecosystem, community support, and open-source nature.

Question: How does R handle statistical analysis compared to other programming languages?
Answer: R is designed for statistical analysis, offering extensive built-in functions and packages that are often more advanced than those in other languages like Python or SAS.

Question: What is the significance of the Tidyverse in the R ecosystem?
Answer: The Tidyverse is a collection of R packages that standardize data manipulation and visualization, promoting a consistent and user-friendly approach.

Question: How has the R language evolved in terms of performance and scalability?
Answer: R has improved in performance and scalability through bytecode compilation, enhanced memory management, and high-performance packages like data.table and Rcpp.

Question: Can you discuss the role of R in the rise of data science?
Answer: R has been pivotal in data science due to its statistical capabilities, extensive packages, and strong support for data analysis and visualization.

Question: What are the challenges associated with using R for large-scale data analysis?
Answer: Challenges include memory management, as R processes data in-memory, but this can be mitigated with packages like data.table or big data integrations.

Question: How has the integration of R with other programming languages and tools evolved over time?
Answer: Integration has evolved with packages like Rcpp (C++), reticulate (Python), and database interfaces, enhancing R's interoperability.

Question: What impact has the open-source nature of R had on its development?
Answer: The open-source nature of R has fostered a collaborative community, driving rapid innovation and the creation of thousands of packages.

Question: How does the R community contribute to the ongoing development of the language?
Answer: The R community contributes by developing and maintaining packages, supporting users, and participating in forums and conferences.

Question: What are some of the most influential packages in the R ecosystem, and why?
Answer: Influential packages include ggplot2 (visualization), dplyr (data manipulation), Shiny (web apps), and caret (machine learning), each setting standards in their domains.

Question: How has the user base of R changed over time?
Answer: R's user base has expanded from statisticians and academics to a broader audience in industries like finance, healthcare, and tech.

Question: What are some of the educational resources available for learning R?
Answer: Educational resources include online courses, books, tutorials, and community-driven content on platforms like Coursera, edX, and DataCamp.

Question: How has the release of RStudio influenced the adoption and use of R?
Answer: RStudio has enhanced R's adoption by providing a user-friendly interface, development tools, and features that streamline workflows.

Question: What are some common criticisms of R, and how have they been addressed?
Answer: Common criticisms include R's learning curve and memory inefficiency, addressed by user-friendly packages and performance tools like data.table.

Question: How does R handle reproducibility in data analysis?
Answer: R supports reproducibility through tools like R Markdown for combining code, text, and output, and Git for version control.

Question: What are some advancements in R related to machine learning and AI?
Answer: Advancements include packages like caret, randomForest, xgboost, and keras, providing robust tools for machine learning and AI.

Question: How has R's package management system evolved over time?
Answer: R's package management has evolved with tools like CRAN, Bioconductor, and devtools, making package development and installation easier.

Question: What role does R play in the bioinformatics field?
Answer: R is crucial in bioinformatics, with packages like Bioconductor enabling analysis of genomic data and other complex biological datasets.

Question: How has R adapted to changes in data privacy and security concerns?
Answer: R has adapted by developing packages that support secure data handling and compliance with privacy regulations.

Question: How does R integrate with cloud computing platforms?
Answer: R integrates with cloud platforms like AWS and Google Cloud through packages and APIs, enabling scalable data processing.

Question: What are some recent developments in R that have expanded its capabilities?
Answer: Recent developments include enhancements in data manipulation, visualization, big data integration, and tools for deep learning.

Question: How does R compare to other programming languages like Python in terms of data analysis?
Answer: R excels in statistical analysis and visualization, while Python is favored for its versatility and broader application in general programming and machine learning.

Question: How have user-contributed packages shaped the evolution of R?
Answer: User-contributed packages have expanded R's functionality, enabling it to adapt to new fields and foster innovation.

Question: What are some future trends in the development and use of R?
Answer: Future trends may include performance enhancements, better AI integration, improved big data tools, and wider industry applications.

Question: How does R support data visualization compared to other tools?
Answer: R supports data visualization through packages like ggplot2, offering high customization and a coherent grammar of graphics.

Question: What challenges exist in maintaining backward compatibility in R, and how are they addressed?
Answer: Challenges include continuous updates and improvements, addressed by release notes, deprecated warnings, and support for older versions.

Question: How has R's role in academia influenced its evolution?
Answer: Academia has driven R's evolution through the development of new methods and packages, solidifying R as a tool for research and education.

Question: How does R handle high-dimensional data?
Answer: R handles high-dimensional data with packages like data.table and bigmemory, optimizing memory usage and computation.

Question: What are some best practices for managing R packages in a production environment?
Answer: Best practices include using version control, managing dependencies, testing in staging environments, and keeping packages updated.

Question: How has the role of R in open science evolved?
Answer: R's open-source nature supports collaboration and transparency in research, with tools like R Markdown and CRAN promoting reproducibility.

Question: How does R handle real-time data processing and what are its limitations?
Answer: R handles real-time data processing through packages like Shiny and Plumber, but may struggle with high-throughput data, requiring specialized systems.

Question: How have advancements in machine learning influenced the development of R packages?
Answer: Machine learning advancements have led to the development of R packages like caret, mlr, and tidymodels, enhancing R's capabilities in this area.

Question: What is the impact of R's community on the continuous improvement of the language?
Answer: R's community drives continuous improvement through active package development, bug reporting, and participation in forums and conferences.

Question: How has the development of R IDEs, like RStudio, enhanced the user experience?
Answer: RStudio has enhanced the R user experience by offering a user-friendly interface, integrated development tools, and features like R Markdown.

Features of R

Question: What are the primary features of R that make it popular for data analysis?
Answer: R is popular for its extensive statistical analysis capabilities, powerful data visualization tools, a vast ecosystem of packages, open-source nature, and strong community support.

Question: How does R handle data visualization?
Answer: R handles data visualization through packages like ggplot2, which offers a high level of customization and implements the Grammar of Graphics for creating complex and publication-quality visualizations.

Question: What role do R packages play in its functionality?
Answer: R packages extend the core functionality of R, providing tools for specialized statistical methods, data manipulation, machine learning, and more, allowing users to tailor R to their specific needs.

Question: How does R support reproducibility in research?
Answer: R supports reproducibility through tools like R Markdown, which allows users to combine code, text, and output in a single document, ensuring that analyses can be replicated exactly.

Question: What are some of the data types supported by R?
Answer: R supports various data types, including vectors, matrices, data frames, lists, factors, and time series, providing flexibility in data manipulation and analysis.

Question: How does R handle large datasets?
Answer: R handles large datasets through packages like data.table and integrations with big data technologies, though it has limitations due to in-memory data storage.

Question: What are the advantages of R being an open-source language?
Answer: As an open-source language, R is freely available, highly customizable, benefits from community contributions, and allows for transparent and collaborative development.

Question: How does R facilitate statistical modeling?
Answer: R provides extensive support for statistical modeling, including linear and nonlinear models, time-series analysis, clustering, and more, with many built-in functions and additional packages available.

Question: What is the significance of the Tidyverse in R?
Answer: The Tidyverse is a collection of R packages designed for data science, offering a consistent syntax and workflow for data manipulation, visualization, and exploration.

Question: How does R handle missing data?
Answer: R has built-in functions like is.na() to detect missing data, and packages like mice and Amelia to perform imputation and handle missing data effectively.

Question: How does R support machine learning?
Answer: R supports machine learning through packages like caret, randomForest, and xgboost, which provide tools for building, training, and evaluating models.

Question: What is R's role in statistical computing?
Answer: R is a leading tool in statistical computing due to its extensive library of statistical functions, flexibility in modeling, and strong visualization capabilities.

Question: How does R integrate with databases?
Answer: R integrates with databases through packages like DBI and dplyr, allowing users to connect to, query, and manipulate data stored in relational databases.

Question: What are some key features of R that support data cleaning?
Answer: R provides powerful data cleaning tools through packages like dplyr for filtering, selecting, and transforming data, and tidyr for tidying messy data.

Question: How does R handle time series data?
Answer: R handles time series data through specialized packages like xts, zoo, and forecast, providing tools for analysis, visualization, and forecasting.

Question: What makes R particularly useful in academic research?
Answer: R is useful in academic research due to its extensive statistical libraries, reproducibility features, open-source nature, and strong support for complex data analysis.

Question: How does R's package ecosystem enhance its functionality?
Answer: R's package ecosystem enhances its functionality by allowing users to extend the base language with specialized tools for diverse applications, from genomics to finance.

Question: How does R support interactive data visualization?
Answer: R supports interactive data visualization through packages like Shiny and plotly, allowing users to create web applications and interactive plots.

Question: What are the benefits of using R for exploratory data analysis?
Answer: R is beneficial for exploratory data analysis (EDA) due to its robust data manipulation functions, extensive plotting capabilities, and packages designed specifically for EDA.

Question: How does R handle parallel computing?
Answer: R handles parallel computing through packages like parallel, foreach, and future, enabling efficient processing of large datasets and computational tasks.

Question: What is the importance of CRAN in the R ecosystem?
Answer: CRAN (Comprehensive R Archive Network) is essential for distributing R and its packages, ensuring users have access to a vast library of tools and updates.

Question: How does R's memory management impact its performance?
Answer: R's memory management, which stores objects in memory, can impact performance with large datasets, but this can be mitigated with packages like data.table or by optimizing code.

Question: How does R support big data analysis?
Answer: R supports big data analysis through integrations with Hadoop, Spark, and big data platforms, and packages like bigmemory for handling large datasets.

Question: What are some visualization techniques supported by R?
Answer: R supports various visualization techniques, including histograms, scatter plots, box plots, bar charts, and more advanced visualizations like heatmaps and 3D plots.

Question: How does R facilitate the creation of reproducible research?
Answer: R facilitates reproducible research with tools like R Markdown, which integrates code and results into a single document, making it easy to reproduce analyses.

Question: What are some of the machine learning algorithms supported by R?
Answer: R supports machine learning algorithms like decision trees, random forests, support vector machines, neural networks, and boosting methods.

Question: How does R handle data manipulation?
Answer: R handles data manipulation through packages like dplyr and data.table, which provide intuitive and efficient tools for transforming and cleaning data.

Question: How does R support text mining and natural language processing?
Answer: R supports text mining and NLP through packages like tm, text2vec, and tidytext, which offer tools for text analysis, sentiment analysis, and topic modeling.

Question: What is the role of R in bioinformatics?
Answer: R plays a significant role in bioinformatics through the Bioconductor project, which provides tools for analyzing genomic data, gene expression, and other biological data.

Question: How does R integrate with other programming languages?
Answer: R integrates with other programming languages like Python, C++, and Java through packages like reticulate (for Python) and Rcpp (for C++), enabling seamless interoperability.

Question: How does R handle geospatial data?
Answer: R handles geospatial data through packages like sp, sf, and raster, providing tools for spatial data analysis, mapping, and visualization.

Question: What are the benefits of using R for statistical simulations?
Answer: R is ideal for statistical simulations due to its powerful random number generation, extensive statistical functions, and ability to simulate complex models.

Question: How does R support the deployment of analytical models?
Answer: R supports the deployment of analytical models through tools like Shiny for web applications, plumber for APIs, and integration with cloud platforms.

Question: What is R's role in financial analysis?
Answer: R's role in financial analysis is significant, with packages like quantmod, PerformanceAnalytics, and TTR providing tools for modeling, backtesting, and analyzing financial data.

Question: How does R handle categorical data?
Answer: R handles categorical data using factors, which are variables that represent categorical data and can be ordered or unordered, with specific levels defined.

Question: How does R support high-performance computing?
Answer: R supports high-performance computing through parallel processing packages, integration with HPC clusters, and the ability to offload computations to GPUs.

Question: What are the advantages of using R for predictive modeling?
Answer: R is advantageous for predictive modeling due to its extensive library of statistical models, machine learning algorithms, and easy-to-use packages for model training and validation.

Question: How does R handle data import/export with various formats?
Answer: R handles data import/export through functions like read.csv(), write.csv(), and packages like readr, haven, and readxl, which support multiple formats like CSV, Excel, and SPSS.

Question: What are some key features of R that support decision-making in business?
Answer: R supports decision-making in business through its powerful data analysis tools, predictive modeling capabilities, and ability to create interactive dashboards and reports with Shiny.

Question: How does R facilitate collaborative work?
Answer: R facilitates collaborative work through version control systems like Git, integration with RStudio Server, and collaborative tools like R Markdown for sharing analyses and results.

Advantages and Disadvantages

Question: What are the key strengths of R for data analysis?
Answer: R offers comprehensive libraries, robust statistical methods, and powerful data visualization capabilities.

Question: How does R support reproducible research?
Answer: R supports reproducibility through RMarkdown, version control with git, and package management tools like renv.

Question: Why is R considered strong for statistical analysis?
Answer: R has extensive statistical packages and is built by statisticians, making it ideal for complex analyses.

Question: How does R handle large datasets?
Answer: R can manage large datasets efficiently with packages like data.table and integration with big data tools.

Question: What makes R a preferred tool for data visualization?
Answer: R's ggplot2 and lattice packages provide flexible and high-quality visualizations.

Question: Why is R favored in academic and research settings?
Answer: R's open-source nature and comprehensive statistical tools make it popular for academic research.

Question: How does the R community contribute to its advantages?
Answer: The active R community continuously develops and maintains a vast array of packages and tools.

Question: What role does CRAN play in R's ecosystem?
Answer: CRAN provides a centralized repository for R packages, ensuring reliability and easy access.

Question: How does R integrate with other programming languages?
Answer: R integrates well with languages like Python, C++, and Java, enhancing its flexibility in projects.

Question: What makes R an attractive choice for statisticians?
Answer: R's comprehensive statistical packages and easy syntax for complex models make it ideal for statisticians.

Question: How does R support exploratory data analysis?
Answer: R's tools for data manipulation and visualization are excellent for exploratory data analysis.

Question: How does R facilitate machine learning?
Answer: R provides packages like caret and randomForest that simplify machine learning model development.

Question: Why is R preferred for data wrangling tasks?
Answer: R's dplyr and tidyr packages streamline data manipulation and cleaning.

Question: How does R's package ecosystem benefit developers?
Answer: R's extensive package ecosystem offers ready-made solutions, saving development time.

Question: How does R handle data visualization customization?
Answer: R allows detailed customization of visualizations, making it versatile for various presentation needs.

Question: What are R's strengths in statistical reporting?
Answer: RMarkdown enables dynamic and reproducible statistical reporting, integrating code with narrative.

Question: How does R's open-source nature benefit users?
Answer: R's open-source nature means it's free to use and constantly improved by its community.

Question: Why is R suitable for handling complex data structures?
Answer: R natively supports vectors, matrices, and data frames, making it adept at handling complex data structures.

Question: How does R's object-oriented programming support complex analysis?
Answer: R's object-oriented nature allows for modular and reusable code, which is essential for complex analyses.

Question: Why is R considered a leader in statistical computing?
Answer: R's rich set of libraries and robust statistical methodologies keep it at the forefront of statistical computing.

Question: How does R support reproducible workflows?
Answer: Tools like renv and RMarkdown promote consistent, reproducible workflows in R.

Question: How does R handle interactive graphics?
Answer: R supports interactive graphics through packages like shiny and plotly, enhancing data exploration.

Question: Why is R preferred for time-series analysis?
Answer: R's specialized packages like xts and zoo are tailored for time-series analysis.

Question: How does R support parallel computing?
Answer: R supports parallel computing through packages like parallel and foreach, speeding up computation.

Question: What makes R scalable for large projects?
Answer: R's ecosystem, including big data packages and cloud integration, makes it scalable for large projects.

Question: How does R's package ecosystem enhance its capabilities?
Answer: The vast ecosystem of specialized packages extends R's functionality across various domains.

Question: How does R's scripting nature benefit data analysis?
Answer: R's scripting nature allows for easy automation and replication of data analysis processes.

Question: Why is R an attractive option for predictive analytics?
Answer: R's robust statistical tools and machine learning packages make it a strong choice for predictive analytics.

Question: How does R's extensibility benefit advanced users?
Answer: Advanced users can extend R's capabilities through custom packages and integration with other languages.

Question: How does R's syntax simplicity benefit beginners?
Answer: R's simple and intuitive syntax makes it accessible to beginners in data analysis.

Question: What are the limitations of R in handling extremely large datasets?
Answer: R can struggle with memory management for extremely large datasets, requiring workarounds like data.table or integration with databases.

Question: How does R's performance compare to other programming languages?
Answer: R can be slower than languages like Python or C++ for certain computational tasks.

Question: What are the challenges of using R in a production environment?
Answer: Managing package dependencies and ensuring reproducibility can be challenging in production with R.

Question: How does the steep learning curve of R affect new users?
Answer: The vast array of packages and functions can overwhelm new users, making the learning curve steep.

Question: What are the limitations of R's object-oriented programming capabilities?
Answer: R's object-oriented system is less powerful and flexible compared to languages like Python or Java.

Question: How does R handle multi-threading and parallelism?
Answer: R's native support for multi-threading is limited, often requiring external packages or integration with other tools.

Question: What are the drawbacks of R's graphical capabilities compared to specialized tools?
Answer: While powerful, R's graphical capabilities can be less performant and harder to use than specialized tools like D3.js.

Question: How does the R ecosystem's reliance on community contributions pose a risk?
Answer: The reliance on community contributions can lead to variability in package quality and support.

Question: What are the challenges of using R for large-scale enterprise applications?
Answer: R is not typically designed for large-scale enterprise applications, making integration with other systems more complex.

Question: How does R's memory management limitations affect performance?
Answer: R's in-memory processing can limit its ability to handle very large datasets, affecting performance and scalability.

Installation of R and R Studio

Question: What are the prerequisites for installing R on a system?
Answer: The prerequisites for installing R include having a compatible operating system (Windows, macOS, or Linux) and sufficient administrative privileges to install software.

Question: How do you download R for installation?
Answer: You can download R from the Comprehensive R Archive Network (CRAN) website, selecting the appropriate version for your operating system.

Question: What is the difference between the R base installation and R Studio?
Answer: The R base installation provides the core R programming language and environment, while RStudio is an Integrated Development Environment (IDE) that provides additional tools and a user-friendly interface for working with R.

Question: Can R be installed on all major operating systems?
Answer: Yes, R can be installed on all major operating systems, including Windows, macOS, and Linux.

Question: What are the steps to install R on Windows?
Answer: To install R on Windows, download the installer from CRAN, run the .exe file, and follow the on-screen instructions to complete the installation.

Question: How do you install R on macOS?
Answer: To install R on macOS, download the .pkg file from CRAN, open it, and follow the installation prompts to install R on your system.

Question: What is the process for installing R on a Linux system?
Answer: On Linux, R can be installed via the system's package manager (e.g., apt-get install r-base on Ubuntu) or by downloading and compiling the source code from CRAN.

Question: How do you verify that R has been successfully installed?
Answer: You can verify R installation by opening the R console (by typing R in the command line) and checking the version information that appears.

Question: What is the purpose of RStudio in the R ecosystem?
Answer: RStudio enhances the R ecosystem by providing a comprehensive IDE that includes tools for script editing, debugging, visualization, and project management.

Question: How do you download RStudio for installation?
Answer: You can download RStudio from the official RStudio website, selecting the appropriate version for your operating system.

Question: What are the installation steps for RStudio on Windows?
Answer: After downloading the RStudio installer for Windows, run the .exe file and follow the on-screen instructions to complete the installation.

Question: How do you install RStudio on macOS?
Answer: Download the .dmg file for RStudio from the official website, open it, and drag the RStudio icon to the Applications folder to install.

Question: How is RStudio installed on Linux?
Answer: On Linux, download the appropriate .deb or .rpm package from the RStudio website and install it using the package manager (e.g., sudo dpkg -i rstudio-x.y.z-amd64.deb on Ubuntu).

Question: What should you do if you encounter an error during R installation?
Answer: If an error occurs during R installation, check the CRAN documentation, ensure system compatibility, and verify that all prerequisites are met. For specific errors, consult forums or the R community for solutions.

Question: How do you verify the installation of RStudio?
Answer: You can verify the installation of RStudio by opening the application and ensuring it launches without errors, and that it detects the installed version of R.

Question: What is the significance of setting up the R environment in RStudio?
Answer: Setting up the R environment in RStudio ensures that the IDE recognizes the R installation and provides all necessary tools and configurations for running R scripts and projects.

Question: How can you customize the RStudio interface after installation?
Answer: You can customize the RStudio interface through the Tools -> Global Options menu, where you can adjust themes, font sizes, pane layouts, and other settings.

Question: What should you check if RStudio doesn't recognize your R installation?
Answer: Ensure that R is correctly installed and check the path configuration in RStudio under Tools -> Global Options -> General to point to the correct R executable.

Question: How do you update R to the latest version?
Answer: To update R, download the latest version from CRAN and install it over the existing installation. On Linux, you can use the package manager to upgrade (sudo apt-get update followed by sudo apt-get upgrade r-base).

Question: How do you update RStudio to the latest version?
Answer: Download the latest version of RStudio from the official website and install it over the existing installation. RStudio will retain your settings and configurations.

Question: What is the function of the RStudio Package Manager?
Answer: The RStudio Package Manager helps manage and install R packages, providing a user-friendly interface for finding, installing, and updating packages within RStudio.

Question: How do you set up RStudio projects?
Answer: RStudio projects can be set up by navigating to File -> New Project, selecting the type of project (e.g., a new directory or an existing directory), and configuring the project settings.

Question: What are some common issues during RStudio installation on Linux?
Answer: Common issues include missing dependencies, incorrect permissions, or conflicts with existing software. These can often be resolved by checking the logs, installing missing libraries, or adjusting permissions.

Question: How do you configure RStudio to work with version control systems?
Answer: RStudio integrates with Git and SVN through Tools -> Global Options -> Git/SVN, where you can set up your version control settings and link your project to a repository.

Question: What is the purpose of RStudio Server?
Answer: RStudio Server allows multiple users to access RStudio through a web browser, enabling collaborative work on R projects hosted on a central server.

Question: How do you install RStudio Server on a Linux machine?
Answer: RStudio Server can be installed on a Linux machine by downloading the appropriate .deb or .rpm file from the RStudio website and installing it using the package manager (e.g., sudo dpkg -i rstudio-server-x.y.z-amd64.deb).

Question: How do you start and stop the RStudio Server service?
Answer: On Linux, you can start the RStudio Server service using sudo systemctl start rstudio-server and stop it using sudo systemctl stop rstudio-server.

Question: How do you check the status of RStudio Server?
Answer: Check the status of RStudio Server using the command sudo systemctl status rstudio-server on Linux.

Question: How do you troubleshoot RStudio installation issues?

Answer: Troubleshoot RStudio installation issues by checking the installation logs, ensuring system compatibility, verifying dependencies, and consulting the RStudio documentation or community forums for solutions.

Question: What are the advantages of using RStudio over the base R console?
Answer: RStudio offers a more user-friendly interface, integrated tools for development, project management, debugging, and enhanced data visualization capabilities, making it more efficient than the base R console.

Question: How do you configure RStudio to use specific R libraries?
Answer: Configure RStudio to use specific R libraries by setting the library path in Tools -> Global Options -> Packages, or by using .libPaths() in your R scripts to specify the location.

Question: What are the steps to install additional R packages in RStudio?
Answer: Install additional R packages in RStudio by using the Packages pane to search and install, or by running install.packages("package_name") in the R console.

Question: How do you install R from source on Linux?
Answer: Install R from source on Linux by downloading the source code from CRAN, extracting it, and running the ./configure, make, and sudo make install commands.

Question: How do you set up RStudio on a virtual machine?
Answer: Set up RStudio on a virtual machine by installing the operating system, followed by the installation of R and RStudio using the same steps as on a physical machine.

Question: How do you install R and RStudio in a Docker container?
Answer: Install R and RStudio in a Docker container by creating a Dockerfile that installs R, RStudio, and any necessary dependencies, then building and running the container.

Question: How do you install RStudio in a non-standard directory?
Answer: Install RStudio in a non-standard directory by downloading the installer, running it from the command line, and specifying the installation directory using the appropriate flags.

Question: How do you configure RStudio to work with R tools like Rcpp?
Answer: Configure RStudio to work with R tools like Rcpp by installing the necessary Rcpp package, ensuring you have a C++ compiler installed, and setting up RStudio to recognize the compiler in Tools -> Global Options.

Question: How do you resolve permission issues when installing R packages in RStudio?
Answer: Resolve permission issues by running RStudio as an administrator or by changing the library path to a directory
where the user has write permissions.

Question: What are the benefits of using RStudio for package development?
Answer: RStudio provides tools for package development, including an integrated package building system, version control integration, and debugging tools, making it easier to develop, test, and deploy R packages.

Question: How do you migrate R and RStudio settings from one machine to another?
Answer: Migrate R and RStudio settings by copying the .Rhistory, .RData, .Rprofile, and .Renviron files, along with RStudio's configuration files, to the new machine's corresponding directories.

Installation and Loading of R Packages

Question: How do you install a package in R?

Answer: You can install a package in R using the install.packages("package_name") function, where "package_name" is the name of the package you want to install.

Question: How can you load a package into the R environment after installation?
Answer: You can load a package into the R environment using the library(package_name) function, where "package_name" is the name of the package.

Question: What is the purpose of the require() function in R?
Answer: The require() function loads a package and returns TRUE if the package is successfully loaded. It is similar to library() but is often used within functions to ensure a package is available.

Question: How do you update an installed package in R?
Answer: You can update an installed package using the update.packages() function, which checks for updates and installs the latest versions of all installed packages.

Question: What is the difference between install.packages() and library() functions?
Answer: install.packages() is used to download and install a package from CRAN, while library() is used to load an already installed package into the current R session.

Question: How do you install a package from a specific repository other than CRAN?
Answer: You can install a package from a specific repository by specifying the repos argument in install.packages(), like install.packages("package_name", repos="https://custom-repo.org").

Question: How can you install a package from a local source file?
Answer: You can install a package from a local source file using the install.packages("path/to/package.tar.gz", repos = NULL, type = "source").

Question: What is the role of the dependencies argument in the install.packages() function?
Answer: The dependencies argument specifies whether to install package dependencies as well. Setting dependencies = TRUE ensures all necessary packages are installed.

Question: How do you check if a package is installed in R?
Answer: You can check if a package is installed by using the installed.packages() function or by checking with if("package_name" %in% rownames(installed.packages())).

Question: How can you remove a package from your R installation?
Answer: You can remove a package using the remove.packages("package_name") function.

Question: What is the purpose of the .libPaths() function in R?
Answer: The .libPaths() function is used to get or set the library trees where R packages are installed.

Question: How do you install a package from GitHub?
Answer: You can install a package from GitHub using the devtools::install_github("username/repository") function after installing the devtools package.

Question: How do you list all installed packages in R?
Answer: You can list all installed packages using the installed.packages() function.

Question: What is the use of the library.dynam() function?
Answer: The library.dynam() function is used to load shared object libraries (dynamic libraries) that are associated with a package.

Question: How do you install multiple packages at once in R?
Answer: You can install multiple packages at once by passing a vector of package names to install.packages(), like install.packages(c("pkg1", "pkg2", "pkg3")).

Question: What are the typical locations where R packages are installed?
Answer: R packages are typically installed in directories listed by .libPaths(), which may include user-specific directories and system-wide directories.

Question: How do you ensure a package is loaded only if it is installed?
Answer: You can ensure a package is loaded only if installed by using if(require(package_name)).

Question: How do you install packages without asking for user input during the installation?
Answer: You can install packages without user input by using install.packages("package_name", ask = FALSE).

Question: What is a "dependency" in the context of R packages?
Answer: A dependency is a package that another package relies on to function correctly. Dependencies are automatically installed when a package is installed if the dependencies argument is set to TRUE.

Question: How do you unload a loaded package in R?
Answer: You can unload a loaded package using the detach("package:package_name", unload = TRUE) function.

Question: What is the NAMESPACE file in an R package?
Answer: The NAMESPACE file controls which functions are exported by a package and which imports are needed from other packages.

Question: How do you handle package installation in environments without internet access?
Answer: In environments without internet access, you can manually download package source files, transfer them to the target machine, and install them using install.packages() with repos = NULL.

Question: What is the purpose of the R CMD INSTALL command?
Answer: The R CMD INSTALL command is used to install a package from source in a command-line environment.

Question: How do you install a specific version of a package in R?
Answer: You can install a specific version of a package using the devtools::install_version("package_name", version = "x.y.z") function.

Question: How do you check the version of a loaded package?
Answer: You can check the version of a loaded package using the packageVersion("package_name") function.

Question: How do you install a package from Bioconductor?
Answer: You can install a package from Bioconductor using the BiocManager::install("package_name") function after installing the BiocManager package.

Question: How do you avoid conflicts between different package versions?
Answer: You can avoid conflicts by using package versioning tools like packrat or renv to manage and isolate package environments.

Question: What are "suggested" packages in R, and how are they installed?
Answer: "Suggested" packages are those that are not essential but provide additional functionality. They can be installed using the dependencies = TRUE argument in install.packages().

Question: How do you check which packages have updates available?

Answer: You can check for package updates using the old.packages() function.

Question: What is the difference between requireNamespace() and require()?
Answer: requireNamespace() loads the namespace of a package without attaching it to the search path, whereas require() loads and attaches the package.

Question: How do you install a package in a non-default library location?
Answer: You can install a package in a non-default location by specifying the lib argument in install.packages(), like install.packages("package_name", lib = "path/to/library").

Question: How do you identify the dependencies of a package?
Answer: You can identify the dependencies of a package using the tools::package_dependencies("package_name") function.

Question: What is the purpose of the DESCRIPTION file in an R package?
Answer: The DESCRIPTION file provides metadata about the package, including its name, version, dependencies, authorship, and other details.

Question: How do you install a package from a tarball file in R?
Answer: You can install a package from a tarball file using install.packages("path/to/package.tar.gz", repos = NULL, type = "source").

Question: What is the significance of the Suggests field in the DESCRIPTION file?
Answer: The Suggests field in the DESCRIPTION file lists packages that are suggested (but not required) for enhancing the functionality of the package.

Question: How do you handle package installation errors?
Answer: Package installation errors can be handled by checking for system dependencies, updating R, or using verbose = TRUE in install.packages() to get detailed error messages.

Question: What is the role of the devtools package in package development and installation?
Answer: The devtools package simplifies package development and installation by providing functions to install packages from various sources, manage dependencies, and automate the development workflow.

Question: How do you list all functions available in a loaded package?
Answer: You can list all functions in a loaded package using the ls("package:package_name") function.

Question: How do you install R packages programmatically within an R script?
Answer: You can programmatically install R packages within an R script using install.packages("package_name") or by checking if the package is installed first and then installing it if not.

Question: How should R packages be managed in a production environment?

Answer: Use tools like renv for isolated environments to ensure version control and reproducibility. Regularly test and validate packages to avoid compatibility issues and maintain stability in production.

R-Basic Syntax

Question: What is the basic structure of an R script?
Answer: The basic structure of an R script includes a series of R expressions and statements that are executed sequentially. Comments can be added using the # symbol.

Question: How do you assign values to variables in R
Answer: Values are assigned to variables using the assignment operator <-, e.g., x <- 10.

Question: What is the difference between <- and = in R?
Answer: Both <- and = can be used for assignment, but <- is the recommended operator in R programming, while = is mainly used for specifying arguments in function calls.

Question: How do you create a sequence of numbers in R?
Answer: You can create a sequence of numbers using the : operator, e.g., 1:10, or the seq() function for more control, e.g., seq(1, 10, by=2).

Question: How do you create comments in R?
Answer: Comments in R are created using the # symbol. Anything following # on a line is considered a comment and is not executed.

Question: How do you print output in R?
Answer: Output can be printed using the print() function, e.g., print("Hello, World!").

Question: How do you create a vector in R?
Answer: A vector can be created using the c() function, e.g., c(1, 2, 3, 4, 5).

Question: How do you create a matrix in R?
Answer: A matrix can be created using the matrix() function, e.g., matrix(1:9, nrow=3, ncol=3).

Question: What is the purpose of the length() function in R?
Answer: The length() function returns the number of elements in an R object, such as a vector.

Question: How do you concatenate strings in R?
Answer: Strings can be concatenated using the paste() or paste0() functions, e.g., paste("Hello", "World").

Question: What is a function in R?
Answer: A function in R is a block of code that performs a specific task. It is created using the function() keyword and can take arguments and return a value.

Question: How do you define a function in R?
Answer: A function is defined using the function() keyword, e.g., my_function <- function(x) { return(x^2) }.

Question: How do you call a function in R?
Answer: A function is called by its name followed by parentheses containing any arguments, e.g., my_function(2).

Question: What are the data structures available in R?
Answer: R provides several data structures, including vectors, matrices, lists, data frames, and factors.

Question: How do you access elements of a vector in R?
Answer: Elements of a vector are accessed using square brackets, e.g., x[1] returns the first element of vector x.

Question: How do you handle missing values in R?
Answer: Missing values in R are represented by NA. Functions like is.na() can be used to identify them, and functions like na.omit() can be used to remove them.

Question: What is the if statement in R?

Answer: The if statement in R is used for conditional execution of code. If the condition is TRUE, the code block inside the if statement is executed.

Question: How do you use if-else statements in R?
Answer: The if-else statement allows for conditional execution of code, with the else block being executed if the if condition is FALSE.

Question: What is a loop in R?
Answer: A loop in R is used to repeatedly execute a block of code. Common loops in R include for, while, and repeat.

Question: How do you create a for loop in R?
Answer: A for loop is created using the for keyword, e.g., for(i in 1:5) { print(i) }.

Question: How do you break out of a loop in R?
Answer: You can break out of a loop using the break statement.

Question: How do you skip to the next iteration of a loop in R?
Answer: You can skip to the next iteration of a loop using the next statement.

Question: What is the while loop in R?
Answer: The while loop in R repeatedly executes a block of code as long as the specified condition is TRUE.

Question: How do you create a while loop in R?
Answer: A while loop is created using the while keyword, e.g., while(x < 10) { x <- x + 1 }.

Question: How do you write a simple conditional statement in R?
Answer: A simple conditional statement can be written using if(condition) { # code to execute }.

Question: What is the switch() function in R?
Answer: The switch() function allows you to choose between multiple options based on the value of an expression.

Question: How do you write an inline if statement in R?
Answer: An inline if statement can be written using the ifelse() function, e.g., ifelse(x > 0, "Positive", "Negative").

Question: What is the use of the return() function in R?
Answer: The return() function is used to explicitly return a value from a function.

Question: How do you comment out multiple lines in R?
Answer: Multiple lines can be commented out by placing # at the beginning of each line.

Question: What is vectorization in R?
Answer: Vectorization in R refers to the ability to perform operations on entire vectors at once, rather than using loops.

Question: How do you perform element-wise operations on vectors in R?
Answer: Element-wise operations on vectors are performed using standard arithmetic operators, e.g., x + y.

Question: How do you define global and local variables in R?
Answer: Global variables are defined outside of functions and are accessible throughout the R session, while local variables are defined within functions and are only accessible within that function.

Question: How do you use the cat() function in R?
Answer: The cat() function concatenates and prints objects, typically for displaying text and variable values together.

Question: What is the str() function used for in R?
Answer: The str() function provides a compact, human-readable summary of an R object, showing its structure.

Question: How do you handle errors in R?
Answer: Errors in R can be handled using try(), tryCatch(), and custom error handling functions.

Data Types

Question: What are the basic data types in R?
Answer: The basic data types in R include numeric, integer, complex, logical, and character.

Question: How do you create a numeric variable in R?
Answer: A numeric variable is created by assigning a decimal number to a variable, e.g., x <- 3.14.

Question: What is the difference between numeric and integer types in R?
Answer: Numeric types in R are floating-point numbers, while integer types are whole numbers. You can explicitly define an integer using the L suffix, e.g., x <- 5L.

Question: How do you check the type of a variable in R?
Answer: The type of a variable can be checked using the typeof() function.

Question: How do you convert a variable from one type to another in R?
Answer: You can convert variables using type conversion functions like as.numeric(), as.integer(), as.character(), etc.

Question: What is a logical data type in R?
Answer: A logical data type in R represents Boolean values, TRUE or FALSE.

Question: How do you create a character string in R?
Answer: A character string is created by enclosing text in quotes, e.g., x <- "Hello".

Question: How do you combine multiple strings into one in R?
Answer: Multiple strings can be combined using the paste() or paste0() functions.

Question: What is a factor in R?
Answer: A factor is a data type used to represent categorical data with a fixed number of possible values (levels).

Question: How do you create a factor in R?
Answer: A factor is created using the factor() function, e.g., x <- factor(c("Male", "Female", "Male")).

Question: How do you change the levels of a factor in R?
Answer: You can change the levels of a factor using the levels() function, e.g., levels(x) <- c("M", "F").

Question: What is a complex number in R?
Answer: A complex number in R has a real and an imaginary part, e.g., z <- 1 + 2i.

Question: How do you create a complex number in R?
Answer: A complex number is created by combining real and imaginary parts using i, e.g., z <- 3 + 4i.

Question: How do you check if a variable is of a specific type in R?
Answer: You can check if a variable is of a specific type using is.numeric(), is.character(), is.factor(), etc.

Question: How do you convert a factor to a numeric type in R?
Answer: To convert a factor to a numeric type in R, first convert the factor to a character using as.character() and then to numeric using as.numeric(). This ensures the correct numeric values are assigned to each level.

Question: How do you subset a data frame in R?
Answer: Subsetting a data frame can be done using indexing, e.g., df[1:3,] for rows and df[, c("column1", "column2")] for columns.

Question: What is the use of the apply() function in R?
Answer: The apply() function is used to apply a function over the margins of an array or matrix, e.g., apply(matrix, 1, sum) to apply the sum function over rows.

Question: How do you handle missing values in R?
Answer: Missing values can be handled using functions like na.omit(), na.rm = TRUE argument in functions, or is.na() to identify them.

Question: How do you save and load objects in R?
Answer: Objects can be saved using the save() function and loaded with load(), e.g., save(my_data, file="my_data.RData") and load("my_data.RData").

Question: What is the purpose of the data.frame() function in R?
Answer: The data.frame() function creates a data frame, a table-like structure that holds data in rows and columns.

Question: How do you merge two data frames in R?
Answer: Data frames can be merged using the merge() function, specifying the common columns for merging.

Question: How do you sort a data frame in R?
Answer: Data frames can be sorted using the order() function along with indexing, e.g., df[order(df$column),].

Question: How do you remove duplicates from a data frame in R?
Answer: Duplicates can be removed using the unique() function or distinct() from the dplyr package.

Question: How do you install a package from GitHub in R?
Answer: You can install a package from GitHub using the devtools package with the install_github() function, e.g., devtools::install_github("username/repository").

Question: How do you create a new R package?
Answer: A new R package can be created using the devtools::create() function, specifying the package name and other details.

Question: How do you check for package updates in R?
Answer: Package updates can be checked using the old.packages() function, which lists packages that have newer versions available.

Question: What is the role of RStudio in managing packages?
Answer: RStudio provides a graphical interface for managing packages, allowing users to install, update, and load packages through the Packages pane.

Question: How do you remove an installed package in R?
Answer: An installed package can be removed using the remove.packages("package_name") function.

Question: What is the use of the sessionInfo() function in R?
Answer: The sessionInfo() function provides details about the R session, including the versions of R, loaded packages, and other session-related information.

Question: How do you check for package dependencies in R?
Answer: Package dependencies can be checked using the packageDescription() function or by examining the DESCRIPTION file of the package.

Question: How do you list all installed packages in R?
Answer: All installed packages can be listed using the installed.packages() function.

Question: How do you install a package from a tarball file?
Answer: A package from a tarball file can be installed using install.packages("path/to/package.tar.gz", repos = NULL, type = "source").

Question: What is the use of install.packages()'s type argument?
Answer: The type argument specifies the type of package to install, such as "source" or "binary".

Question: How can you find out the package version in R?
Answer: You can find the package version using the packageVersion("package_name") function.

Question: How do you get help on a specific package in R?
Answer: You can get help on a specific package using the help(package="package_name") function.

Question: What is the role of CRAN in the R ecosystem?
Answer: CRAN (Comprehensive R Archive Network) is a repository that hosts R packages and their documentation.

Question: How do you manage package versions in R?
Answer: Package versions can be managed using the packageVersion() function to check the version and update.packages() to update to the latest version.

Question: How do you use the install.packages() function to install multiple packages at once?
Answer: Multiple packages can be installed at once by passing a vector of package names, e.g., install.packages(c("pkg1", "pkg2")).

Question: What is the BiocManager package used for in R?
Answer: The BiocManager package is used to install and manage packages from Bioconductor, a project that provides tools for the analysis of genomic data.

Question: How do you install packages from Bioconductor?
Answer: Packages from Bioconductor can be installed using BiocManager::install("package_name").

Variables and Constants

Question: What is a variable in R?
Answer: A variable in R is a symbolic name for a storage location that can hold data of various types, such as numeric,
character, or logical.

Question: How do you declare a variable in R?
Answer: A variable is declared by assigning a value using the <- or = operator, e.g., x <- 10.

Question: What is a constant in R?
Answer: A constant in R refers to a value that does not change during the execution of a program. Constants can be numeric, character, or logical values.

Question: How do you define a constant in R?
Answer: R does not have a built-in constant type, but you can create a constant by assigning a value to a variable and
ensuring it is not modified, e.g., PI <- 3.14159.

Question: What is the scope of a variable in R?
Answer: The scope of a variable in R refers to the region of code where the variable is accessible. Variables defined within
functions have local scope, while variables defined outside have global scope.

Question: How do you create a global variable in R?
Answer: A global variable is created by defining it outside of any function, making it accessible throughout the R session.

Question: How do you create a local variable in R?
Answer: A local variable is created within a function, and it is only accessible within that function.

Question: What is the difference between local and global variables in R?
Answer: Local variables are defined within a function and only accessible within that function, while global variables are
defined outside of functions and accessible throughout the entire R session.

Question: How do you check if a variable exists in R?
Answer: You can check if a variable exists using the exists() function, e.g., exists("x").

Question: How do you remove a variable in R?
Answer: A variable can be removed using the rm() function, e.g., rm(x).

Question: What is variable assignment in R?
Answer: Variable assignment in R refers to the process of assigning a value to a variable using the <- or = operator.

Question: How do you perform multiple assignments in R?
Answer: Multiple assignments can be done by assigning the same value to multiple variables, e.g., a <- b <- c <- 5.

Question: What is the assign() function in R?
Answer: The assign() function assigns a value to a variable, where the variable name is provided as a string, e.g., assign("x", 10).

Question: How do you prevent a variable from being modified in R?
Answer: While R does not have immutable variables, you can prevent modification by avoiding reassignment and by not
exporting it from its environment.

Question: What is the purpose of the globalenv() function in R?

Answer: The globalenv() function returns the global environment in R, where global variables are stored.

Question: How do you use the get() function in R?
Answer: The get() function retrieves the value of a variable by its name, provided as a string, e.g., get("x").

Question: How do you list all variables in the global environment?
Answer: All variables in the global environment can be listed using the ls() function.

Question: How do you create a variable name dynamically in R?
Answer: A variable name can be created dynamically using the paste() function combined with assign(), e.g., assign(paste("var", i, sep=""), i).

Question: What are reserved words in R?
Answer: Reserved words in R are words that have special meaning in the language, such as if, else, for, while, and cannot
be used as variable names.

Question: How do you assign a NULL value to a variable?
Answer: A NULL value is assigned using the NULL keyword, e.g., x <- NULL.

Question: What is the difference between NULL and NA in R?
Answer: NULL represents the absence of a value, while NA represents a missing value within a data structure.

Question: How do you handle large numbers in R?
Answer: Large numbers can be handled in R using the numeric type, but for very large numbers, the gmp package can be
used for arbitrary-precision arithmetic.

Question: What is variable shadowing in R?
Answer: Variable shadowing occurs when a local variable in a function has the same name as a global variable, causing
the global variable to be inaccessible within the function.

Question: How do you pass variables by reference in R?
Answer: R does not support passing variables by reference directly, but environments can be used to achieve similar behavior.

Question: What is a reference class in R?
Answer: Reference classes in R allow for object-oriented programming with mutable state, where objects can be modified
directly.

Question: How do you enforce a specific data type for a variable in R?
Answer: You can enforce a specific data type using type conversion functions like as.numeric(), as.character(), etc., or by
checking types with stopifnot(is.numeric(x)).

Question: How do you create a variable in a specific environment?
Answer: A variable can be created in a specific environment using the assign() function with the envir argument, e.g.,
assign("x", 10, envir=env).

Question: How do you save and load variables in R?
Answer: Variables can be saved using the save() function and loaded with the load() function, e.g., save(x, file="x.RData")
and load("x.RData").

Question: How do you check if a variable is numeric?
Answer: A variable can be checked for being numeric using the is.numeric() function.

Question: How do you check if a variable is a factor?
Answer: A variable can be checked for being a factor using the is.factor() function.

Question: How do you concatenate variables in R?
Answer: Variables can be concatenated using the paste() or paste0() functions.

Question: How do you create a logical variable in R?
Answer: A logical variable can be created by assigning TRUE or FALSE to a variable, e.g., x <- TRUE.

Question: How do you determine the length of a vector in R?
Answer: The length of a vector can be determined using the length() function.

Question: What is variable interpolation in R?
Answer: Variable interpolation allows embedding variables directly within strings using the glue() function from the glue
package.

Question: How do you handle infinite values in R?
Answer: Infinite values are represented by Inf in R and can be checked using is.infinite().

Question: How do you remove all variables from the environment in R?
Answer: All variables can be removed using rm(list=ls()).

Question: What are the limitations of variable names in R?
Answer: Variable names in R cannot start with a digit, contain spaces, or be reserved words, and should only include letters,
numbers, and underscores.

Online Resources

Online Practice Paper Link: https://forms.gle/dLedFXPVhFgcbceC9

QR Code:

YouTube Video Link:
https://www.youtube.com/playlist?list=PLzlh_31VWEFrbD40dOF1n0fUG9hgq3NyY

QR Code :

Chapter 2: Operators in R

Introduction to Operators

Question: What is an operator in R?
Answer: An operator in R is a symbol that performs operations on one or more operands. R supports arithmetic, relational,
logical, assignment, and other operators.

Question: How many types of operators are there in R?
Answer: R supports five primary types of operators: arithmetic, relational, logical, assignment, and miscellaneous operators.

Question: What is the purpose of operators in R programming?
Answer: Operators are used to perform various calculations and comparisons, manipulate data, and assign values to variables.

Question: What is the precedence of operators in R?
Answer: Operator precedence determines the order in which operations are performed in an expression, with certain operators being evaluated before others.

Question: How do you perform addition in R?
Answer: Addition is performed using the + operator, e.g., x + y.

Question: What is the difference between unary and binary operators in R?
Answer: Unary operators operate on a single operand (e.g., -x), while binary operators operate on two operands (e.g., x + y).

Question: How does the precedence of operators affect expressions?
Answer: The precedence of operators dictates the order in which parts of an expression are evaluated. Operators with higher precedence are evaluated first.

Question: How do you change the precedence of operators in an expression?
Answer: Parentheses can be used to change the precedence of operators in an expression, ensuring certain operations are performed first.

Question: Can operators in R be overloaded?
Answer: Yes, operators in R can be overloaded by defining specific methods for S3 or S4 classes.

Question: What is operator associativity in R?
Answer: Associativity determines the direction in which an expression is evaluated when operators of the same precedence are used. Most operators in R are left-associative.

Question: What is the %in% operator used for in R?
Answer: The %in% operator is used to check if elements of one vector are present in another vector.

Question: How do you perform exponentiation in R?
Answer: Exponentiation is performed using the ^ operator, e.g., x^2.

Question: What does the : operator do in R?
Answer: The : operator generates a sequence of integers, e.g., 1:10.

Question: How do you check if an object is of a specific type using an operator?
Answer: You can check an object's type using functions like is.numeric().

Question: What is the difference between & and && in R?
Answer:& is used for element-wise logical AND, while && is used for logical AND that only evaluates the first element of each vector.

Question: How do you use the assign() function in R?
Answer: The assign() function assigns a value to a variable, where the variable name is provided as a string.

Question: What is operator overloading?
Answer: Operator overloading allows custom behavior to be defined for operators when applied to objects of specific classes.
Question: What is the role of the = operator in R?
Answer: The = operator is primarily used for assignment, though it is generally recommended to use <- for assignment in R.

Question: How do you use the paste() function in R?
Answer: The paste() function concatenates strings with a specified separator.

Question: What does the ~ operator represent in R?
Answer: The ~ operator is used to define formulas in statistical modeling, e.g., y ~ x.

Question: What is the use of the c() function in R?
Answer: The c() function is used to combine values into a vector.

Question: How do you check for equality in R?
Answer: Equality is checked using the == operator.

Question: How do you perform logical negation in R?
Answer: Logical negation is performed using the ! operator.

Question: What is the purpose of the %*% operator in R?
Answer: The %*% operator performs matrix multiplication.

Question: How do you perform element-wise operations in R?
Answer: Element-wise operations are performed directly on vectors using operators like +, -, *, and /.

Question: What is the use of the : operator in loops?
Answer: The : operator is commonly used to generate a sequence of numbers for looping.

Question: How do you check for inequality in R?
Answer: Inequality is checked using the != operator.

Question: How do you create a matrix in R?
Answer: A matrix is created using the matrix() function.

Question: What is the purpose of the seq() function in R?
Answer: The seq() function generates sequences with more control over the increment, start, and end points compared to the : operator.

Question: How do you use the rep() function in R?
Answer: The rep() function repeats elements of a vector a specified number of times.

Question: How do you perform integer division in R?
Answer: Integer division is performed using the %/% operator.

Question: What is the modulus operator in R?
Answer: The modulus operator is %, which returns the remainder of a division.

Question: What is the purpose of the outer() function in R?
Answer: The outer() function applies a vectorized function to all combinations of elements of two vectors.

Question: How do you use the match() function in R?
Answer: The match() function returns the positions of matches of its first argument in its second argument.

Question: How do you perform conditional operations in R?
Answer: Conditional operations can be performed using if, else, and ifelse() constructs.

Question: What is the use of the with() function in R?
Answer: The with() function simplifies code by allowing expressions to be evaluated within the context of a specific data frame.

Question: How do you concatenate strings in R?
Answer: Strings can be concatenated using paste() or paste0().

Question: What is vector recycling in R?
Answer: Vector recycling is the process where shorter vectors are automatically repeated to match the length of longer Vectors in operations.

Arithmetic Operators

Question: What are the basic arithmetic operators in R?
Answer: The basic arithmetic operators in R are +, -, *, /, and ^.

Question: How do you perform addition in R?
Answer: Addition is performed using the + operator, e.g., x + y.

Question: How do you perform subtraction in R?
Answer: Subtraction is performed using the - operator, e.g., x - y.

Question: How do you perform multiplication in R?
Answer: Multiplication is performed using the * operator, e.g., x * y.

Question: How do you perform division in R?
Answer: Division is performed using the / operator, e.g., x / y.

Question: What does the ^ operator do in R?
Answer: The ^ operator raises a number to the power of another, e.g., x^2.

Question: How do you perform integer division in R?
Answer: Integer division is performed using the %/% operator, which returns the quotient without the remainder.

Question: What is the modulus operator in R?
Answer: The modulus operator is %, which returns the remainder of a division, e.g., 7 %% 3 returns 1.

Question: How do arithmetic operators work with vectors in R?
Answer: Arithmetic operators are applied element-wise to vectors, e.g., c(1, 2, 3) + c(4, 5, 6) results in 5, 7, 9.

Question: How do you handle NA values in arithmetic operations in R?
Answer: NA values propagate through the result unless handled with functions like na.rm = TRUE.

Question: How do you perform arithmetic operations on matrices in R?
Answer: Arithmetic operations on matrices are performed element-wise using standard arithmetic operators, e.g., matrix1 + matrix2.

Question: How do you perform matrix multiplication in R?
Answer: Matrix multiplication is performed using the %*% operator, not the * operator, which performs element-wise multiplication.

Question: How do you calculate the square root of a number in R?
Answer: The square root is calculated using the sqrt() function, e.g., sqrt(16) returns 4.

Question: How do you calculate the absolute value in R?
Answer: The absolute value is calculated using the abs() function, e.g., abs(-5) returns 5.

Question: How do you calculate the exponential in R?
Answer: The exponential function is calculated using the exp() function, e.g., exp(1) returns 2.71828.

Question: How do you calculate the logarithm in R?
Answer: The logarithm is calculated using the log() function, with options for base 2, base 10, or natural log.

Question: What happens when you apply arithmetic operators to vectors of different lengths in R?
Answer: R recycles the shorter vector to match the length of the longer vector, which may generate a warning if the length is not a multiple.

Question: How do you sum all elements of a vector in R?
Answer: The sum of all elements in a vector is calculated using the sum() function.

Question: How do you find the mean of a numeric vector in R?
Answer: The mean is calculated using the mean() function, e.g., mean(c(1, 2, 3)) returns 2.

Question: How do you calculate the cumulative sum in R?
Answer: The cumulative sum is calculated using the cumsum() function, e.g., cumsum(c(1, 2, 3)) returns 1, 3, 6.

Question: How do you calculate the product of elements in a vector in R?
Answer: The product of elements is calculated using the prod() function, e.g., prod(c(1, 2, 3)) returns 6.

Question: How do you calculate the difference between consecutive elements in a vector in R?
Answer: The difference is calculated using the diff() function, e.g., diff(c(1, 2, 4)) returns 1, 2.

Question: How do you round numbers in R?
Answer: Numbers are rounded using the round() function, which can specify the number of decimal places, e.g., round(3.14159, 2) returns 3.14.

Question: How do you truncate numbers in R?
Answer: Numbers are truncated using the trunc() function, which removes the fractional part, e.g., trunc(3.99) returns 3.

Question: How do you calculate the ceiling of a number in R?
Answer: The ceiling of a number is the smallest integer greater than or equal to the number, calculated using ceiling(),
e.g.,ceiling(3.1) returns 4.

Question: How do you calculate the floor of a number in R?
Answer: The floor of a number is the largest integer less than or equal to the number, calculated using floor(), e.g., floor(3.9) returns 3.

Question: How do you generate a sequence of numbers in R?
Answer: A sequence of numbers is generated using the seq() function or the : operator, e.g., seq(1, 10, by=2) returns 1, 3,
5,7, 9.

Question: How do you use arithmetic operators with complex numbers in R?
Answer: Arithmetic operators work with complex numbers similarly to real numbers, e.g., (1+2i) + (2+3i) returns 3+5i.

Question: How do you raise a matrix to a power in R?
Answer: Raising a matrix to a power is done element-wise with the ^ operator, or by matrix exponentiation using the %*% operator.

Question: How do you calculate the inverse of a matrix in R?
Answer: The inverse of a matrix is calculated using the solve() function, e.g., solve(matrix).

Question: How do you transpose a matrix in R?
Answer: The transpose of a matrix is obtained using the t() function, e.g., t(matrix).

Question: How do you apply a function to each element of a matrix in R?
Answer: A function can be applied to each element of a matrix using the apply() function, e.g., apply(matrix, 1, sum) sums
the rows.

Question: What is vector recycling in the context of arithmetic operations in R?
Answer: Vector recycling occurs when R repeats the elements of a shorter vector to match the length of a longer vector in arithmetic operations.

Question: How do you use the outer() function for element-wise operations on two vectors in R?
Answer: The outer() function applies a function to all combinations of elements from two vectors, e.g., outer(1:3, 1:3, "*") performs element-wise multiplication.

Relational Operators

Question: What are relational operators in R?
Answer: Relational operators in R include >, <, >=, <=, ==, and !=, used for comparing values.

Question: How do you check for equality between two variables in R?
Answer: Equality is checked using the == operator, e.g., x == y.

Question: What operator is used to check if one value is greater than another in R?
Answer: The > operator checks if one value is greater than another, e.g., x > y.

Question: How do you check if one value is less than or equal to another in R?
Answer: The <= operator checks if one value is less than or equal to another, e.g., x <= y.

Question: What does the != operator do in R?
Answer: The != operator checks if two values are not equal, e.g., x != y.

Question: How do relational operators work with vectors in R?
Answer: Relational operators are applied element-wise to vectors, returning a logical vector, e.g., c(1, 2, 3) > c(0, 2, 4) results in TRUE, FALSE, FALSE.

Question: How do you combine multiple relational conditions in R?
Answer: Multiple relational conditions can be combined using logical operators like & (AND) and | (OR).

Question: How do you check if a value falls within a range in R?
Answer: You can check if a value falls within a range using combined relational operators, e.g., x >= 1 & x <= 10.

Question: What is the output of a relational operation when comparing different types?
Answer: Relational operations between different types may result in an error or a comparison based on coercion, e.g., comparing a number to a character string.

Question: How do you use relational operators with factors in R?
Answer: Relational operators can compare factors based on their underlying integer codes, considering the order of levels.

Question: How do you check if two vectors are identical in R?
Answer: Two vectors can be checked for exact equality using the identical() function.

Question: How do you perform a greater than or equal to comparison in R?
Answer: A greater than or equal to comparison is performed using the >= operator, e.g., x >= y.

Question: What does the < operator do in R?
Answer: The < operator checks if the value on the left is less than the value on the right, e.g., x < y.

Question: How do you compare character strings in R?
Answer: Character strings are compared lexicographically using relational operators, e.g., "apple" < "banana" returns TRUE.

Question: How do you handle NA values in relational operations in R?
Answer: NA values result in NA in relational operations, indicating that the comparison is undefined.

Question: How do you perform relational operations on matrices in R?
Answer: Relational operations on matrices are performed element-wise, returning a logical matrix.

Question: How do you check if any element of a vector satisfies a condition in R?
Answer: The any() function checks if any element of a vector satisfies a condition, e.g., any(x > 0).

Question: How do you check if all elements of a vector satisfy a condition in R?
Answer: The all() function checks if all elements of a vector satisfy a condition, e.g., all(x > 0).

Question: How do you find the position of the first match of a condition in R?
Answer: The which() function returns the positions of elements that match a condition, e.g., which(x == 5).

Question: How do you use the %in% operator to check membership in R?
Answer: The %in% operator checks if elements of one vector are present in another, e.g., x %in% y.

Question: How do you compare two lists element-wise in R?
Answer: Lists can be compared element-wise using relational operators in combination with mapply().

Question: How do you use the isTRUE() function in R?
Answer: The isTRUE() function checks if an expression is TRUE, useful for explicit logical checks.

Question: How do you check if a value is missing or NA in R?
Answer: The is.na() function checks if a value is missing or NA.

Question: How do you perform vectorized comparisons in R?
Answer: Vectorized comparisons are performed using relational operators directly on vectors, returning logical vectors.

Question: How do you filter a data frame based on a condition in R?
Answer: A data frame can be filtered using relational operators in combination with the subset() function or square bracket indexing.

Question: How do you sort a vector based on a relational condition in R?
Answer: A vector can be sorted based on a relational condition using the order() function.

Question: How do you check if elements of one vector are greater than the elements of another vector in R?
Answer: Element-wise comparison is performed using the > operator, e.g., x > y.

Question: How do you compare dates in R?
Answer: Dates are compared using relational operators like >, <, ==, etc.

Question: How do you compare times in R?
Answer: Times, like dates, are compared using relational operators, taking into account hours, minutes, and seconds.

Question: What is the result of comparing two factors with different levels in R?
Answer: Comparing factors with different levels may result in an error or NA if the levels are incompatible.

Question: How do you check if two objects are equal, including attributes, in R?
Answer: The all.equal() function checks if two objects are equal, including their attributes.

Question: How do you perform relational comparisons with complex numbers in R?
Answer: Relational comparisons of complex numbers are not directly supported and may require comparing the real or imaginary parts separately.

Question: How do you combine relational operations with logical operators in R?
Answer: Relational operations can be combined with logical operators like & and | to create compound conditions.

Question: How do you use the match() function in relational operations?
Answer: The match() function can be used to find the position of elements in one vector that match elements in another, facilitating relational comparisons.

Question: How do you perform a relational operation across columns in a data frame in R?
Answer: Relational operations across columns can be performed using apply() or dplyr functions like mutate().

Question: How do you ensure that a relational operation does not produce NA in R?
Answer: Ensure that NA values are handled using is.na() or na.omit() before performing relational operations.

Question: How do you use relational operators to subset a list in R?
Answer: Subsetting a list based on relational operators can be done using lapply() or sapply() to apply the condition to each element.

Question: How do you compare the lengths of two vectors using a relational operator in R?
Answer: The lengths of two vectors can be compared using length(x) > length(y).

Question: What is the effect of coercion in relational operations between different data types in R?
Answer: Coercion converts data types to a common type before performing relational operations, which can affect the result.

Logical Operators

Question: What are the logical operators in R?
Answer: The logical operators in R are & (AND), | (OR), and ! (NOT).

Question: How do you perform a logical AND operation in R?
Answer: A logical AND operation is performed using the & operator, e.g., x & y.

Question: How do you perform a logical OR operation in R?
Answer: A logical OR operation is performed using the | operator, e.g., x | y.

Question: What does the ! operator do in R?
Answer: The ! operator negates a logical value, e.g., !TRUE results in FALSE.

Question: How do logical operators work with vectors in R?
Answer: Logical operators are applied element-wise to vectors, returning a logical vector, e.g., c(TRUE, FALSE) & c(FALSE, TRUE) results in FALSE, FALSE.

Question: What is the difference between & and && in R?
Answer:& performs element-wise logical AND, while && evaluates only the first element of each vector.

Question: What is the difference between | and || in R?
Answer: | performs element-wise logical OR, while || evaluates only the first element of each vector.

Question: How do you use logical operators in conditional statements in R?
Answer: Logical operators are used in if, else, and while statements to control the flow of execution based on conditions.

Question: How do you combine multiple logical conditions in R?
Answer: Multiple logical conditions can be combined using & for AND and | for OR, e.g., x > 0 & x < 10.

Question: What is the output of logical operations with NA values in R?
Answer: Logical operations with NA values result in NA unless handled specifically, e.g., using na.rm = TRUE in logical functions.

Question: How do you check if a vector contains only TRUE values in R?
Answer: The all() function checks if all elements of a vector are TRUE, e.g., all(x).

Question: How do you check if a vector contains at least one TRUE value in R?
Answer: The any() function checks if at least one element of a vector is TRUE, e.g., any(x).

Question: How do you negate a logical condition in R?
Answer: A logical condition is negated using the ! operator, e.g., !TRUE results in FALSE.

Question: How do you use the ifelse() function in R?
Answer: The ifelse() function is a vectorized conditional function that returns values based on a logical test, e.g., ifelse(x > 0, "Positive", "Negative").

Question: How do you apply logical operators to data frames in R?
Answer: Logical operators can be applied to data frames for element-wise comparison or filtering, e.g., df[df$col1 > 0 & df$col2 < 10,].

Question: How do you evaluate a logical condition across multiple vectors in R?
Answer: Multiple vectors can be evaluated using logical operators combined with functions like mapply().

Question: How do you use the xor() function in R?
Answer: The xor() function performs a logical exclusive OR operation, returning TRUE if one, but not both, of the inputs is TRUE.

Question: How do you filter data in R using logical conditions?
Answer: Data is filtered using logical conditions within the subset() function or square bracket indexing, e.g., df[df$col > 5,].

Question: How do you create a logical vector in R?
Answer: A logical vector is created using logical expressions or by directly assigning TRUE/FALSE values, e.g., x <- c(TRUE, FALSE, TRUE).

Question: How do you check if a logical vector contains any FALSE values in R?
Answer: The any() function combined with the ! operator checks if a logical vector contains any FALSE values, e.g., any(!x).

Question: How do you perform a logical AND operation on two matrices in R?
Answer: A logical AND operation on two matrices is performed element-wise using the & operator.

Question: How do you use the which() function with logical vectors in R?
Answer: The which() function returns the indices of TRUE values in a logical vector, e.g., which(x == TRUE).

Question: How do you check if a condition is FALSE using logical operators in R?
Answer: You can check if a condition is FALSE using the ! operator, e.g., if(!condition).

Question: How do you use logical operators to subset a list in R?
Answer: A list can be subset using logical operators with lapply() or sapply() functions to apply the condition to each element.

Question: How do you check if a vector is entirely FALSE in R?
Answer: The all() function combined with the ! operator checks if a vector is entirely FALSE, e.g., all(!x).

Question: How do you use the match() function with logical conditions in R?
Answer: The match() function can be used to find the positions of elements in one vector that match a logical condition in another vector.

Question: How do you check for NULL values using logical operators in R?
Answer: The is.null() function checks for NULL values, which can be combined with logical operators for more complex conditions.

Question: How do you combine logical conditions across different columns in a data frame in R?
Answer: Logical conditions across columns can be combined using & and |, e.g., df[df$col1 > 0 & df$col2 < 10,].

Question: How do you use the isTRUE() function in logical operations in R?
Answer: The isTRUE() function is used to check if an expression is exactly TRUE, useful for explicit logical checks.

Question: How do you handle logical operations in conjunction with loops in R?
Answer: Logical operations can be used within loops to control iteration, such as breaking out of a loop when a condition is met.

Question: How do you create a truth table in R using logical operators?
Answer: A truth table can be created by applying logical operators to all combinations of TRUE and FALSE values.

Question: How do you use logical operators with the ifelse() function in vectorized operations?
Answer: Logical operators can be used within ifelse() to apply conditional logic across entire vectors, e.g., ifelse(x > 0 & y < 10, "Valid", "Invalid").

Question: How do you compare the logical output of two functions in R?
Answer: The logical output of two functions can be compared using identical() or all.equal().

Question: How do you check if all values in a logical vector are TRUE using a logical operator?
Answer: The all() function checks if all values in a logical vector are TRUE, e.g., all(x).

Question: How do you use the && operator in conditional statements in R?
Answer: The && operator is used in conditional statements to evaluate the first element of each logical vector and short-circuit the evaluation if FALSE.

Question: How do you combine multiple logical vectors into one in R?
Answer: Multiple logical vectors can be combined using &, |, or xor() operators, depending on the desired outcome.

Question: How do you perform a logical OR operation on multiple conditions in R?
Answer: A logical OR operation on multiple conditions is performed using the | operator, e.g., x > 5 | y < 10 | z == 3.

Question: How do you check if none of the elements in a vector satisfy a condition using logical operators in R?
Answer: Use !any() combined with the condition to check if none of the elements satisfy it, e.g., !any(x > 10).

Assignment Operators

Question: What are the assignment operators in R?
Answer: The primary assignment operators in R are <-, =, and ->.

Question: How do you assign a value to a variable in R?
Answer: A value is assigned to a variable using the <- or = operator, e.g., x <- 5 or x = 5.

Question: What is the difference between <- and = in R?
Answer: Both <- and = can be used for assignment, but <- is the preferred assignment operator in R, while = is typically used for specifying function arguments.

Question: How do you assign a value from right to left in R?
Answer: A value can be assigned from right to left using the -> operator, e.g., 5 -> x.

Question: How do you perform multiple assignments in a single statement in R?
Answer: Multiple assignments can be performed by chaining assignment operators, e.g., a <- b <- c <- 10.

Question: Can you assign values to variables within a function call in R?
Answer: Yes, values can be assigned to variables within a function call using the = operator for named arguments.

Question: How do you use the assign() function in R?
Answer: The assign() function assigns a value to a variable whose name is provided as a string, e.g., assign("x", 10).

Question: What does the <<- operator do in R?
Answer: The <<- operator assigns a value to a variable in the parent environment, not just the local environment.

Question: How do you ensure that a variable is assigned globally in R?
Answer: To assign a variable globally, you can use the <<- operator or explicitly assign it in the global environment using assign("x", 10, envir = .GlobalEnv).

Question: How do you use assignment operators with lists or data frames in R?
Answer: Assignment operators can assign values to specific elements or columns in lists or data frames, e.g., df$column <- value.

Question: What is the effect of using <<- within a function in R?
Answer: Using <<- within a function modifies the variable in the parent environment rather than creating a new local variable.

Question: How do you assign a value to an element of a vector in R?
Answer: A value is assigned to an element of a vector using indexing, e.g., x[1] <- 10.

Question: How do you use the assign() function with dynamic variable names in R?
Answer: The assign() function can create variables with names generated at runtime, e.g., assign(paste("var", i, sep=""), i).

Question: How do you remove a variable from the environment in R?
Answer: A variable is removed using the rm() function, e.g., rm(x).

Question: How do you assign a value to multiple variables at once in R?
Answer: Multiple variables can be assigned the same value using chained assignment, e.g., x <- y <- z <- 5.

Question: What is the purpose of the .Last.value variable in R?
Answer: .Last.value stores the result of the last evaluated expression in R.

Question: How do you prevent a variable from being reassigned in R?
Answer: While R does not have a built-in mechanism to make variables immutable, avoiding reassignment or using environments can help control variable scope.

Question: How do you copy a variable in R without linking to the original?
Answer: Variables are copied by value in R, so assigning one variable to another creates a new copy unless dealing with reference classes.

Question: How do you set default values for function arguments using assignment operators in R?
Answer: Default values are set using the = operator in function definitions, e.g., function(x = 10).

Question: How do you swap the values of two variables in R?
Answer: Values can be swapped using a temporary variable, e.g., temp <- x; x <- y; y <- temp.

Question: What is the role of the environment() function in assignment?
Answer: The environment() function returns the environment in which the assignment occurs, useful for controlling scope.

Question: How do you use assignment operators to modify a specific element in a list in R?
Answer: An element in a list is modified by specifying its index, e.g., list[[1]] <- new_value.

Question: How do you assign NULL to a variable in R?
Answer: NULL is assigned to a variable using the assignment operator, e.g., x <- NULL.

Question: How do you check if a variable is assigned in R?
Answer: The exists() function checks if a variable is assigned, e.g., exists("x").

Question: How do you perform assignment within an if statement in R?
Answer: Assignment within an if statement is performed using <- or =, e.g., if (x <- condition) { ... }.

Question: What is the purpose of the globalenv() function in R?
Answer: The globalenv() function returns the global environment where global variables are stored.

Question: How do you save and load variables in R?
Answer: Variables can be saved using the save() function and loaded with the load() function, e.g., save(x, file="x.RData") and load("x.RData").

Question: How do you list all assigned variables in the global environment in R?
Answer: All assigned variables in the global environment can be listed using the ls() function.

Question: How do you dynamically assign values in a loop in R?
Answer: Dynamic assignment in a loop can be achieved using assign() with a variable name generated at each iteration.

Question: How do you assign values to multiple elements of a vector simultaneously in R?
Answer: Multiple elements of a vector can be assigned using vectorized operations or indexing, e.g., x[1:3] <- c(1, 2, 3).

Question: How do you assign a list of values to a vector in R?
Answer: A list of values is assigned to a vector using indexing, ensuring that the length of the list matches the length of the selected elements.

Question: How do you use the <<- operator to modify a variable in a parent function in R?
Answer: The <<- operator can be used within a nested function to modify a variable in the parent function, affecting its value outside the nested function.

Question: How do you assign values from a data frame to a new variable in R?
Answer: Values from a data frame are assigned to a new variable using indexing or column selection, e.g., new_var <- df$column.

Question: How do you prevent unintended global assignments in R functions?
Answer: Unintended global assignments can be prevented by carefully managing the use of <<- and using environments to control variable scope.

Question: How do you initialize multiple variables to the same value in R?
Answer: Multiple variables can be initialized to the same value using chained assignment, e.g., a <- b <- c <- 0.

Question: How do you assign values to variables using the with() function in R?
Answer: The with() function allows you to assign values within the context of a data frame, simplifying access to its columns.

Miscellaneous Operators

Question: What is the %in% operator used for in R?
Answer: The %in% operator checks if elements of one vector are present in another, returning a logical vector.

Question: How do you use the : operator in R?
Answer: The : operator generates a sequence of integers between two values, e.g., 1:10.

Question: What is the purpose of the %*% operator in R?
Answer: The %*% operator performs matrix multiplication in R.

Question: How do you use the %/% operator in R?
Answer: The %/% operator performs integer division, returning the quotient without the remainder.

Question: What does the %% operator do in R?
Answer: The %% operator returns the remainder of a division, known as the modulus.

Question: How do you use the ~ operator in R?
Answer: The ~ operator is used in formula notation for statistical models, e.g., y ~ x represents a linear model with y as the dependent variable and x as the independent variable.

Question: What is the : operator's role in defining ranges in R?
Answer: The : operator is used to define ranges or sequences, typically for looping or vector creation, e.g., for (i in 1:10).

Question: How do you use the -> operator in R?
Answer: The -> operator assigns a value to a variable on the right-hand side, e.g., value -> x.

Question: How do you combine elements into a vector in R using an operator?
Answer: Elements are combined into a vector using the c() function, not an operator, e.g., c(1, 2, 3).

Question: How do you use the : operator with logical conditions in R?
Answer: The : operator itself is not typically used with logical conditions, but sequences it creates can be used in loops or indexing for logical operations.

Question: What is the purpose of the @ operator in R?
Answer: The @ operator is used to access slots in S4 objects, e.g., object@slot.

Question: How do you use the <<- operator for assignments in parent environments in R?
Answer: The <<- operator assigns a value to a variable in the parent environment rather than the local environment.

Question: How do you apply the : operator to a range of dates in R?
Answer: The : operator can be used with dates by creating a sequence from start to end dates, e.g., seq(as.Date("2021-01-01"), as.Date("2021-01-10"), by="day").

Question: How do you use the %o% operator for outer product in R?
Answer: The %o% operator computes the outer product of two vectors, e.g., 1:3 %o% 4:6.

Question: How do you use the %>% operator in R?
Answer: The %>% operator, from the magrittr package, is used to pipe the result of one expression into the next, e.g., data %>% filter(col > 0) %>% summarise(mean = mean(col)).

Question: How do you use the %x% operator in R?
Answer: The %x% operator performs the Kronecker product of two matrices, e.g., matrix1 %x% matrix2.

Question: How do you use the ? operator in R?
Answer: The ? operator provides help on a specific function or topic, e.g., ?mean opens the documentation for the mean function.

Question: How do you use the * operator for element-wise multiplication in R?
Answer: The * operator multiplies corresponding elements of two vectors or matrices, e.g., c(1, 2, 3) * c(4, 5, 6) results in 4, 10, 18.

Question: How do you use the :: operator in R?
Answer: The :: operator is used to access a function from a specific package, e.g., package::function.

Question: How do you use the ::: operator in R?
Answer: The ::: operator is used to access non-exported functions from a package, e.g., package:::hidden_function.

Question: What is the purpose of the attr() function in R?
Answer: The attr() function is used to get or set the attributes of an R object, such as names, dimensions, or class.

Question: How do you extract elements from a list using the $ operator in R?
Answer: The $ operator is used to extract elements from a list by name, e.g., list$element.

Question: How do you use the [and [[operators in R?
Answer: The [operator extracts subsets of objects, while [[extracts individual elements. For example, list[1] returns a list, whereas list[[1]] returns the first element of the list.

Question: How do you use the |> operator in R?
Answer: The |> operator is the native pipe operator in R, introduced in R 4.1.0, used to pass the output of one expression to the next.

Question: How do you use the %<>% operator in R?
Answer: The %<>% operator from the magrittr package is a compound assignment pipe, which pipes the result of the right-hand side expression back into the left-hand side variable.

Question: How do you use the matrix() function in conjunction with operators in R?
Answer: The matrix() function creates matrices that can be used with operators like %*%, *, and + for matrix operations.

Question: How do you use the as.vector() function in R?
Answer: The as.vector() function converts an object to a vector, which can then be used with vectorized operators.

Question: How do you perform scalar multiplication with a vector in R?
Answer: Scalar multiplication with a vector is performed using the * operator, e.g., 2 * c(1, 2, 3) results in 2, 4, 6.

Question: How do you use the : operator with factors in R?
Answer: The : operator creates interactions between factors, often used in modeling, e.g., factor1:factor2.

Question: What is the purpose of the cut() function in conjunction with relational operators in R?
Answer: The cut() function is used to divide continuous data into intervals, which can then be compared using relational operators.

Question: How do you use the outer() function with operators in R?
Answer: The outer() function applies a specified function (e.g., *, +) to all combinations of two vectors, producing a matrix.

Question: How do you use the %dopar% operator in parallel computing in R?
Answer: The %dopar% operator, used with the foreach package, allows for parallel execution of loops.

Question: How do you use the == operator with data frames in R?
Answer: The == operator compares each element of a data frame to a specified value or another data frame, returning a logical matrix.

Question: How do you use the rowSums() function with logical operators in R?
Answer: The rowSums() function can sum the results of logical operations applied across rows, e.g., rowSums(df > 0) returns the number of positive values per row.

Question: How do you use the isTRUE() function with logical vectors in R?
Answer: The isTRUE() function checks if an entire logical vector is TRUE, useful for confirming conditions across multiple elements.

Question: How do you use the anyNA() function in conjunction with logical operators in R?
Answer: The anyNA() function checks if there are any NA values in an object, often combined with logical operators to filter or clean data.

Question: How do you use the Reduce() function with operators in R?
Answer: The Reduce() function applies a binary function (e.g., +, *) successively to the elements of a vector, reducing it to a single value.

Online Resources

Online Practice Paper Link : https://forms.gle/4oR8d63Cgi3dkCE17

QR Code:

YouTube Video Link: https://www.youtube.com/playlist?list=PLzlh_31VWEFpv-ZOWtwcktU04Swa9YUCI

QR Code:

Chapter 3: Conditional operation, loops and functions

Conditional Statements

Question: What are conditional statements in R?
Answer: Conditional statements in R allow the execution of code blocks based on whether a condition is TRUE or FALSE. The primary conditional statements in R are if, else if, and else.

Question: How do you write a basic if statement in R?
Answer: A basic if statement is written as if (condition) { # code }, where the code block executes if the condition is TRUE.

Question: What is the purpose of the else statement in R?
Answer: The else statement provides an alternative block of code that executes if the if condition is FALSE.

Question: How do you use else if in R?
Answer: The else if statement is used to specify a new condition if the previous if condition is FALSE, allowing multiple conditional checks.

Question: How do you combine multiple conditions in an if statement?
Answer: Multiple conditions in an if statement can be combined using logical operators like & (AND) and | (OR).

Question: Can if statements be nested in R?
Answer: Yes, if statements can be nested, meaning you can place an if statement inside another if statement.

Question: What happens if you omit the else clause in an if statement?
Answer: If the else clause is omitted and the if condition is FALSE, the code block within the if statement will not execute, and the program will continue with the next line of code.

Question: How do you handle complex conditions in if statements?
Answer: Complex conditions can be handled using a combination of logical operators, parentheses for grouping, and nested if statements.

Question: What is the difference between ifelse() and if in R?
Answer: The ifelse() function is vectorized and returns a value for each element of a vector, while if handles single conditions.

Question: How does R handle NA values in conditional statements?
Answer: NA values in conditional statements cause the condition to be evaluated as NA, which is treated as neither TRUE nor FALSE, potentially leading to unexpected results.

Question: How do you use conditional statements with data frames in R?
Answer: Conditional statements can be used to filter or modify data frames by applying conditions to columns or rows.

Question: What is the role of the switch() function in conditional logic?
Answer: The switch() function allows branching based on the value of an expression, similar to a series of if-else statements.

Question: How do you write an if statement to check multiple independent conditions in R?
Answer: Multiple independent conditions can be checked using separate if, else if, and else statements.

Question: How do you execute different blocks of code based on the value of a variable in R?
Answer: Different blocks of code can be executed based on a variable's value using if-else statements or the switch() function.

Question: What is the purpose of using the ifelse() function?
Answer: The ifelse() function is used to perform vectorized conditional operations, returning values based on a condition for each element of a vector.

Question: How do you handle nested conditional statements effectively?
Answer: Nested conditional statements can be handled effectively by clearly indenting code, using comments, and minimizing nesting depth for readability.

Question: How do you avoid deeply nested if statements?
Answer: Deeply nested if statements can be avoided by using ifelse() for vectorized operations, the switch() function for multi-way branching, or breaking down complex conditions into separate functions.

Question: Can ifelse() handle multiple conditions?
Answer: ifelse() handles a single condition, but multiple conditions can be managed by chaining or nesting ifelse() calls.

Question: How do you use conditional statements to manage missing data in R?
Answer: Conditional statements can be used to check for missing data with is.na() and apply appropriate handling strategies, such as imputation or removal.

Question: How does switch() differ from ifelse()?
Answer: switch() is used for multi-way branching based on a single expression's value, while ifelse() is used for element-wise conditional operations in vectors.

Question: How do you execute code based on multiple variables in R?
Answer: Code execution based on multiple variables can be handled using multiple if statements, logical operators, or the switch() function.

Question: How do you ensure that all possible conditions are covered in conditional statements?
Answer: To ensure all possible conditions are covered, use else as a catch-all for any conditions not explicitly handled by if or else if.

Question: What happens when multiple if statements are true?
Answer: In a series of if, else if, and else statements, only the first true condition block is executed; subsequent else if or else blocks are ignored.

Question: How do you perform actions based on specific character strings in R?
Answer: Actions based on specific character strings can be performed using if statements or switch() with string comparisons.

Question: How do you use conditional statements within loops in R?
Answer: Conditional statements within loops allow for different actions to be performed in each iteration based on varying conditions.

Question: How do you exit a loop early using a conditional statement?
Answer: You can exit a loop early using a conditional statement combined with the break function when a certain condition is met.

Question: How do you write an if statement to check for multiple conditions simultaneously?
Answer: Multiple conditions can be checked simultaneously using logical operators within a single if statement, e.g., if (x > 0 & y < 10).

Question: How does the switch() function improve code readability compared to multiple ifelse() statements?
Answer: The switch() function improves readability by organizing code into a clear, concise structure for handling multiple discrete cases, reducing the need for complex, nested ifelse() statements.

Question: Can you use ifelse() for factor levels?
Answer: Yes, ifelse() can be used to return different factor levels based on a condition applied to a factor variable.

Question: How do you handle conditions with numeric ranges in R?
Answer: Numeric ranges can be handled using comparison operators combined with logical operators within an if statement, e.g., if (x > 10 & x <= 20).

Question: How do you use ifelse() to replace values in a vector?
Answer: ifelse() can replace values in a vector by returning the replacement values for elements that meet a specified condition, e.g., ifelse(x > 5, "High", "Low").

Question: What are common pitfalls in using conditional statements in R?
Answer: Common pitfalls include not accounting for NA values, misusing logical operators, and incorrectly nesting if statements, leading to unexpected results.

Question: How do you ensure that a condition in an if statement is always evaluated as TRUE or FALSE?
Answer: Ensure that conditions in an if statement are always logical expressions, and handle any NA or missing values that could cause ambiguity.

Question: How do you test multiple conditions on the same variable?
Answer: Multiple conditions on the same variable can be tested using else if or logical operators within a single if statement.

Question: How do you write conditional statements that return multiple values?
Answer: Conditional statements that return multiple values can be written using ifelse() for vectors or if-else blocks that return different data structures like lists or data frames.

Question: How do you use ifelse() to handle multiple conditions with different return values?
Answer: Multiple conditions with different return values can be handled by nesting ifelse() statements, though this can become complex and hard to read.

Looping Statements

Question: What are looping statements in R?
Answer: Looping statements in R are used to repeat a block of code multiple times. The main types are for, while, and repeat loops.

Question: How does a for loop work in R?
Answer: A for loop iterates over a sequence (like a vector or list) and executes a block of code for each element in the sequence.

Question: What is the syntax for a for loop in R?
Answer: The syntax for a for loop is for (variable in sequence) { # code }, where the code block is executed for each element of the sequence.

Question: How does a while loop work in R?
Answer: A while loop repeatedly executes a block of code as long as a specified condition remains TRUE.

Question: What is the syntax for a while loop in R?
Answer: The syntax for a while loop is while (condition) { # code }, where the code block is executed as long as the condition is TRUE.

Question: How does a repeat loop work in R?
Answer: A repeat loop repeatedly executes a block of code until a break statement is encountered.

Question: What is the syntax for a repeat loop in R?
Answer: The syntax for a repeat loop is repeat { # code; if (condition) break }, where the loop runs indefinitely until break is called.

Question: How do you exit a loop early in R?
Answer: You can exit a loop early using the break statement when a certain condition is met.

Question: How do you skip an iteration in a loop in R?
Answer: You can skip an iteration in a loop using the next statement, which immediately jumps to the next iteration.

Question: How do you loop over a list in R?
Answer: You can loop over a list using a for loop, e.g., for (element in list) { # code }.

Question: How do you handle loops with large datasets in R?
Answer: Handling loops with large datasets can be optimized by pre-allocating memory for results, minimizing operations within the loop, or using vectorized alternatives.

Question: How do you use nested loops in R?
Answer: Nested loops involve placing one loop inside another, allowing you to iterate over multiple sequences or dimensions simultaneously.

Question: What are the common uses of for loops in R?
Answer: Common uses of for loops include iterating over vectors, lists, or data frame rows to perform calculations, data manipulation, or apply functions.
Question: How can you loop over the columns of a data frame in R?
Answer: You can loop over the columns of a data frame using for (col in names(df)) { # code }.

Question: How do you ensure that a loop terminates in R?
Answer: Ensure that loops terminate by setting appropriate conditions for while or repeat loops, or using a break statement when a specific condition is met.

Question: How do you combine looping with conditional statements in R?
Answer: Combine looping with conditional statements by using if, else if, or switch() inside a loop to perform different actions based on the iteration's state.

Question: How do you iterate over a sequence of numbers in R?
Answer: You can iterate over a sequence of numbers using a for loop with a numeric vector, e.g., for (i in 1:10) { # code }.

Question: How do you apply a function to each element in a vector using a loop in R?
Answer: Apply a function to each element in a vector by using a for loop to iterate over the vector and call the function within the loop.

Question: What is the difference between while and repeat loops?
Answer: A while loop continues as long as a condition is TRUE, whereas a repeat loop runs indefinitely until a break statement is encountered.

Question: How do you create a loop that counts down in R?
Answer: A loop that counts down can be created using a for loop with a decreasing sequence, e.g., for (i in 10:1) { # code }.

Question: How do you use the seq() function in a loop?
Answer: The seq() function generates a sequence of numbers that can be used as the iteration sequence in a for loop, e.g., for (i in seq(1, 10, by=2)) { # code }.

Question: How do you loop through multiple vectors simultaneously in R?
Answer: Loop through multiple vectors simultaneously by using indexing within a for loop or by using mapply() for a vectorized approach.

Question: How do you accumulate results in a loop in R?
Answer: Accumulate results by initializing a variable outside the loop and updating it within each iteration, e.g., result <- result + value.

Question: How do you handle performance issues with loops in R?
Answer: Improve performance by using vectorized functions, avoiding unnecessary computations, and minimizing the use of loops when possible.

Question: How do you iterate over a matrix in R?
Answer: Iterate over a matrix by using nested for loops for rows and columns, e.g., for (i in 1:nrow(matrix)) { for (j in 1:ncol(matrix)) { # code } }.

Question: How do you loop over a data frame row by row in R?
Answer: Loop over a data frame row by row using for (i in 1:nrow(df)) { # code }.

Question: What is vectorization, and how does it relate to loops?
Answer: Vectorization is the process of applying operations directly on entire vectors without explicit loops, making code more efficient and concise.

Question: How do you avoid infinite loops in R?
Answer: Avoid infinite loops by ensuring that loop conditions will eventually be FALSE, or by using break statements to terminate the loop.

Question: How do you implement a loop that runs until a specific condition is met in R?
Answer: Implement such a loop using a while or repeat loop with the condition checked within the loop body.

Question: How do you use the lapply() function as an alternative to loops?
Answer: The lapply() function applies a function to each element of a list, returning a list of results, often used as a loop alternative.
Question: How do you iterate over a character vector in R?
Answer: Iterate over a character vector using a for loop, e.g., for (char in c("a", "b", "c")) { # code }.

Question: How do you terminate a loop when a condition is met within the loop?
Answer: Terminate the loop using a break statement when the specified condition is met.

Question: How do you update a variable within a loop in R?
Answer: Update a variable within a loop by reassigning it in each iteration, e.g., sum <- sum + value.

Question: How do you create a loop that repeats a specific number of times in R?
Answer: Create such a loop using a for loop with a predefined sequence, e.g., for (i in 1:n) { # code }.

Question: How do you check loop progress in R?
Answer: Check loop progress by printing the iteration number or a status message within the loop, e.g., print(paste("Iteration", i)).

Jump Statements

Question: What are jump statements in R?
Answer: Jump statements in R control the flow of loops by allowing you to skip iterations or exit the loop early. The primary jump statements are break and next.

Question: How do you use the break statement in R?
Answer: The break statement exits a loop immediately when encountered, skipping any remaining iterations.

Question: How do you use the next statement in R?
Answer: The next statement skips the current iteration of a loop and moves to the next iteration.

Question: What happens when a break statement is executed in a loop?
Answer: When a break statement is executed, the loop terminates immediately, and the program continues with the code following the loop.

Question: How do you exit a loop based on a condition using break?
Answer: Exit a loop based on a condition by placing a break statement inside an if condition within the loop.

Question: What is the difference between break and next in R?
Answer: break exits the loop entirely, while next skips the current iteration and continues with the next one.

Question: Can you use break and next in the same loop?
Answer: Yes, you can use both break and next in the same loop to control the flow based on different conditions.

Question: How do you handle multiple break conditions in a loop?
Answer: Handle multiple break conditions by using separate if statements for each condition within the loop.

Question: How do you prevent a loop from running indefinitely?
Answer: Prevent a loop from running indefinitely by ensuring that the loop's exit condition will eventually be met or by using a break statement.

Question: How do you skip the first few iterations of a loop in R?
Answer: Skip the first few iterations using an if condition combined with next, e.g., if (i <= n) next.

Question: How do you exit nested loops using break?
Answer: Exiting nested loops requires a break statement in each loop level or restructuring the code to allow for a single break to exit all loops.

Question: Can you use break in functions other than loops?
Answer: No, break is specifically designed for use within loops in R.

Question: What is the purpose of the return statement in a function, and how does it differ from break?
Answer: The return statement exits a function and returns a value, while break exits a loop without returning a value.

Question: How do you ensure that a loop runs a minimum number of times before checking for a break condition?
Answer: Ensure the loop runs a minimum number of times by structuring the loop's condition or using a counter that allows break only after a certain number of iterations.

Question: How do you continue a loop after handling an error using next?
Answer: Continue a loop after handling an error by placing error-handling code before the next statement, ensuring the loop can proceed to the next iteration.

Question: How do you handle loops with multiple next statements for different conditions?
Answer: Handle loops with multiple next statements by using separate if conditions for each scenario that requires skipping an iteration.

Question: What is a practical use case for the next statement in R?
Answer: A practical use case for next is skipping invalid or missing data points in a loop that processes elements of a vector or data frame.

Question: How do you use break to exit a loop after a certain number of successful iterations?
Answer: Track the number of successful iterations with a counter and use break when the counter reaches the desired number.

Question: Can break be used in repeat loops?
Answer: Yes, break is commonly used in repeat loops to exit the loop when a specific condition is met.

Question: How do you implement a loop that continues running until a condition is met, using break?
Answer: Implement such a loop using while(TRUE) or repeat, and include a break statement inside an if condition to exit the loop when the condition is satisfied.

Question: How do you skip even-numbered iterations in a loop using next?
Answer: Skip even-numbered iterations by checking the iteration index with if (i %% 2 == 0) next.

Question: How do you use next in a loop to avoid processing NA values?
Answer: Use next in combination with if (is.na(value)) next to skip iterations with NA values.

Question: How do you control the execution flow in nested loops using break and next?
Answer: Control execution flow by strategically placing break and next statements in the inner and outer loops based on the desired logic.

Question: How do you handle the loop index when using next?
Answer: The loop index automatically increments when using next, so no additional handling is required.

Question: How do you ensure that break only exits the current loop in nested loops?
Answer: Ensure that break only exits the current loop by using it in the innermost loop, allowing the outer loop to continue.

Question: How do you optimize loop performance when using next frequently?
Answer: Optimize loop performance by minimizing unnecessary computations before the next statement and using vectorized operations where possible.

Question: How do you avoid infinite loops when using break?
Answer: Avoid infinite loops by ensuring that the break condition is correctly defined and will eventually be met.

Question: How do you use break to exit a loop based on a user input condition?
Answer: Use break within an if condition that checks for user input, allowing the loop to exit when the user specifies.

Question: Can break be used in combination with tryCatch for error handling in loops?
Answer: Yes, break can be used within a tryCatch block to exit the loop if an error occurs, depending on the error handling logic.

Question: How do you resume a loop after an error using next?
Answer: Resume the loop after an error by using next within the catch block of tryCatch, allowing the loop to skip the problematic iteration.

Question: How do you manage loop counters when using break and next?
Answer: Loop counters are automatically managed by R; however, you may need to manually adjust counters or indices if you implement complex loop logic.

Question: How do you handle situations where both break and next might be triggered in the same loop?
Answer: Prioritize the conditions for break and next by placing the break condition first to exit the loop entirely if necessary, and next for skipping iterations when the loop continues.

Question: How do you use next to avoid processing specific data points in a loop?
Answer: Use next within an if statement that identifies the data points to be skipped, allowing the loop to continue with the remaining data.

Question: How do you exit a loop based on multiple criteria using break?
Answer: Exit the loop using break within an if statement that checks for all criteria, combining conditions with logical operators as needed.

Functions in R

Question: What is a function in R?
Answer: A function in R is a block of code designed to perform a specific task. Functions can take arguments, process them, and return a result.

Question: How do you define a function in R?
Answer: A function is defined using the function keyword, e.g., my_function <- function(arg1, arg2) { # code }.

Question: What is the purpose of the return() function in R?
Answer: The return() function specifies the value that a function should return to the caller.

Question: Can a function in R return multiple values?
Answer: Yes, a function in R can return multiple values by combining them in a list or a vector.

Question: How do you call a function in R?
Answer: A function is called by using its name followed by parentheses enclosing any required arguments, e.g., result <- my_function(1, 2).

Question: How do you pass arguments to a function in R?
Answer: Arguments are passed to a function by specifying them within the parentheses when calling the function.

Question: What are default arguments in a function, and how are they used?
Answer: Default arguments are specified in the function definition, allowing the function to use those values if no argument is provided by the caller.

Question: How do you create a function with optional arguments in R?
Answer: Optional arguments are created by assigning default values in the function definition, e.g., my_function <- function(x, y=10) { # code }.

Question: What is an anonymous function in R?
Answer: An anonymous function is a function without a name, often used in situations where a function is needed temporarily, e.g., lapply(1:5, function(x) x^2).

Question: How do you document a function in R?
Answer: Functions are documented using comments within the function code or by creating a help file if the function is part of a package.

Question: What is the difference between return() and simply placing a value at the end of a function in R?
Answer: In R, a function returns the last evaluated expression by default, but using return() makes the return behavior explicit and allows for early returns.

Question: Can functions in R have no arguments?
Answer: Yes, functions can be defined without arguments, e.g., my_function <- function() { # code }.

Question: How do you handle variable arguments in a function?
Answer: Variable arguments are handled using the ... notation, allowing a function to accept any number of additional arguments.

Question: How do you create a recursive function in R?
Answer: A recursive function is created by defining a function that calls itself within its own definition.

Question: What are the advantages of using functions in R?
Answer: Functions promote code reuse, modularity, and clarity, making code easier to manage, test, and debug.

Question: How do you pass a function as an argument to another function in R?
Answer: A function is passed as an argument by providing the function name without parentheses, e.g., apply(X, MARGIN, sum).

Question: How do you define a function inside another function in R?
Answer: A function can be defined inside another function by including the inner function's definition within the body of the outer function.

Question: What is the scope of a variable inside a function in R?
Answer: Variables inside a function have local scope, meaning they are only accessible within the function and do not affect variables outside the function.

Question: How do you create a function that returns another function in R?
Answer: A function that returns another function can be created by defining the inner function and returning it from the outer function.

Question: How do you handle errors within a function in R?
Answer: Errors within a function can be handled using tryCatch() or by validating input arguments and returning informative error messages.

Question: Can a function modify a global variable in R?
Answer: Yes, a function can modify a global variable using the <<- operator, although this is generally discouraged in favor of returning values and reassigning them.

Question: How do you make a function return early in R?
Answer: A function can return early using the return() function when a certain condition is met.

Question: How do you pass named arguments to a function in R?
Answer: Named arguments are passed by specifying the argument names in the function call, e.g., my_function(x=1, y=2).

Question: How do you create a function that operates on multiple data types?
Answer: A function can operate on multiple data types by using conditional checks or generic functions that handle different types within the function body.

Question: How do you check the arguments passed to a function in R?
Answer: The arguments passed to a function can be checked using the missing() function or by manually validating each argument.

Question: How do you write a function that works with both vectors and lists?
Answer: Write a function that checks the input type using is.vector() or is.list() and processes the input accordingly.

Question: What is the use of the environment() function in relation to functions in R?
Answer: The environment() function returns the environment in which a function was created, which can be useful for understanding variable scope and closures.

Question: How do you use closures in R functions?
Answer: Closures in R are functions that capture the environment in which they were created, allowing them to retain access to local variables even after the outer function has exited.

Question: How do you define a function that accepts a data frame as an argument in R?
Answer: Define the function with a data frame as an argument and use typical data frame operations within the function body.

Question: How do you handle different return types in a function in R?
Answer: Handle different return types by using conditional statements to return the appropriate data structure based on input or processing.

Question: How do you write a function that returns a plot in R?
Answer: A function that returns a plot can be written by including the plotting code within the function and returning the plot object if necessary.
Question: How do you create a function that applies a specific transformation to a data set?
Answer: Create a function that takes the data set as an argument and includes the transformation logic within the function body, returning the transformed data.

Question: How do you optimize the performance of a function in R?
Answer: Optimize function performance by minimizing unnecessary computations, using vectorized operations, and avoiding side effects like modifying global variables.

Question: How do you write a function that handles missing data in R?
Answer: Write a function that checks for missing data using is.na() and applies the appropriate handling strategy, such as imputation or removal, before processing the data.

Question: How do you create a function that outputs multiple results?
Answer: A function can output multiple results by returning a list, where each element of the list represents a different result.

Actual Arguments

Question: What are actual arguments in R?
Answer: Actual arguments are the values or variables passed to a function when it is called. These are the inputs that the function processes.

Question: How do you pass actual arguments to a function in R?
Answer: Actual arguments are passed to a function by specifying them in the parentheses during the function call, e.g., my_function(arg1, arg2).

Question: Can actual arguments be expressions in R?
Answer: Yes, actual arguments can be expressions that are evaluated before being passed to the function.

Question: How do you handle missing actual arguments in a function call in R?
Answer: Missing actual arguments can be handled by defining default values in the function signature or by checking for missing arguments within the function using missing().

Question: How do you pass multiple arguments to a function in R?
Answer: Multiple arguments are passed by separating them with commas in the function call, e.g., my_function(arg1, arg2, arg3).

Question: How are actual arguments matched to formal parameters in R?
Answer: Actual arguments are matched to formal parameters by position or by name. If names are provided, they take precedence over position.

Question: How do you ensure that actual arguments match the expected data type in R?
Answer: Ensure that actual arguments match the expected data type by validating them within the function using is.numeric(), is.character(), etc.

Question: What happens if too few actual arguments are provided in R?
Answer: If too few actual arguments are provided, and there are no defaults, R will generate an error indicating that some arguments are missing.

Question: How do you handle excess actual arguments in a function call in R?
Answer: Excess actual arguments can be handled by including ... in the function signature, allowing the function to accept additional arguments.

Question: Can actual arguments be modified within a function in R?
Answer: Actual arguments can be modified within the function, but these changes do not affect the original variables outside the function unless passed by reference.

Question: How do you pass a data frame as an actual argument in R?
Answer: A data frame is passed as an actual argument by specifying it in the function call, e.g., my_function(df).

Question: How do you handle actual arguments that are functions themselves in R?
Answer: Actual arguments that are functions can be passed and invoked within the function body using their names, e.g., result <- fun(arg).

Question: How do you pass a variable number of actual arguments in R?
Answer: A variable number of actual arguments can be passed using ... in the function signature, and accessed within the function using list(...).

Question: What is lazy evaluation of actual arguments in R?
Answer: Lazy evaluation means that actual arguments are not evaluated until they are actually used within the function body.

Question: How do you use do.call() with actual arguments in R?
Answer: do.call() is used to call a function with a list of actual arguments, e.g., do.call("my_function", list(arg1, arg2)).

Question: How do you pass named actual arguments in R?
Answer: Named actual arguments are passed by specifying the parameter name followed by =, e.g., my_function(x=1, y=2).

Question: Can actual arguments be passed as a list in R?
Answer: Yes, actual arguments can be passed as a list using do.call() or by using list(...) within the function.

Question: How do you pass a matrix as an actual argument in R?
Answer: A matrix is passed as an actual argument in the same way as other objects, e.g., my_function(matrix).

Question: How do you handle actual arguments with missing values in R?
Answer: Handle actual arguments with missing values by checking for NA or NULL within the function and applying appropriate handling strategies.

Question: How do you specify default values for actual arguments in R?
Answer: Default values for actual arguments are specified in the function definition, e.g., my_function(x=10).

Question: How do you modify actual arguments within a function and return the modified values in R?
Answer: Modify actual arguments within the function and return the modified values by including them in the return() statement or as part of a list.

Question: How do you pass actual arguments by reference in R?
Answer: In R, arguments are passed by value, but you can simulate pass-by-reference by modifying elements of objects like lists or environments.

Question: How do you pass an actual argument conditionally in R?
Answer: Pass an actual argument conditionally by using an if statement or ifelse() to determine which argument to pass.

Question: How do you validate actual arguments within a function in R?
Answer: Validate actual arguments by using checks like is.numeric(), is.character(), and custom error messages to ensure that the function receives the correct input.

Question: How do you pass actual arguments that are vectors in R?
Answer: Pass vector arguments in the same way as other types, e.g., my_function(c(1, 2, 3)).

Question: How do you use match.call() to retrieve the actual arguments passed to a function in R?
Answer: match.call() retrieves the function call with the actual arguments, which can be used for debugging or logging.

Question: How do you handle missing actual arguments in a custom way in R?
Answer: Handle missing actual arguments by using the missing() function to check for their presence and provide default behavior or values if absent.

Question: How do you pass an environment as an actual argument in R?
Answer: Pass an environment as an actual argument by specifying it in the function call, allowing the function to access or modify the environment's variables.

Question: How do you handle conflicts between actual arguments and default values in R?
Answer: Handle conflicts by giving precedence to actual arguments passed by the user over default values specified in the function definition.

Question: Can actual arguments be passed as symbols in R?
Answer: Yes, actual arguments can be passed as symbols and then evaluated within the function using eval().

Question: How do you use formals() to inspect the formal parameters of a function before passing actual arguments in R?
Answer: Use formals() to retrieve the list of formal parameters and their default values, helping to match actual arguments correctly.

Question: How do you pass a list of actual arguments to a function expecting multiple parameters in R?
Answer: Pass a list of actual arguments using do.call(), which unpacks the list and matches its elements to the function's parameters.

Question: How do you use on.exit() in relation to actual arguments in R?
Answer: on.exit() can be used to perform actions after a function has completed, such as cleaning up resources related to actual arguments.

Question: How do you ensure that actual arguments are passed in the correct order in R?
Answer: Ensure correct order by either relying on positional matching or explicitly naming the arguments when passing them to the function.

Question: How do you pass a factor as an actual argument in R?
Answer: Pass a factor in the same way as other objects, ensuring that the function is designed to handle factors appropriately.

Named Arguments

Question: What are named arguments in R?
Answer: Named arguments are arguments passed to a function by explicitly naming them, allowing for more readable code and flexibility in the order of arguments.

Question: How do you pass named arguments to a function in R?
Answer: Named arguments are passed by specifying the parameter name followed by =, e.g., my_function(arg1=10, arg2=20).

Question: What is the advantage of using named arguments in R?
Answer: Named arguments improve code readability and make it easier to understand the function call, especially when there are multiple or optional parameters.

Question: Can named arguments be used out of order in a function call?
Answer: Yes, named arguments can be provided in any order when calling a function, as long as they are named correctly.

Question: How do you combine named and positional arguments in a function call?
Answer: Named and positional arguments can be combined, but positional arguments must come before any named arguments.

Question: What happens if you use the wrong name for an argument in R?
Answer: If the wrong name is used for an argument, R will generate an error indicating that the argument is not recognized.

Question: Can you omit some arguments when using named arguments?
Answer: Yes, you can omit arguments that have default values when using named arguments, allowing the function to use the defaults.

Question: How does R handle partially matched named arguments?
Answer: R allows partial matching of named arguments, where a unique prefix of the argument name is sufficient to identify it, although this can lead to ambiguity.

Question: How do you avoid ambiguity with partially matched named arguments?
Answer: Avoid ambiguity by fully specifying the argument names or using named arguments that do not overlap in their prefixes.

Question: How do named arguments interact with the ... parameter in R?
Answer: Named arguments can be passed through the ... parameter to other functions, allowing for flexible and dynamic argument handling.

Question: How do you specify default values for named arguments in R?
Answer: Default values are specified in the function definition, e.g., my_function(arg1=10).

Question: Can you use named arguments with the apply() family of functions?
Answer: Yes, named arguments can be passed to the apply() family of functions, either directly or through .

Question: How do you document named arguments in a function?
Answer: Named arguments are documented in the function's help file or comments, specifying their purpose and any default values.

Question: What is the impact of named arguments on function flexibility?
Answer: Named arguments increase function flexibility by allowing users to specify only the arguments they need and to provide them in any order.

Question: How do you handle named arguments with match.call()?
Answer: match.call() captures the named arguments as they were passed to the function, which can be useful for debugging or re-evaluating the function call.

Question: How do you ensure that named arguments are used correctly in large functions?
Answer: Ensure correct use by clearly documenting each named argument, using meaningful names, and validating arguments within the function.

Question: How do named arguments affect the order of argument matching in R?
Answer: Named arguments are matched by name first, followed by positional matching for any unnamed arguments, ensuring that the correct parameters receive the intended values.

Question: Can named arguments be used with anonymous functions in R?
Answer: Yes, named arguments can be used with anonymous functions, allowing you to specify which arguments are being passed even in short, inline functions.

Question: How do you pass named arguments to a function inside a loop in R?
Answer: Named arguments can be passed inside a loop by including them in the function call within the loop, ensuring that each iteration uses the correct values.

Question: How do you deal with conflicting named arguments in nested function calls?
Answer: Handle conflicts by explicitly naming all arguments in the nested function calls and ensuring that each function receives the correct arguments.

Question: Can named arguments be used with S3 and S4 methods in R?
Answer: Yes, named arguments can be used with S3 and S4 methods, and they are particularly useful for dispatching the correct method based on argument names.

Question: How do you check if a named argument was passed to a function?
Answer: Check if a named argument was passed using the missing() function or by checking the argument's value against its default.

Question: How do named arguments interact with default arguments in R?
Answer: Named arguments override default arguments if provided by the user, while any arguments not explicitly passed will use their default values.

Question: How do you use named arguments to improve the clarity of function calls?
Answer: Improve clarity by always using named arguments in function calls, especially when dealing with functions that have many parameters or where the purpose of each parameter is not immediately obvious.

Question: How do you validate named arguments within a function?
Answer: Validate named arguments by checking their types, values, and ensuring they meet the function's requirements using conditional statements.

Question: Can named arguments be passed as a list in R?
Answer: Yes, named arguments can be passed as a list and unpacked within the function using do.call().

Question: How do you ensure that named arguments are correctly matched in functions with ...?
Answer: Ensure correct matching by clearly documenting which arguments are expected in ... and validating them within the function.

Question: How do named arguments affect function overloading in R?
Answer: Named arguments can be used to differentiate between overloaded functions, allowing the same function name to handle different argument sets.

Question: How do you handle optional named arguments in R?
Answer: Handle optional named arguments by providing default values and using conditional checks to see if they were provided by the user.

Question: How do you override default named arguments in a function call?
Answer: Override default named arguments by explicitly specifying new values when calling the function, e.g., my_function(arg1=20).

Question: How do named arguments interact with ... in recursive functions?
Answer: In recursive functions, named arguments passed through ... can be forwarded to subsequent recursive calls, allowing for flexible argument passing.

Question: How do you ensure compatibility when passing named arguments between functions?
Answer: Ensure compatibility by using consistent naming conventions and argument types across functions that are intended to work together.

Question: Can named arguments be combined with partial matching in R?
Answer: Yes, named arguments can be combined with partial matching, though it's recommended to use full names to avoid ambiguity.

Question: How do you document the expected named arguments in a function's help file?
Answer: Document the expected named arguments by listing them under the "Arguments" section of the help file, including their purpose, type, and default values if applicable.

Question: How do you pass named arguments from one function to another?
Answer: Pass named arguments from one function to another using ..., or by explicitly naming and passing each argument.

Question: How do you handle named arguments in functions that accept ...?
Answer: Handle named arguments in functions with ... by unpacking them using list(...) or by passing them to another function using do.call().

Question: How do you ensure that named arguments are consistent across related functions?
Answer: Ensure consistency by using the same names, types, and default values for arguments that serve the same purpose across related functions.

Global & Local Variables

Question: What is a global variable in R?
Answer: A global variable is a variable that is defined in the global environment and can be accessed from anywhere in the R session.

Question: What is a local variable in R?
Answer: A local variable is a variable that is defined within a function and is only accessible within that function's scope.

Question: How do you create a global variable in R?
Answer: A global variable is created by assigning a value to a variable in the global environment, typically by direct assignment outside of any function.

Question: How do you create a local variable in R?
Answer: A local variable is created by assigning a value to a variable inside a function. It is only accessible within that function.

Question: What happens if a global and a local variable have the same name in R?
Answer: If a global and a local variable have the same name, the local variable takes precedence within the function, while the global variable remains unchanged outside the function.

Question: How do you modify a global variable within a function in R?
Answer: A global variable can be modified within a function using the <<- operator.

Question: Can a function return a local variable in R?
Answer: Yes, a function can return a local variable, and the returned value can be stored in a global variable or used elsewhere.

Question: How do you list all global variables in R?
Answer: All global variables can be listed using the ls() function in the global environment.

Question: How do you check the value of a global variable inside a function?
Answer: You can check the value of a global variable inside a function by referencing it directly, as long as the variable is not overwritten locally.

Question: How do you avoid unintended modification of global variables in R?
Answer: Avoid unintended modification of global variables by using local variables within functions, returning values explicitly, and avoiding the use of <<-.

Question: What is the environment() function used for in relation to variables?
Answer: The environment() function returns the environment in which a variable or function was created, helping to understand its scope.

Question: How do you explicitly create a variable in the global environment from within a function?
Answer: A variable can be explicitly created in the global environment from within a function using the <<- operator or assign() with envir = .GlobalEnv.

Question: How do you check if a variable is global or local in R?
Answer: Check if a variable is global or local by examining its environment using environment() or by checking for its existence in the global environment with exists().

Question: How do you pass global variables to a function in R?
Answer: Global variables can be passed to a function by including them as arguments in the function call.

Question: How do you ensure that changes to a variable inside a function do not affect the global variable with the same name?
Answer: Ensure that changes do not affect the global variable by using a different name for the local variable or by explicitly returning the modified value without using <<-.

Question: How do you access global variables from within nested functions in R?
Answer: Access global variables from within nested functions by referencing them directly, as long as they are not overwritten by local variables of the same name.

Question: How do you create a local variable within a function that has the same name as a global variable?
Answer: Create a local variable with the same name as a global variable by simply assigning a value to that name within the function. The local variable will shadow the global variable within the function.

Question: What is the difference between <<- and ->> operators in R?
Answer: Both operators are used to assign values in the parent environment, but <<- assigns from left to right, while ->> assigns from right to left.

Question: How do you remove a global variable in R?
Answer: A global variable can be removed using the rm() function, e.g., rm(variable_name).

Question: How do you debug issues with global and local variable conflicts?
Answer: Debug conflicts by using the ls() function to list variables in the current environment, environment() to check scope, and print() statements to track variable values.

Question: How do you use environments to manage global and local variables in R?
Answer: Use environments to create isolated scopes where variables are managed independently, helping to prevent conflicts and unintended modifications.

Question: How do you ensure that a variable remains local within a function?
Answer: Ensure that a variable remains local by defining and using it exclusively within the function, and avoiding <<- for assignments.

Question: How do you share variables between functions without making them global?
Answer: Share variables between functions by passing them as arguments or by using closures to capture and retain the variable's environment.

Question: How do you modify a variable in the parent function from a nested function?
Answer: Modify a variable in the parent function by using the <<- operator or by returning the modified value from the nested function and reassigning it in the parent function.

Question: How do you use with() or within() to manage variable scope in R?
Answer: Use with() or within() to evaluate expressions within a specific environment, allowing for temporary variable creation and modification without affecting the global environment.

Question: How do you avoid side effects when working with global variables in functions?
Answer: Avoid side effects by minimizing the use of global variables, using local variables within functions, and returning results explicitly instead of modifying global state.

Question: Can local variables be accessed outside the function after the function has been executed?
Answer: No, local variables are not accessible outside the function after it has been executed unless they are returned or assigned to a global variable.

Question: How do you use get() to access a global variable from within a function?
Answer: Use get("variable_name", envir = .GlobalEnv) to access a global variable from within a function.

Question: How do you use assign() to create a global variable from within a function?
Answer: Use assign("variable_name", value, envir = .GlobalEnv) to create or modify a global variable from within a function.

Question: How do you manage variable scope when using lapply() or sapply()?
Answer: Manage variable scope by ensuring that variables needed inside the applied function are passed as arguments or are globally accessible.

Question: How do you handle variable conflicts when using loops that modify global variables?
Answer: Handle conflicts by using local variables within the loop, or by carefully managing updates to global variables to avoid unintended side effects.

Question: How do you track the creation and modification of global variables during script execution?
Answer: Track global variables by periodically using ls() to list them, and print() statements to output their values at key points in the script.

Question: How do you encapsulate functionality to avoid global variable pollution in R?
Answer: Encapsulate functionality by writing functions that use local variables and return results, minimizing the creation of global variables.

Question: How do you handle complex data structures that require both global and local variable management?
Answer: Handle complex data structures by passing them explicitly between functions, using environments to manage scope, and avoiding direct modification of global variables.

Argument & Lazy Evaluation

Question: What is lazy evaluation in R?
Answer: Lazy evaluation in R means that function arguments are not evaluated until they are actually used within the function body.

Question: How does lazy evaluation affect function performance in R?
Answer: Lazy evaluation can improve function performance by avoiding unnecessary computations, as arguments are only evaluated when needed.

Question: How do you trigger the evaluation of an argument in R?
Answer: An argument is triggered for evaluation when it is referenced within the function body.

Question: What is the advantage of lazy evaluation in R?
Answer: The advantage of lazy evaluation is that it allows for efficient execution by deferring the computation of arguments until absolutely necessary, potentially skipping unnecessary computations.

Question: Can lazy evaluation lead to unexpected behavior in R?
Answer: Yes, lazy evaluation can lead to unexpected behavior if arguments that are never used contain errors or if their expected side effects are not triggered.

Question: How do you force the evaluation of an argument in R?
Answer: Force the evaluation of an argument by explicitly using it within the function, or by calling force(argument).

Question: How does lazy evaluation interact with default arguments in R?
Answer: Default arguments are also lazily evaluated, meaning they are only computed when the argument is not provided and is used within the function.

Question: How do you handle side effects in functions that use lazy evaluation?
Answer: Handle side effects by ensuring that arguments with important side effects are evaluated as soon as possible within the function.

Question: How do you use force() to ensure an argument is evaluated in R?
Answer: Use force(argument) at the beginning of the function to ensure that the argument is evaluated immediately upon function execution.

Question: What happens if an argument is never used in a function with lazy evaluation?
Answer: If an argument is never used, it is never evaluated, which can lead to improved performance but may also skip important computations or side effects.

Question: How does lazy evaluation interact with the ... argument in R?
Answer: Lazy evaluation applies to each argument passed through ..., with each being evaluated only when referenced within the function.

Question: How do you debug issues related to lazy evaluation in R?
Answer: Debug lazy evaluation issues by explicitly forcing evaluation with force(), using print statements to track when arguments are evaluated, and checking for unexpected behavior.

Question: Can lazy evaluation be disabled in R?
Answer: No, lazy evaluation is a core feature of R's function evaluation model and cannot be disabled, but you can force evaluation when needed.

Question: How do you ensure that all arguments are evaluated in a function?
Answer: Ensure all arguments are evaluated by referencing each one within the function or by using force() on each argument at the beginning of the function.

Question: How does lazy evaluation affect the use of functions with side effects?
Answer: Lazy evaluation can delay or prevent the execution of functions with side effects, so it's important to ensure that such functions are called directly within the function body.

Question: How do you manage dependencies between arguments in a function with lazy evaluation?
Answer: Manage dependencies by carefully ordering the evaluation of arguments within the function body and using force() if necessary to ensure proper sequence.

Question: How does lazy evaluation work with vectorized operations in R?
Answer: Lazy evaluation defers the computation of vectorized operations until they are actually used, potentially optimizing performance by avoiding unnecessary calculations.

Question: How do you test for lazy evaluation in R?
Answer: Test for lazy evaluation by creating functions where arguments are conditionally used, and observing when and if they are evaluated.

Question: How do you handle errors in lazily evaluated arguments?
Answer: Handle errors by ensuring that arguments are evaluated early if their correctness is critical, or by using error handling techniques to catch issues when they are evaluated.

Question: What are the limitations of lazy evaluation in R?
Answer: Limitations include potential confusion about when arguments are evaluated, delayed detection of errors, and the need to explicitly manage side effects.

Question: How do you document functions that rely on lazy evaluation?
Answer: Document such functions by clearly explaining which arguments are lazily evaluated, and providing guidance on when and how they will be used.

Question: Can you control the order of argument evaluation in R?
Answer: The order of argument evaluation is controlled by the order in which they are used within the function body, with earlier references leading to earlier evaluation.

Question: How do you use lazy evaluation to optimize functions with optional arguments?
Answer: Optimize functions by only evaluating optional arguments when they are actually needed, thereby saving computational resources if they are not used.

Question: How does lazy evaluation impact recursive functions in R?
Answer: In recursive functions, lazy evaluation can delay the evaluation of arguments until the base case is reached, potentially optimizing the recursive process.

Question: How do you ensure that arguments with side effects are evaluated in the correct order?
Answer: Ensure the correct order by explicitly evaluating arguments with side effects early in the function, or by structuring the function logic to control the sequence.

Question: How do you pass lazily evaluated arguments to another function in R?
Answer: Pass lazily evaluated arguments by using force() if you need them evaluated before passing, or by passing them as-is and allowing the receiving function to evaluate them as needed.

Question: How does lazy evaluation interact with conditionally executed code?
Answer: Lazy evaluation interacts with conditionally executed code by only evaluating arguments when their condition is met, potentially skipping evaluation entirely if the condition is false.

Question: How do you use lazy evaluation to defer computation in performance-critical functions?
Answer: Defer computation by structuring the function so that only the necessary arguments are evaluated based on the input, allowing for optimized performance in critical scenarios.

Question: How do you handle lazy evaluation in functions that rely on external data sources?
Answer: Handle it by ensuring that any necessary data is available before the argument is used, or by forcing evaluation early if access to the external source is time-sensitive.

Question: How do you explain lazy evaluation to someone new to R?
Answer: Explain lazy evaluation as a feature where R delays computing an argument until it's actually needed in the function, which can make programs more efficient but requires careful consideration of when things happen.

Question: How does lazy evaluation interact with debugging tools in R?
Answer: Lazy evaluation can complicate debugging by delaying the appearance of errors; using debugging tools like trace() or debug() can help identify when arguments are evaluated.

Question: Can lazy evaluation be used to create more flexible functions?
Answer: Yes, lazy evaluation allows for more flexible functions by enabling conditional and delayed computation, which can adapt to the specific needs of the function's usage.

Question: How do you prevent unintended consequences of lazy evaluation?
Answer: Prevent unintended consequences by carefully designing functions to control when arguments are evaluated, using force() for critical arguments, and thoroughly testing the function's behavior.

Question: How do you optimize functions for lazy evaluation?
Answer: Optimize functions by minimizing the number of arguments that need to be evaluated, using conditional logic to skip unnecessary evaluations, and ensuring that side effects are properly managed.

Question: How do you compare the behavior of functions with and without lazy evaluation?
Answer: Compare behaviors by creating two versions of a function, one that uses lazy evaluation and one that forces all arguments, and then testing them with various inputs to observe differences in performance and outcomes.

Question: How do you manage lazy evaluation in functions that are part of a larger workflow?
Answer: Manage it by ensuring that the workflow accounts for when arguments are evaluated, potentially using force() to synchronize evaluations across functions in the workflow.

Recursive Function

Question: What is a recursive function in R?
Answer: A recursive function is a function that calls itself within its own definition to solve a problem by breaking it down into smaller, more manageable sub-problems.

Question: How do you define a recursive function in R?
Answer: A recursive function is defined like any other function, but it includes a call to itself within its body, typically with modified arguments to progress toward a base case.

Question: What is the base case in a recursive function?
Answer: The base case is the condition under which the recursion stops, preventing infinite recursion and allowing the function to return a result.

Question: How do you prevent infinite recursion in R?
Answer: Prevent infinite recursion by ensuring that the recursive function has a well-defined base case that will eventually be met.

Question: Can a recursive function return multiple values in R?
Answer: Yes, a recursive function can return multiple values by combining them into a list or vector as it unwinds the recursion.

Question: How do you handle large inputs in a recursive function?
Answer: Handle large inputs by ensuring that the recursion depth does not exceed the system's stack limit, or by converting the recursion to an iterative process if necessary.

Question: What is tail recursion, and how is it used in R?
Answer: Tail recursion is a special case of recursion where the recursive call is the last operation in the function. It can be optimized by the compiler to reduce the overhead of repeated function calls.

Question: How do you debug a recursive function in R?
Answer: Debug a recursive function by using print statements to track the flow of recursion, or by using R's debugging tools like trace() and debug().

Question: How do you ensure that a recursive function converges to a solution?
Answer: Ensure convergence by carefully designing the recursive logic to move closer to the base case with each recursive call.

Question: Can recursive functions be used with lists in R?
Answer: Yes, recursive functions can process lists by recursing through list elements or nested lists, handling each level of the list structure.

Question: How do you optimize a recursive function in R?
Answer: Optimize a recursive function by minimizing redundant calculations, using memoization to store intermediate results, or converting it to an iterative solution if possible.

Question: What are the performance considerations for using recursion in R?
Answer: Performance considerations include stack depth limitations, the overhead of repeated function calls, and the potential inefficiency of solving large problems without optimization techniques.

Question: How do you convert a recursive function to an iterative one in R?
Answer: Convert recursion to iteration by using loops to simulate the recursive process, maintaining a stack or queue to manage state across iterations.

Question: How do you apply recursion to solve a factorial problem in R?
Answer: Apply recursion to a factorial problem by defining the factorial function as factorial(n) = n * factorial(n-1), with a base case of factorial(1) = 1.

Question: How does recursion work with tree structures in R?
Answer: Recursion works with tree structures by recursively processing each node, typically handling left and right children in binary trees or multiple children in more complex structures.

Question: How do you use recursion to traverse a directory structure in R?
Answer: Use recursion to traverse a directory structure by defining a function that processes a directory, then recursively calls itself on each subdirectory.

Question: What is mutual recursion in R?
Answer: Mutual recursion occurs when two or more functions call each other in a cyclical manner, often used to solve problems where different parts of the problem require different processing logic.

Question: How do you track the depth of recursion in R?
Answer: Track the depth by including a counter argument in the recursive function that increments with each call, allowing you to monitor or limit the recursion depth.

Question: How do you use recursion to implement a Fibonacci sequence generator in R?
Answer: Implement a Fibonacci sequence generator by defining a function that returns the sum of the previous two Fibonacci numbers, with base cases for the first two numbers.

Question: How do you handle recursive functions that require backtracking in R?
Answer: Handle backtracking by carefully managing the state within each recursive call and using conditional logic to explore different paths or options.

Question: How does recursion compare to iteration in terms of readability in R?
Answer: Recursion can often be more readable for problems naturally suited to recursive thinking, such as tree traversal, while iteration may be clearer for straightforward loops.

Question: What are common pitfalls when using recursion in R?
Answer: Common pitfalls include missing base cases, causing infinite recursion; exceeding stack limits; and inefficiently handling large inputs without optimization.

Question: How do you write a recursive function to solve a maze in R?
Answer: Write a recursive function to solve a maze by defining a function that checks each possible move, recursively exploring paths until the exit is found or all paths are exhausted.

Question: How do you return a complex data structure from a recursive function in R?
Answer: Return a complex data structure by combining results from recursive calls into a list, vector, or other suitable structure, building the final result as the recursion unwinds.

Question: How do you manage memory usage in recursive functions?
Answer: Manage memory by minimizing the creation of large intermediate structures, reusing objects where possible, and considering iterative alternatives for deep recursion.

Question: How do you write a recursive function to compute the power of a number in R?
Answer: Write the function by defining power(x, n) as x * power(x, n-1) with a base case of power(x, 0) = 1.

Question: How do you handle edge cases in recursive functions?
Answer: Handle edge cases by carefully defining base cases and including conditional logic to manage unusual or boundary conditions, such as empty input or extreme values.

Question: How do you use recursion to flatten a nested list in R?
Answer: Use recursion to flatten a list by checking if each element is itself a list and recursively flattening it, combining all elements into a single flat list.

Question: How do you ensure that a recursive function is tail-recursive in R?
Answer: Ensure tail recursion by structuring the function so that the recursive call is the last operation, with no further computation needed after the call returns.

Question: How do you visualize the recursion tree of a function in R?
Answer: Visualize the recursion tree by using print statements or a custom visualization function to output the recursive calls and their relationships, or by using tools like DiagrammeR for graphical representation.

Question: How do you use recursion to generate permutations of a set in R?
Answer: Use recursion to generate permutations by fixing one element and recursively permuting the remaining elements, collecting all possible arrangements.

Question: How do you write a recursive function to compute the greatest common divisor (GCD) in R?
Answer: Write the function using the Euclidean algorithm, where gcd(a, b) is gcd(b, a %% b) with a base case of gcd(a, 0) = a.

Question: How do you handle recursion in functions that involve complex calculations in R?
Answer: Handle it by breaking down the calculations into smaller, manageable parts, ensuring that the recursive calls progress toward the base case, and optimizing as needed.

Question: How do you decide between using recursion or iteration for a problem in R?
Answer: Decide based on the problem's nature: use recursion for problems that naturally fit a recursive approach (like tree traversal or divide-and-conquer algorithms) and iteration for simpler, linear problems where recursion may introduce unnecessary complexity.

Question: How do you use recursion to implement a binary search algorithm in R?
Answer: Implement binary search by defining a recursive function that checks the middle element of a sorted array and recursively searches the left or right half based on the comparison, with a base case of finding the target or exhausting the search range.

Question: How do you test the correctness of a recursive function in R?
Answer: Test correctness by using a variety of test cases, including edge cases, to ensure the function returns correct results for all inputs, and by carefully checking the base cases and recursive logic.

Question: How do you measure the performance of a recursive function in R?
Answer: Measure performance using tools like system.time(), microbenchmark, or profvis to track execution time, memory usage, and identify bottlenecks or inefficiencies.

Types of Functions

Question: What are the different types of functions in R?
Answer: The main types of functions in R are built-in functions, user-defined functions, anonymous functions, and closures.

Question: How do you create a user-defined function in R?
Answer: A user-defined function is created using the function keyword, e.g., my_function <- function(arg1, arg2) { # code }.

Question: What is an anonymous function in R?
Answer: An anonymous function is a function without a name, often used temporarily in places where a function is needed for a short period, e.g., function(x) x^2.

Question: What is a closure in R?
Answer: A closure is a function that retains access to the variables in its environment, even after the environment where it was created has been destroyed.

Question: How do you use built-in functions in R?
Answer: Built-in functions are used by calling them with the necessary arguments, e.g., sum(1:10).

Question: How do you pass functions as arguments in R?
Answer: Functions can be passed as arguments by providing the function name without parentheses, e.g., apply(X, MARGIN, FUN).

Question: How do you create a function that returns another function in R?
Answer: A function that returns another function can be created by defining the inner function within the outer function and returning it, e.g., function_factory <- function() { return(function(x) x^2) }.

Question: What is the difference between S3, S4, and reference classes in R?
Answer: S3 is an informal class system based on generic functions and method dispatch, S4 is a more formal system with explicit class definitions and method signatures, and reference classes are used for object-oriented programming with mutable objects.

Question: How do you create a higher-order function in R?
Answer: A higher-order function is created by defining a function that takes one or more functions as arguments or returns a function, e.g., apply() or lapply().

Question: What are generic functions in R?
Answer: Generic functions are functions that use method dispatch to determine the appropriate method to apply based on the class of the object passed to them, e.g., print() or summary().

Question: How do you use the UseMethod() function to create S3 methods?
Answer: UseMethod() is used in an S3 generic function to dispatch the appropriate method based on the class of the object, e.g., print <- function(x) UseMethod("print").

Question: How do you define a method for an S4 class in R?
Answer: A method for an S4 class is defined using setMethod() in conjunction with setGeneric() to create the generic function, e.g., setMethod("show", "MyClass", function(object) { # code }).

Question: What is the purpose of the NextMethod() function in S3?
Answer: NextMethod() calls the next method in the method chain for an S3 generic, allowing for method inheritance and extended behavior.

Question: How do you override a built-in function in R?
Answer: Override a built-in function by defining a new function with the same name in the global environment, though this should be done with caution to avoid unintended side effects.

Question: How do you use lapply() as a higher-order function in R?
Answer: lapply() applies a function to each element of a list and returns a list of results, making it a common higher-order function.

Question: How do you define a recursive function in R?
Answer: A recursive function is defined by having the function call itself within its own body, progressing toward a base case.

Question: How do you write a function that accepts a varying number of arguments in R?
Answer: A function that accepts a varying number of arguments uses the ... parameter, which captures additional arguments as a list.

Question: How do you use closures to encapsulate state in R?
Answer: Closures encapsulate state by defining a function inside another function, with the inner function retaining access to the outer function's environment even after the outer function has finished executing.

Question: How do you create a reference class in R?
Answer: A reference class is created using setRefClass(), allowing for object-oriented programming with mutable objects, e.g., MyClass <- setRefClass("MyClass", fields = list(x = "numeric")).

Question: What is the purpose of the Recall() function in recursion?
Answer: Recall() is used in recursive functions to call the function again with the same arguments, simplifying the recursion logic.

Question: How do you create a function with default arguments in R?
Answer: A function with default arguments is created by specifying default values in the function signature, e.g., my_function <- function(x=1, y=2) { # code }.

Question: What is the purpose of the base::identity() function?
Answer: identity() is a function that returns its input unchanged, often used in higher-order functions or as a default argument for other functions.

Question: How do you write a function that operates on different data types in R?
Answer: Write a function that checks the type of its arguments using class() or typeof(), and branches the logic accordingly.

Question: How do you use the formals() function to inspect a function's arguments?
Answer: formals() returns a list of the formal arguments of a function, which can be used for introspection or dynamic function creation.

Question: How do you create a custom generic function in R?
Answer: A custom generic function is created using UseMethod() in S3 or setGeneric() in S4, allowing for method dispatch based on object class.

Question: How do you define a method for a reference class in R?
Answer: Define a method for a reference class within the methods field of setRefClass(), allowing the class to include functions that operate on its fields.

Question: How do you handle errors within a function in R?
Answer: Handle errors using tryCatch() or by validating input arguments and providing informative error messages.

Question: How do you write a function that returns multiple outputs in R?
Answer: Return multiple outputs by combining them into a list or a named vector, allowing the caller to access each result separately.

Question: How do you document a function in R for use in packages?
Answer: Document a function using Roxygen comments or by creating a .Rd help file, specifying details like the function's purpose, arguments, and return value.

Question: How do you test the behavior of a function with different inputs in R?
Answer: Test a function using unit tests with packages like testthat, providing a range of inputs and verifying that the outputs match expected results.

Question: How do you create a function that modifies its inputs in R?
Answer: In R, functions do not typically modify their inputs unless the inputs are mutable objects like environments or reference classes; otherwise, return the modified values explicitly.

Question: How do you create a function that works with both numeric and character data?
Answer: Create a function that checks the type of its input and processes numeric and character data differently, or uses generic functions that can handle multiple types.

Question: How do you optimize a function for speed in R?
Answer: Optimize for speed by minimizing loops, using vectorized operations, avoiding redundant calculations, and profiling the function with tools like microbenchmark or profvis.

Question: How do you create a function that is compatible with parallel processing in R?
Answer: Ensure the function is stateless and does not rely on global variables, making it suitable for parallel execution with packages like parallel or foreach.

Question: How do you use ... to create flexible functions in R?
Answer: Use ... to pass additional arguments to other functions within your function, allowing for flexible and dynamic behavior based on user input.

Online Resources

Online Practice Paper Link: https://forms.gle/4T5YFMfTNC4syCLJA

QR Code :

YouTube Video Link:
https://www.youtube.com/playlist?list=PLzlh_31VWEFq981M6tjkByIlEi13qlb84

QR Code:

Chapter 4: Vector

Create Vector

Question: How do you create a numeric vector in R?
Answer: Use the c() function to combine numbers into a vector, e.g., c(1, 2, 3).

Question: How do you create a character vector in R?
Answer: Use the c() function with character strings, e.g., c("apple", "banana", "cherry").

Question: How can you create a vector of repeating values in R?
Answer: Use the rep() function, e.g., rep(1, times = 5) creates a vector with five 1s.

Question: How do you create a sequence of numbers in R?
Answer: Use the : operator for simple sequences, e.g., 1:10, or seq() for more control, e.g., seq(1, 10, by = 2).

Question: How do you create a logical vector in R?
Answer: Use c() with logical values, e.g., c(TRUE, FALSE, TRUE).

Question: How do you create a vector using the vector() function?
Answer: Use vector() to create an empty vector of a specified type and length, e.g., vector("numeric", length = 5).

Question: How do you initialize a vector with NA values?
Answer: Use rep(NA, times = n) or vector("logical", length = n) for logical NAs.

Question: How do you concatenate two vectors in R?
Answer: Use the c() function to concatenate, e.g., c(vec1, vec2).

Question: How do you create a named vector in R?
Answer: Assign names using the names() function, e.g., x <- c(1, 2, 3); names(x) <- c("a", "b", "c").

Question: How do you create a factor vector in R?
Answer: Use the factor() function, e.g., factor(c("low", "medium", "high")).

Question: How do you create a vector with mixed data types in R?
Answer: R will coerce all elements to the most flexible type, usually character.

Question: How do you create a vector by sampling from another vector?
Answer: Use the sample() function, e.g., sample(1:10, size = 5).

Question: How do you create a vector with a specific range of values in R?
Answer: Use the seq() function, e.g., seq(1, 100, by = 10).

Question: How do you create a vector with random values in R?
Answer: Use rnorm() for normal distribution or runif() for uniform distribution.

Question: How do you create a vector by repeating an existing vector multiple times?
Answer: Use the rep() function with the each or times parameter, e.g., rep(c(1, 2, 3), times = 3).

Question: How do you convert a list to a vector in R?
Answer: Use unlist() to flatten a list into a vector.

Question: How do you create a vector from a data frame column in R?
Answer: Use the $ or [[operator, e.g., df$column or df[[1]].

Question: How do you check the type of a vector in R?
Answer: Use the typeof() or class() function, e.g., typeof(vec).

Question: How do you create a vector with elements from an existing vector based on a condition?
Answer: Use logical indexing, e.g., vec[vec > 5].

Question: How do you create a vector using as.vector()?
Answer: Convert another data type to a vector, e.g., as.vector(matrix).

Question: How do you generate a vector from a matrix's diagonal elements?
Answer: Use diag() to extract or set diagonal elements as a vector.

Question: How do you ensure a vector is of a specific length?
Answer: Use length() to check and rep() or slicing to adjust.

Question: How do you fill a vector with a specific pattern?
Answer: Use rep() with the pattern vector, e.g., rep(c(1, 2), times = 5).

Question: How do you create a vector of indices for elements in a vector that match a condition?
Answer: Use which(), e.g., which(vec > 5).

Question: How do you create a sparse vector in R?
Answer: Manually set most elements to zero or use specialized packages like Matrix.

Question: How do you create a vector by taking a difference between consecutive elements?
Answer: Use the diff() function, e.g., diff(vec).

Question: How do you create a vector with unique elements from another vector?
Answer: Use the unique() function, e.g., unique(vec).

Question: How do you create a vector that combines elements from multiple vectors?
Answer: Use c(), e.g., c(vec1, vec2, vec3).

Question: How do you create a vector with elements in reverse order?
Answer: Use the rev() function, e.g., rev(vec).

Question: How do you create a vector from an existing one by filtering out specific values?
Answer: Use negative indexing, e.g., vec[vec != value].

Question: How do you replicate elements of a vector a specific number of times?
Answer: Use rep(vec, times = n).

Question: How do you create a vector by repeating each element a specific number of times?
Answer: Use rep(vec, each = n).

Question: How do you create a vector of random integers within a specified range?
Answer: Use sample() with replace = TRUE if needed, e.g., sample(1:100, size = 10, replace = TRUE).

Question: How do you create a vector with missing values in R?
Answer: Include NA in the vector, e.g., c(1, 2, NA, 4).

Question: How do you create a vector from the row names or column names of a data frame?
Answer: Use rownames() or colnames().

Question: How do you create a vector by applying a function to each element of another vector?
Answer: Use sapply() or lapply().

Question: How do you convert a vector of factors to their corresponding numeric values?
Answer: Use as.numeric(as.character(factor)).

Question: How do you create a vector by extracting a specific attribute from a list of objects?
Answer: Use sapply() or lapply() combined with [.

Access Element of Vector

Question: How do you access the first element of a vector in R?
Answer: Use the index 1, e.g., vec[1].

Question: How do you access the last element of a vector in R?
Answer: Use the length() function, e.g., vec[length(vec)].

Question: How do you access a specific range of elements in a vector?
Answer: Use the : operator, e.g., vec[2:5].

Question: How do you access elements of a vector by their names?
Answer: Use named indexing, e.g., vec["name"].

Question: How do you access multiple non-consecutive elements in a vector?
Answer: Use a vector of indices, e.g., vec[c(1, 3, 5)].

Question: How do you access elements in a vector based on a logical condition?
Answer: Use logical indexing, e.g., vec[vec > 10].

Question: How do you access elements in a vector based on another vector of indices?
Answer: Use the second vector as indices, e.g., vec[indices].

Question: How do you extract all but the first element of a vector?
Answer: Use negative indexing, e.g., vec[-1].

Question: How do you access elements in reverse order in R?
Answer: Use the rev() function, or indexing like vec[length(vec):1].

Question: How do you access elements of a vector using which() in R?
Answer: Use which() to find indices based on a condition, e.g., vec[which(vec > 10)].

Question: How do you replace specific elements in a vector?
Answer: Use indexing to assign new values, e.g., vec[2:4] <- c(10, 20, 30).

Question: How do you access elements of a vector inside a loop?
Answer: Use indexing within the loop, e.g., for (i in 1:length(vec)) { print(vec[i]) }.

Question: How do you access the length of a vector in R?
Answer: Use the length() function, e.g., length(vec).

Question: How do you access elements of a vector conditionally?
Answer: Combine logical conditions with indexing, e.g., vec[vec > 5 & vec < 10].

Question: How do you access vector elements that are NA?
Answer: Use is.na(), e.g., vec[is.na(vec)].

Question: How do you access the elements of a vector that match a specific pattern?
Answer: Use grep() for pattern matching, e.g., vec[grep("pattern", vec)].

Question: How do you access vector elements by skipping a specific value?
Answer: Use negative indexing, e.g., vec[vec != value].

Question: How do you access and modify elements of a vector simultaneously?
Answer: Use indexing to directly modify elements, e.g., vec[vec > 5] <- 10.

Question: How do you access a subvector from a vector?
Answer: Use indexing to create a subvector, e.g., subvec <- vec[3:7].

Question: How do you access vector elements using a loop with an if statement?
Answer: Inside the loop, use if to conditionally access elements, e.g., for (i in 1:length(vec)) { if (vec[i] > 5) print(vec[i]) }.

Question: How do you access elements of a named vector using names?
Answer: Use names as indices, e.g., vec["name1"].

Question: How do you access elements of a vector using a logical vector?
Answer: Index the vector with a logical vector, e.g., vec[logical_vec].

Question: How do you access elements of a vector excluding NA values?
Answer: Use !is.na() to filter out NAs, e.g., vec[!is.na(vec)].

Question: How do you access elements of a vector by matching them with elements of another vector?
Answer: Use %in% operator, e.g., vec[vec %in% other_vec].

Question: How do you access the middle element(s) of a vector?
Answer: Calculate the middle index and use it, e.g., mid <- ceiling(length(vec)/2); vec[mid].

Question: How do you access elements of a vector using a sequence?
Answer: Use the seq() function for indexing, e.g., vec[seq(1, length(vec), by = 2)].

Question: How do you access vector elements by converting them to another type?
Answer: Use as.*() functions, e.g., as.character(vec[1:3]).

Question: How do you access the elements of a vector and apply a function to them?
Answer: Combine indexing with function application, e.g., log_vec <- log(vec[vec > 1]).

Question: How do you access the minimum and maximum elements of a vector?
Answer: Use min() and max(), e.g., min_val <- min(vec); max_val <- max(vec).

Question: How do you access the sum of selected vector elements?
Answer: Use sum() with indexing, e.g., sum(vec[1:5]).

Question: How do you access elements of a vector based on rank order?
Answer: Use order() to get indices and then index the vector, e.g., vec[order(vec)].

Question: How do you access the first and last elements of a vector simultaneously?
Answer: Use c() with indexing, e.g., c(vec[1], vec[length(vec)]).

Question: How do you access elements of a vector that are greater than a certain threshold?
Answer: Use logical indexing, e.g., vec[vec > threshold].

Question: How do you access the indices of elements that satisfy a condition?
Answer: Use which(), e.g., which(vec > 10).

Question: How do you access vector elements in a custom order?
Answer: Use a vector of indices in the desired order, e.g., vec[c(3, 1, 4)].

Question: How do you access elements of a vector to create a cumulative sum?
Answer: Use cumsum() function, e.g., cumsum(vec).

Question: How do you access vector elements that fall within a specific range?
Answer: Use logical indexing, e.g., vec[vec > 5 & vec < 15].

Operators of Vector

Question: What is the purpose of the + operator in vector arithmetic in R?
Answer: The + operator performs element-wise addition between two vectors.

Question: How does the - operator work with vectors in R?
Answer: The - operator subtracts corresponding elements of one vector from another.

Question: How do you use the * operator with vectors in R?
Answer: The * operator multiplies corresponding elements of two vectors.

Question: What is the function of the / operator in vector operations?
Answer: The / operator divides corresponding elements of one vector by another.

Question: How does the ^ operator work with vectors?
Answer: The ^ operator raises each element of a vector to the power of the corresponding element in another vector.

Question: What does the %% operator do when applied to vectors?
Answer: The %% operator calculates the element-wise remainder of division between two vectors.

Question: How do you use the %/% operator with vectors in R?
Answer: The %/% operator performs element-wise integer division between two vectors.

Question: What is the purpose of the == operator in vector comparisons?
Answer: The == operator checks element-wise equality between two vectors.

Question: How do you use the != operator with vectors?
Answer: The != operator checks for element-wise inequality between two vectors.

Question: How does the < operator work with vectors?
Answer: The < operator checks if elements of one vector are less than the corresponding elements of another vector.

Question: What is the function of the > operator in vector operations?
Answer: The > operator checks if elements of one vector are greater than the corresponding elements of another vector.

Question: How do you use the <= operator with vectors in R?
Answer: The <= operator checks if elements of one vector are less than or equal to the corresponding elements of another vector.

Question: What does the >= operator do when applied to vectors?
Answer: The >= operator checks if elements of one vector are greater than or equal to the corresponding elements of another vector.

Question: How do you apply the & operator to vectors in R?
Answer: The & operator performs element-wise logical AND between two vectors.

Question: What is the function of the | operator in vector operations?
Answer: The | operator performs element-wise logical OR between two vectors.

Question: How does the ! operator work with vectors in R?
Answer: The ! operator negates each element of a logical vector, turning TRUE to FALSE and vice versa.

Question: What is the purpose of the %in% operator in vector comparisons?
Answer: The %in% operator checks if elements of one vector are present in another vector.

Question: How do you use the : operator with vectors?
Answer: The : operator generates a sequence of integers between two numbers, often used for indexing or sequence creation.

Question: How does the * operator differ from %*% in vector operations?
Answer: The * operator performs element-wise multiplication, while %*% is used for matrix multiplication.

Question: What is the function of the is.na() operator when applied to vectors?
Answer: The is.na() operator returns a logical vector indicating which elements of the vector are NA.

Question: How do you use the na.rm = TRUE argument with vector operations?
Answer: The na.rm = TRUE argument is used in functions like sum() to remove NA values before performing the operation.

Question: What is the purpose of the all() operator when applied to a logical vector?
Answer: The all() operator checks if all elements of a logical vector are TRUE.

Question: How does the any() operator work with logical vectors?
Answer: The any() operator checks if any element of a logical vector is TRUE.

Question: What is the purpose of the which() function in vector operations?
Answer: The which() function returns the indices of TRUE elements in a logical vector.

Question: How do you apply the abs() function to a vector in R?
Answer: The abs() function returns a vector of the absolute values of the elements of the input vector.

Question: What does the sqrt() function do when applied to a vector?
Answer: The sqrt() function returns a vector with the square roots of the elements of the input vector.

Question: How do you use the round() function with vectors in R?
Answer: The round() function rounds the elements of a numeric vector to the specified number of decimal places.

Question: How does the sum() function work with vectors?
Answer: The sum() function returns the sum of all the elements in a numeric vector.

Question: What is the purpose of the mean() function in vector operations?
Answer: The mean() function calculates the arithmetic mean of the elements in a numeric vector.

Question: How do you apply the min() and max() functions to a vector?
Answer: The min() function returns the smallest element, and max() returns the largest element in a numeric vector.

Question: How does the range() function work with vectors?
Answer: The range() function returns a vector containing the minimum and maximum values of the input vector.

Question: What is the purpose of the diff() function in vector operations?
Answer: The diff() function calculates the differences between consecutive elements in a numeric vector.

Question: How do you use the cumsum() function with vectors?
Answer: The cumsum() function returns a cumulative sum of the elements in a numeric vector.

Question: How does the prod() function work with vectors?
Answer: The prod() function returns the product of all elements in a numeric vector.

Question: What is the function of the rep() operator in vector manipulation?
Answer: The rep() function replicates the elements of a vector a specified number of times.

Question: How do you apply the tapply() function to a vector?
Answer: The tapply() function applies a function to subsets of a vector defined by a factor or a list of factors.

Question: What is the use of the match() function in vector operations?
Answer: The match() function returns a vector of the positions of the first matches of its first argument in its second argument.

Question: How do you use the unique() function with vectors?
Answer: The unique() function returns a vector with the duplicate elements removed.

Vector Arithmetic and Manipulation

Question: How do you add two vectors in R?
Answer: Use the + operator for element-wise addition, e.g., vec1 + vec2.

Question: How do you subtract one vector from another in R?
Answer: Use the - operator for element-wise subtraction, e.g., vec1 - vec2.

Question: How do you multiply two vectors in R?
Answer: Use the * operator for element-wise multiplication, e.g., vec1 * vec2.

Question: How do you divide one vector by another in R?
Answer: Use the / operator for element-wise division, e.g., vec1 / vec2.

Question: How do you raise a vector to a power in R?
Answer: Use the ^ operator, e.g., vec1 ^ 2 or vec1 ^ vec2.

Question: How do you calculate the cumulative sum of a vector in R?
Answer: Use the cumsum() function, e.g., cumsum(vec).

Question: How do you calculate the cumulative product of a vector in R?
Answer: Use the cumprod() function, e.g., cumprod(vec).

Question: How do you find the cumulative maximum of a vector in R?
Answer: Use the cummax() function, e.g., cummax(vec).

Question: How do you find the cumulative minimum of a vector in R?
Answer: Use the cummin() function, e.g., cummin(vec).

Question: How do you reverse the elements of a vector in R?
Answer: Use the rev() function, e.g., rev(vec).

Question: How do you sort a vector in ascending order in R?
Answer: Use the sort() function, e.g., sort(vec).

Question: How do you sort a vector in descending order in R?
Answer: Use sort(vec, decreasing = TRUE).

Question: How do you find the unique elements of a vector in R?
Answer: Use the unique() function, e.g., unique(vec).

Question: How do you remove duplicates from a vector in R?
Answer: Use the unique() function to keep only distinct elements.

Question: How do you replicate the elements of a vector in R?
Answer: Use the rep() function, e.g., rep(vec, times = 3).

Question: How do you repeat each element of a vector in R?
Answer: Use rep(vec, each = 2) to repeat each element twice.

Question: How do you shift elements of a vector to the left in R?
Answer: Use indexing, e.g., vec <- c(vec[-1], NA).

Question: How do you shift elements of a vector to the right in R?
Answer: Use indexing, e.g., vec <- c(NA, vec[-length(vec)]).

Question: How do you normalize a vector in R?
Answer: Divide by the vector's magnitude or range, e.g., (vec - min(vec)) / (max(vec) - min(vec)).

Question: How do you compute the dot product of two vectors in R?
Answer: Use the sum(vec1 * vec2) expression for the dot product.

Question: How do you find the length of a vector in R?
Answer: Use the length() function, e.g., length(vec).

Question: How do you concatenate two vectors in R?
Answer: Use the c() function, e.g., c(vec1, vec2).

Question: How do you generate a sequence from a vector in R?
Answer: Use seq_along(vec) to generate a sequence based on the vector length.

Question: How do you apply a function to each element of a vector in R?
Answer: Use sapply() or lapply(), e.g., sapply(vec, sqrt).

Question: How do you filter elements of a vector based on a condition in R?
Answer: Use logical indexing, e.g., vec[vec > 0].

Question: How do you merge two vectors element-wise in R?
Answer: Use mapply(FUN, vec1, vec2) for element-wise operations.

Question: How do you remove NA values from a vector in R?
Answer: Use na.omit(vec) or vec[!is.na(vec)].

Question: How do you apply cumulative operations to a vector in R?
Answer: Use Reduce(), e.g., Reduce(f, vec) for cumulative operations with custom functions.

Question: How do you scale a vector to have a mean of 0 and a standard deviation of 1 in R?
Answer: Use scale(vec) to standardize the vector.

Question: How do you compute the running total of a vector in R?
Answer: Use cumsum(vec) for a running total.

Question: How do you reverse the sign of all elements in a vector in R?
Answer: Use -vec to negate each element.

Question: How do you access every nth element of a vector in R?
Answer: Use vec[seq(1, length(vec), by = n)].

Question: How do you create a vector of indices for elements that meet a condition in R?
Answer: Use which(vec > threshold) to get the indices.

Question: How do you compute the square of each element in a vector in R?
Answer: Use vec^2 to square each element.

Question: How do you convert a vector to a matrix in R?
Answer: Use matrix(vec, nrow = n, ncol = m) to reshape the vector.

Question: How do you rotate elements of a vector circularly in R?
Answer: Use a combination of indexing and concatenation, e.g., vec <- c(vec[n:1], vec[1:(n-1)]).

Deleting a Vector

Question: How do you delete a vector in R?
Answer: Use the rm() function, e.g., rm(vec).

Question: How do you delete multiple vectors at once in R?
Answer: Use rm() with multiple arguments, e.g., rm(vec1, vec2).

Question: What happens if you try to access a vector after it has been deleted?
Answer: An error will occur, indicating that the object is not found.

Question: How do you remove a vector and clear memory in R?
Answer: Use rm(vec) followed by gc() to clear memory.

Question: How do you remove all vectors from the workspace in R?
Answer: Use rm(list = ls()) to remove all objects.

Question: How do you remove a vector if its name is stored in another variable?
Answer: Use rm(list = name_of_vector) where name_of_vector is a character string.

Question: How do you check if a vector exists before attempting to delete it in R?
Answer: Use exists("vec") to check for existence before using rm().

Question: How do you prevent accidental deletion of a vector in R?
Answer: Avoid using rm(list = ls()) unless you are sure, and consider renaming critical vectors.

Question: Can you delete specific elements of a vector in R?
Answer: You cannot delete elements, but you can create a new vector without them using negative indexing, e.g., vec <- vec[-c(1, 2)].

Question: How do you remove vectors that start with a specific pattern in their names in R?
Answer: Use rm(list = ls(pattern = "^prefix")) to remove vectors with names that match the pattern.

Question: How do you delete a vector and all related objects in R?
Answer: Use rm() for the vector and any related objects, followed by gc() to clear memory.

Question: How do you delete a vector inside a function in R?
Answer: Use rm() within the function to delete local vectors, but it will not affect the global environment unless you use <<-.
Question: How do you delete a vector within a loop in R?
Answer: Use rm() within the loop, but be careful as it may affect the loop's execution if not managed properly.

Question: What is the impact of deleting a vector on other objects in R?
Answer: Deleting a vector removes only that object unless other objects depend on it (e.g., in the case of references or pointers).

Question: How do you delete a vector conditionally in R?
Answer: Use an if statement to check a condition before using rm(), e.g., if (length(vec) > 100) rm(vec).

Question: How do you recover a deleted vector in R?
Answer: You cannot recover a deleted vector unless it was saved to a file or another environment before deletion.

Question: How do you remove vectors after they are used in a function?
Answer: Use rm() within the function or after the function call to clean up.

Question: How do you delete vectors that were created within a script in R?
Answer: Use rm(list = ls()) at the end of the script to clean up all objects.

Question: How do you prevent the accidental deletion of important vectors in R?
Answer: Use careful naming conventions, and avoid using rm(list = ls()) unless necessary.

Question: How do you delete a vector but retain its name for reuse in R?
Answer: Use vec <- NULL to clear the contents but keep the name available for future assignments.

Question: How do you remove a vector from a specific environment in R?
Answer: Use rm(vec, envir = env_name) to remove a vector from a particular environment.

Question: How do you delete vectors based on their size in R?
Answer: Use a loop or sapply() with object.size() to delete vectors over a certain size.

Question: How do you delete a vector after saving it to a file in R?
Answer: Use save(vec, file = "filename.RData") followed by rm(vec).

Question: How do you delete a vector without affecting other vectors in R?
Answer: Use rm() specifically for that vector, ensuring no dependencies.

Question: How do you remove vectors with a specific length in R?
Answer: Use a conditional check with length() before using rm().

Question: How do you delete vectors that are no longer needed in R?
Answer: Regularly clean up the workspace with rm() for vectors that are not needed for further analysis.

Question: How do you delete vectors with a specific value or content in R?
Answer: Loop through the vectors and use conditional checks before using rm().

Question: How do you ensure that a vector is completely deleted from memory in R?
Answer: Use rm() followed by gc() to ensure the vector is removed from memory.

Question: How do you delete a vector and reset the workspace in R?
Answer: Use rm(vec) followed by rm(list = ls()) and gc() to clear everything.

Question: How do you delete vectors created during data processing in R?
Answer: Identify and remove them after processing, or use a script that ends with rm(list = ls()).

Question: How do you delete vectors with names matching a pattern in R?
Answer: Use rm(list = ls(pattern = "pattern")) to remove all matching vectors.

Question: How do you prevent deletion of essential vectors in R?
Answer: Avoid using global deletion commands and consider saving essential vectors to a file before any mass deletion.

Vector Element Sorting

Question: How do you sort a vector in ascending order in R?
Answer: Use the sort() function, e.g., sort(vec).

Question: How do you sort a vector in descending order in R?
Answer: Use sort(vec, decreasing = TRUE).

Question: How do you sort a vector of character strings in R?
Answer: Use sort() for character vectors, e.g., sort(c("apple", "banana", "cherry")).

Question: How do you sort a vector of factors in R?
Answer: Use sort() after converting factors to character or numeric, e.g., sort(as.character(factor_vec)).

Question: How do you sort a vector by the absolute values of its elements in R?
Answer: Use sort() with abs(), e.g., sort(vec, key = abs).

Question: How do you perform a partial sort in R?
Answer: Use order() with indexing, e.g., vec[order(vec)].

Question: How do you sort a vector with missing values (NA) in R?
Answer: Use sort() with the na.last argument, e.g., sort(vec, na.last = TRUE).

Question: How do you sort a vector of dates in R?
Answer: Convert dates to Date class and use sort(), e.g., sort(as.Date(vec)).

Question: How do you sort a vector by a custom order in R?
Answer: Use order() with custom logic, e.g., vec[order(custom_order)].

Question: How do you reverse sort a vector in R?
Answer: Use sort() with decreasing = TRUE, or rev(sort(vec)).

Question: How do you sort a vector of logical values in R?
Answer: Use sort() directly; FALSE values come before TRUE.

Question: How do you sort a vector of complex numbers in R?
Answer: Sort by modulus using Mod(), e.g., vec[order(Mod(vec))].

Question: How do you sort a vector using rank() in R?
Answer: Use rank() to get ranks and then order by rank, e.g., vec[order(rank(vec))].

Question: How do you sort a vector in a custom function in R?
Answer: Use sort() within the function body to sort the vector.

Question: How do you sort a vector and keep track of the original order in R?
Answer: Use order() to get sorted indices, then index the vector, e.g., vec[order(vec)].

Question: How do you sort a vector of numeric and character elements together in R?
Answer: Convert to a consistent type (usually character) before sorting, e.g., sort(as.character(vec)).

Question: How do you sort a vector of integers in R?
Answer: Use sort() directly on the integer vector.

Question: How do you sort a vector with duplicate values in R?
Answer: Use sort(); duplicates will be retained in their natural order.

Question: How do you sort a vector and remove duplicates in R?
Answer: Combine sort() with unique(), e.g., sort(unique(vec)).

Question: How do you sort a vector of mixed data types in R?
Answer: Convert to a common type (usually character) before sorting, e.g., sort(as.character(vec)).

Question: How do you sort a vector of names in R?
Answer: Use sort() directly on the vector of names.

Question: How do you sort a vector and return the sorted indices in R?
Answer: Use order(), e.g., order(vec).

Question: How do you sort a vector with ties in R?
Answer: Ties will be sorted based on their order in the vector unless specified otherwise.

Question: How do you sort a vector and limit the output to the top n values in R?
Answer: Use head(sort(vec, decreasing = TRUE), n).

Question: How do you sort a vector by multiple criteria in R?
Answer: Use order() with multiple arguments, e.g., vec[order(crit1, crit2)].

Question: How do you sort a vector that includes Inf or -Inf values in R?
Answer: Inf values will be sorted as the largest and -Inf as the smallest by default.

Question: How do you sort a vector of integers as strings in R?
Answer: Convert integers to character and then sort, e.g., sort(as.character(vec)).

Question: How do you sort a vector of months or days of the week in R?
Answer: Use factor() with specified levels, then sort.

Question: How do you sort a vector of elements that are a result of a function in R?
Answer: Apply the function within sort(), e.g., sort(f(vec)).

Question: How do you sort a vector of numeric values that includes NAs in R?
Answer: Use sort(vec, na.last = TRUE) to place NAs last.

Question: How do you sort a vector within a data frame in R?
Answer: Use order() within with(), e.g., df <- df[order(df$vec),].

Question: How do you sort a vector and match the order with another vector in R?
Answer: Use order() to get indices from one vector and apply them to the other, e.g., vec2[order(vec1)].

Question: How do you sort a vector of factor levels in R?
Answer: Use factor() with levels specified in the desired order, then use sort().

Question: How do you sort a vector of elements with mixed upper and lower case in R?
Answer: Convert to all lower or upper case using tolower() or toupper() before sorting.

Question: How do you sort a vector with a large number of elements efficiently in R?
Answer: Use sort() as it is optimized for large vectors.

Question: How do you sort a vector and keep track of the original positions in R?
Answer: Use order() to get the original indices, e.g., order(vec).

Question: How do you sort a vector using a custom function for comparison in R?
Answer: Use order() with the custom function to generate sorting indices.

Question: How do you sort a vector and perform additional operations on sorted elements in R?
Answer: Chain sort() with additional operations, e.g., log(sort(vec)).

Question: How do you sort a vector in descending order and get the top elements in R?
Answer: Use sort(vec, decreasing = TRUE) followed by head() to get the top elements.

Online Resources

Online Practice Paper Link: https://forms.gle/uFs94N4vfg9PW5S46

QR Code:

YouTube Video Link: https://www.youtube.com/playlist?list=PLzlh_31VWEFp6_N-rIl5LQXyCEG6dr3V4

QR Code :

Chapter 5: List

Creating a List

Question: How do you create a list in R?
Answer: Use the list() function to create a list, e.g., my_list <- list(a = 1, b = "text", c = TRUE).

Question: Can a list in R contain elements of different types?
Answer: Yes, a list can contain elements of different types, such as numeric, character, logical, and even other lists.

Question: How do you create a list with named elements in R?
Answer: Provide names to the elements inside list(), e.g., my_list <- list(name1 = 1, name2 = "text").

Question: How do you access the length of a list in R?
Answer: Use the length() function, e.g., length(my_list).

Question: How do you access an element of a list by its position?
Answer: Use double square brackets, e.g., my_list[[1]].

Question: How do you access a named element of a list?
Answer: Use the $ operator or double square brackets with the name, e.g., my_list$name1 or my_list[["name1"]].

Question: How do you create an empty list in R?
Answer: Use list() without any arguments, e.g., empty_list <- list().

Question: How do you add an element to a list?
Answer: Assign a new value to a new or existing name, e.g., my_list$new_element <- 5.

Question: How do you remove an element from a list in R?
Answer: Set the element to NULL, e.g., my_list$name1 <- NULL.

Question: Can a list contain other lists as elements in R?
Answer: Yes, lists in R can be nested by including other lists as elements.

Question: How do you combine multiple lists into one list?
Answer: Use the c() function, e.g., combined_list <- c(list1, list2).

Question: How do you check if an element exists in a list?
Answer: Use the is.null() function combined with element access, e.g., !is.null(my_list$name1).

Question: How do you create a list from a vector in R?
Answer: Use as.list(), e.g., list_from_vec <- as.list(c(1, 2, 3)).

Question: How do you update an element in a list?
Answer: Reassign the element, e.g., my_list$name1 <- 10.

Question: How do you create a list with a specific length?
Answer: Use vector("list", length = n) to create a list of a specified length.

Question: How do you iterate over a list in R?
Answer: Use a for loop, e.g., for (item in my_list) { print(item) }.

Question: How do you apply a function to each element of a list?
Answer: Use lapply(), e.g., lapply(my_list, FUN).

Question: How do you convert a list to a data frame in R?
Answer: Use as.data.frame(), e.g., df <- as.data.frame(my_list).

Question: How do you convert a list to a vector in R?
Answer: Use unlist(), e.g., vec <- unlist(my_list).
Question: How do you create a list from the columns of a data frame?
Answer: Use as.list(df) to convert each column of a data frame into a list element.

Question: How do you merge two lists by name in R?
Answer: Use modifyList(list1, list2) to merge two lists based on names.

Question: How do you access multiple elements of a list by their names?
Answer: Use single square brackets with a vector of names, e.g., my_list[c("name1", "name2")].

Question: How do you create a list with repeated elements in R?
Answer: Use rep() inside list(), e.g., my_list <- list(rep(1, times = 3)).

Question: How do you flatten a nested list in R?
Answer: Use unlist(), e.g., flat_list <- unlist(nested_list).

Question: How do you preserve the structure of a list when subsetting it?
Answer: Use single square brackets, e.g., sub_list <- my_list[1:2].

Question: How do you check the type of each element in a list?
Answer: Use lapply() with class(), e.g., lapply(my_list, class).

Question: How do you create a list with an initial set of NULL elements?
Answer: Use vector("list", length = n) and leave the elements as NULL.

Question: How do you replace multiple elements in a list simultaneously?
Answer: Use indexing and assignment, e.g., my_list[c(1, 2)] <- list(10, "new_value").

Question: How do you create a list from an existing list by extracting certain elements?
Answer: Use single square brackets, e.g., new_list <- my_list[c("name1", "name3")].

Question: How do you filter elements in a list based on a condition?
Answer: Use Filter(), e.g., filtered_list <- Filter(function(x) x > 1, my_list).

Question: How do you handle lists with different element lengths when creating a data frame?
Answer: Use rbind.fill() from the plyr package or tibble() from the tibble package.

Question: How do you create a list with elements generated by a function?
Answer: Use lapply() with a function, e.g., my_list <- lapply(1:3, function(x) x^2).

Question: How do you replace NULL elements in a list with a default value?
Answer: Use lapply() with a conditional function, e.g., lapply(my_list, function(x) if (is.null(x)) 0 else x).

Question: How do you combine lists with different lengths in R?
Answer: Use mapply() to apply a function across lists, recycling shorter ones.

Question: How do you create a list from user input in R?
Answer: Use list() with readline() or scan() for interactive input.

Question: How do you convert a list of vectors into a matrix in R?
Answer: Use do.call(rbind, my_list) or do.call(cbind, my_list) depending on the orientation.

Question: How do you extract specific elements from a nested list?
Answer: Use recursive indexing, e.g., nested_list[[1]][[2]].

Question: How do you identify the names of all elements in a list?
Answer: Use names() function, e.g., names(my_list).

Naming a List

Question: How do you assign names to the elements of a list in R?
Answer: Use the names() function, e.g., names(my_list) <- c("name1", "name2", "name3").

Question: How do you create a list with named elements directly in R?
Answer: Use the list() function with named arguments, e.g., my_list <- list(name1 = 1, name2 = 2).

Question: How do you retrieve the names of the elements in a list?
Answer: Use the names() function, e.g., names(my_list).

Question: Can you change the names of a list after it has been created?
Answer: Yes, you can change the names using names() again, e.g., names(my_list) <- c("new_name1", "new_name2").

Question: How do you remove the names from a list in R?
Answer: Set names(my_list) to NULL, e.g., names(my_list) <- NULL.

Question: How do you assign names to a subset of a list?
Answer: Use names() on the subset, e.g., names(my_list[1:2]) <- c("first", "second").

Question: How do you create a list with partially named elements?
Answer: Use names() to assign names only to certain elements, e.g., names(my_list) <- c("name1", "name2", NULL).

Question: What happens if you assign fewer names than the number of elements in a list?
Answer: Only the specified elements will be named; the rest will remain unnamed.

Question: How do you access a list element by its name?
Answer: Use the $ operator or double square brackets with the name, e.g., my_list$name1 or my_list[["name1"]].

Question: Can list names contain special characters in R?
Answer: Yes, but you should use backticks if the names contain spaces or special characters, e.g., my_list$"name with spaces"`.

Question: How do you check if a list element has a name?
Answer: Use !is.null(names(my_list)[index]) or check with names(my_list) directly.

Question: How do you rename a single element of a list?
Answer: Use indexing with names(), e.g., names(my_list)[1] <- "new_name1".

Question: How do you assign names to a list using the setNames() function?
Answer: Use setNames(), e.g., my_list <- setNames(list(1, 2, 3), c("name1", "name2", "name3")).

Question: Can you have duplicate names in a list in R?
Answer: Yes, but it's generally discouraged because it can lead to confusion when accessing elements.

Question: How do you assign names to a list while preserving existing names?
Answer: Assign names only to the unnamed elements, leaving the others unchanged, e.g., names(my_list)[is.na(names(my_list))] <- c("new_name").

Question: How do you combine two named lists in R?
Answer: Use c() and ensure the names are preserved, e.g., combined_list <- c(list1, list2).

Question: How do you assign names to a list when creating it from a vector?
Answer: Use setNames() after converting the vector to a list, e.g., my_list <- setNames(as.list(vec), c("name1", "name2")).

Question: How do you handle names when subsetting a list?
Answer: The names are preserved when subsetting, e.g., sub_list <- my_list[1:2].

Question: How do you rename all elements in a list simultaneously?
Answer: Use names() with a complete vector of new names, e.g., names(my_list) <- c("name1", "name2", "name3").

Question: What is the impact of assigning NULL to list names?
Answer: Assigning NULL removes all names from the list elements.

Question: How do you access multiple elements of a list by their names?
Answer: Use single square brackets with a vector of names, e.g., my_list[c("name1", "name2")].

Question: How do you copy the names from one list to another?
Answer: Assign names(list2) <- names(list1) to copy names from one list to another.

Question: How do you set default names for elements in a list if they are not named?
Answer: Use a conditional approach, e.g., if(is.null(names(my_list))) names(my_list) <- c("default1", "default2").

Question: Can you mix named and unnamed elements in a list?
Answer: Yes, you can have a mix of named and unnamed elements in a list.

Question: How do you assign names to a list that was created with repeated elements?
Answer: Use setNames() after list creation, e.g., names(repeated_list) <- c("name1", "name2").

Question: How do you ensure unique names in a list?
Answer: Use the make.names() function to create unique names automatically.

Question: How do you convert the names of a list into a separate vector?
Answer: Use names_vec <- names(my_list) to create a vector of names.

Question: How do you assign names based on the contents of the list?
Answer: Use a loop or sapply() to assign names dynamically based on content, e.g., names(my_list) <- sapply(my_list, function(x) paste0("Element_", x)).

Question: How do you create a list with names corresponding to data frame column names?
Answer: Use as.list() on the data frame and names(), e.g., list_from_df <- as.list(df); names(list_from_df) <- colnames(df).

Question: How do you replace the names of a list with sequential numbers?
Answer: Use names(my_list) <- as.character(1:length(my_list)).

Question: Can you assign names to a list using a named vector?
Answer: Yes, use names(my_list) <- names(named_vector) to assign names based on a named vector.

Question: How do you assign names conditionally based on a list element's value?
Answer: Use ifelse() within names(), e.g., names(my_list) <- ifelse(sapply(my_list, is.numeric), "numeric", "non-numeric").

Question: How do you convert the names of a list to upper or lower case?
Answer: Use toupper(names(my_list)) or tolower(names(my_list)).

Question: How do you append a new named element to an existing list?
Answer: Use the $ operator or [[ ]] with assignment, e.g., my_list$new_name <- new_value.

Question: How do you assign names to a list based on another list's names?
Answer: Use names(my_list) <- names(other_list).

Question: How do you check if a list has names assigned to it?
Answer: Use !is.null(names(my_list)) to check if the list has names.

Question: How do you sort a list based on its names?
Answer: Use my_list <- my_list[order(names(my_list))].

Question: How do you convert the names of a list into a separate data frame column?
Answer: Use df <- data.frame(names = names(my_list), values = unlist(my_list)).

Question: How do you assign names to a list based on the results of a function?
Answer: Use names(my_list) <- sapply(my_list, function(x) function_result(x)).

Accessing and Updating List

Question: How do you access a specific element in a list by its index in R?
Answer: Use double square brackets, e.g., my_list[[1]] to access the first element.

Question: How do you access a named element in a list in R?
Answer: Use the $ operator or double square brackets with the name, e.g., my_list$name or my_list[["name"]].

Question: How do you access multiple elements of a list by their indices?
Answer: Use single square brackets with a vector of indices, e.g., my_list[c(1, 3)].

Question: How do you update an element in a list by its index?
Answer: Use double square brackets for assignment, e.g., my_list[[1]] <- "new_value".

Question: How do you update a named element in a list?
Answer: Use the $ operator or double square brackets, e.g., my_list$name <- "new_value" or my_list[["name"]] <- "new_value".

Question: How do you access the length of a list in R?
Answer: Use the length() function, e.g., length(my_list).

Question: Can you update multiple elements of a list at once?
Answer: Yes, use single square brackets with a vector of indices or names, e.g., my_list[c(1, 2)] <- list("new1", "new2").

Question: How do you access elements of a list conditionally?
Answer: Use a loop or lapply() with a conditional function to access elements based on a condition.

Question: How do you access the last element of a list?
Answer: Use my_list[[length(my_list)]] to access the last element.

Question: How do you replace an element in a list with NULL?
Answer: Assign NULL to the element, e.g., my_list[[1]] <- NULL.

Question: How do you access a list element that is itself a list?
Answer: Use double indexing, e.g., my_list[[1]][[2]] if the first element is a list.

Question: How do you update an element in a nested list?
Answer: Use double indexing to access and update the element, e.g., my_list[[1]][[2]] <- "new_value".

Question: How do you append a new element to a list in R?
Answer: Use the c() function or assign it to a new index, e.g., my_list[[length(my_list) + 1]] <- "new_element".

Question: How do you remove an element from a list?
Answer: Assign NULL to the element, e.g., my_list[[2]] <- NULL.

Question: How do you update the names of elements in a list?
Answer: Use the names() function, e.g., names(my_list) <- c("new_name1", "new_name2").

Question: How do you access a list element by its name in a vector?
Answer: Use single square brackets with the name, e.g., my_list["name"].

Question: How do you access elements in a list that are themselves lists?
Answer: Use multiple layers of indexing, e.g., my_list[[1]][[2]].

Question: How do you combine accessing and updating elements in a list?
Answer: Access the element using double brackets and then assign a new value, e.g., my_list[[1]] <- my_list[[1]] + 1.

Question: How do you access elements of a list inside a loop?
Answer: Use indexing inside the loop, e.g., for (i in 1:length(my_list)) { print(my_list[[i]]) }.

Question: How do you update elements of a list inside a loop?
Answer: Use indexing and assignment within the loop, e.g., for (i in 1:length(my_list)) { my_list[[i]] <- my_list[[i]] + 1 }.

Question: How do you access elements of a list using a custom function?
Answer: Use lapply() or sapply(), e.g., lapply(my_list, custom_function).

Question: How do you replace all elements in a list with new values?
Answer: Use a loop or lapply() to reassign values, e.g., my_list <- lapply(my_list, function(x) "new_value").

Question: How do you extract multiple elements from a list by their names?
Answer: Use single square brackets with a vector of names, e.g., my_list[c("name1", "name2")].
Question: How do you conditionally update elements in a list?
Answer: Use lapply() or a loop with an if statement, e.g., my_list <- lapply(my_list, function(x) if (x > 10) x + 1 else x).

Question: How do you access the names of all elements in a list?
Answer: Use the names() function, e.g., names(my_list).

Question: How do you access a subset of a list?
Answer: Use single square brackets, e.g., sub_list <- my_list[1:3].

Question: How do you convert a list element to a different type?
Answer: Use type conversion functions, e.g., my_list[[1]] <- as.numeric(my_list[[1]]).

Question: How do you replace NA values in a list with a default value?
Answer: Use lapply() to replace NA, e.g., my_list <- lapply(my_list, function(x) ifelse(is.na(x), 0, x)).

Question: How do you access elements of a list with different types?
Answer: Access normally with indexing, but handle different types within functions using class() or typeof().

Question: How do you access and update a list element based on its content?
Answer: Use conditional logic to access and update, e.g., if (my_list[[1]] == "old_value") my_list[[1]] <- "new_value".

Question: How do you access elements of a list that match a specific condition?
Answer: Use Filter() or lapply() with a conditional function, e.g., Filter(function(x) x > 10, my_list).

Question: How do you merge two lists by updating existing elements?
Answer: Use modifyList() to update one list with elements from another, e.g., merged_list <- modifyList(list1, list2).

Question: How do you access and update elements of a list in a custom order?
Answer: Use a vector of indices in the desired order, e.g., for (i in c(2, 1, 3)) { my_list[[i]] <- my_list[[i]] + 1 }.

Question: How do you access an element of a list that contains another list?
Answer: Use multiple indexing, e.g., my_list[[1]][[2]] if the first element is a list.

Question: How do you update all elements of a list to have the same value?
Answer: Use a loop or lapply(), e.g., my_list <- lapply(my_list, function(x) "new_value").

Question: How do you access and update list elements that are functions?
Answer: Use indexing to access the function and assign a new one, e.g., my_list[[1]] <- function(x) x * 2.

Question: How do you handle errors when accessing list elements that may not exist?
Answer: Use conditional checks like if (!is.null(my_list[[1]])) before accessing or updating.

Question: How do you swap elements in a list?
Answer: Temporarily store one element and reassign, e.g., temp <- my_list[[1]]; my_list[[1]] <- my_list[[2]]; my_list[[2]] <- temp.

Sorting and Searching

Question: How do you sort a vector in ascending order in R?
Answer: Use the sort() function, e.g., sort(vec).

Question: How do you sort a vector in descending order in R?
Answer: Use sort(vec, decreasing = TRUE).

Question: How do you sort a data frame by a specific column in R?
Answer: Use the order() function within data.frame[], e.g., df[order(df$column),].

Question: How do you sort a vector of character strings in R?
Answer: Use sort() for character vectors, e.g., sort(c("apple", "banana", "cherry")).

Question: How do you sort a data frame by multiple columns in R?
Answer: Use order() with multiple columns, e.g., df[order(df$column1, df$column2),].

Question: How do you search for a specific value in a vector in R?
Answer: Use the which() function, e.g., which(vec == "value").

Question: How do you sort a list of vectors in R?
Answer: Use lapply() with sort(), e.g., sorted_list <- lapply(my_list, sort).

Question: How do you find the index of the maximum value in a vector in R?
Answer: Use which.max(), e.g., which.max(vec).

Question: How do you find the index of the minimum value in a vector in R?
Answer: Use which.min(), e.g., which.min(vec).

Question: How do you sort a vector by the absolute values of its elements in R?
Answer: Use order() with abs(), e.g., vec[order(abs(vec))].

Question: How do you search for multiple values in a vector in R?
Answer: Use which() with %in%, e.g., which(vec %in% c("value1", "value2")).

Question: How do you perform a binary search in a sorted vector in R?
Answer: Use findInterval() or implement a custom binary search function.

Question: How do you sort a factor variable in R?
Answer: Use factor() with levels specified in the desired order.

Question: How do you search for NA values in a vector in R?
Answer: Use is.na() within which(), e.g., which(is.na(vec)).

Question: How do you sort a matrix by a specific column in R?
Answer: Use order() within matrix indexing, e.g., matrix[order(matrix[, column_index]),].

Question: How do you check if a value exists in a vector in R?
Answer: Use %in%, e.g., "value" %in% vec.

Question: How do you sort a data frame by row names in R?
Answer: Use order() on rownames(), e.g., df[order(rownames(df)),].

Question: How do you find the unique elements in a sorted vector in R?
Answer: Use unique() after sorting, e.g., unique(sort(vec)).

Question: How do you sort a list of data frames in R?
Answer: Use lapply() with order() for each data frame.

Question: How do you perform a case-insensitive sort in R?
Answer: Convert to lower case with tolower() before sorting, e.g., sort(tolower(vec)).

Question: How do you search for a substring in a character vector in R?
Answer: Use grep() or grepl(), e.g., grep("pattern", vec).

Question: How do you sort a vector and keep the original indices in R?
Answer: Use order() and store the result, e.g., indices <- order(vec).

Question: How do you sort a list of lists in R?
Answer: Use lapply() with sort() on each sub-list.

Question: How do you find the rank of elements in a vector in R?
Answer: Use the rank() function, e.g., rank(vec).

Question: How do you sort a data frame by a factor column in its natural order?
Answer: Convert the factor to numeric order with as.numeric(), then use order().

Question: How do you search for a pattern in a vector of strings and replace it in R?
Answer: Use gsub() for replacement, e.g., gsub("pattern", "replacement", vec).

Question: How do you sort a vector with missing values in R?
Answer: Use sort() with the na.last argument, e.g., sort(vec, na.last = TRUE).

Question: How do you find all occurrences of a value in a vector in R?
Answer: Use which(vec == value) to get all indices of occurrences.

Question: How do you sort a vector of dates in R?
Answer: Convert to Date class and use sort(), e.g., sort(as.Date(date_vec)).

Question: How do you search for a value in a list of vectors in R?
Answer: Use lapply() with which() or %in% to search within each vector.

Question: How do you sort a data frame in descending order by a specific column in R?
Answer: Use order() with decreasing = TRUE, e.g., df[order(df$column, decreasing = TRUE),].

Question: How do you perform a partial sort on a vector in R?
Answer: Use sort() with indexing for the required portion, e.g., sort(vec)[1:n].

Question: How do you search for values greater than a threshold in a vector in R?
Answer: Use which(vec > threshold) to find indices of values greater than the threshold.

Question: How do you sort a character vector numerically in R?
Answer: Convert the character vector to numeric before sorting, e.g., sort(as.numeric(vec)).

Question: How do you find the first occurrence of a value in a vector in R?
Answer: Use match(), e.g., match(value, vec).

Question: How do you sort a vector of logical values in R?
Answer: Use sort() directly; FALSE values come before TRUE.

Question: How do you search for multiple patterns in a character vector in R?
Answer: Use grep() with | for multiple patterns, e.g., grep("pattern1|pattern2", vec).

Question: How do you sort a list of mixed data types in R?
Answer: Use a custom sorting function within lapply() or order().

Question: How do you find the positions of the top n values in a vector in R?
Answer: Use order() with indexing, e.g., order(vec, decreasing = TRUE)[1:n].

Merging List

Question: How do you merge two lists in R?
Answer: Use the c() function to concatenate two lists, e.g., merged_list <- c(list1, list2).

Question: Can you merge lists with different lengths in R?
Answer: Yes, the c() function can merge lists of different lengths without any issues.

Question: How do you merge multiple lists at once in R?
Answer: Use c() with multiple list arguments, e.g., merged_list <- c(list1, list2, list3).

Question: How do you preserve the names of elements when merging two named lists?
Answer: The names are automatically preserved when using c(), e.g., merged_list <- c(named_list1, named_list2).

Question: How do you handle duplicate names when merging lists?
Answer: When merging lists with duplicate names, the resulting list will have duplicate names unless you handle them manually.

Question: How do you merge lists by appending elements from one list to another?
Answer: Use c() to append one list to another, e.g., appended_list <- c(list1, list2).

Question: How do you merge lists and create a unique set of elements?
Answer: Convert the merged list to a vector using unlist(), then apply unique(), e.g., unique_elements <- unique(unlist(c(list1, list2))).

Question: How do you merge lists containing lists as elements?
Answer: Use c() to merge the outer lists, which will include the nested lists as elements, e.g., merged_list <- c(list1, list2).

Question: How do you merge lists with different types of elements?
Answer: Use c() directly; R will handle the different types automatically in the merged list.

Question: How do you merge lists without flattening them?
Answer: Use c() to merge the lists without using unlist(), so the list structure remains intact.

Question: How do you merge lists while removing NULL elements?
Answer: Use lapply() with Filter() to remove NULL elements before merging, e.g., filtered_list <- Filter(Negate(is.null), c(list1, list2)).

Question: How do you merge lists into a data frame?
Answer: Use data.frame() with c() or mapply() if the lists have elements of equal length.

Question: How do you merge named lists and ensure no names are duplicated?
Answer: Use modifyList() to update one list with elements from another, e.g., merged_list <- modifyList(list1, list2).

Question: Can you merge lists with different structures?
Answer: Yes, c() can merge lists with different structures, but the resulting list will contain elements in their original structure.

Question: How do you merge lists and sort the resulting list?
Answer: Use c() to merge and sort() or order() to sort the elements, e.g., sorted_list <- sort(c(list1, list2)).

Question: How do you merge lists conditionally based on element values?
Answer: Use lapply() with a custom function to merge only elements that meet a condition.

Question: How do you merge lists into a single vector?
Answer: Use unlist() after merging with c(), e.g., merged_vector <- unlist(c(list1, list2)).

Question: How do you merge lists by combining elements with the same name?
Answer: Use modifyList() or lapply() to combine elements with matching names from different lists.

Question: How do you merge two lists and retain only the common elements?
Answer: Use intersect() on the unlisted versions of the lists, e.g., common_elements <- intersect(unlist(list1), unlist(list2)).

Question: How do you merge lists and remove specific elements by name?
Answer: Use c() to merge, followed by names() and indexing to remove specific elements.

Question: How do you merge two lists and overwrite elements with the same name?
Answer: Use modifyList() where elements in the second list overwrite those in the first list, e.g., merged_list <- modifyList(list1, list2).

Question: How do you merge lists that contain both named and unnamed elements?
Answer: Use c() to merge the lists; unnamed elements will be appended without names.

Question: How do you merge lists and exclude certain elements by condition?
Answer: Use Filter() to exclude elements that do not meet the condition before merging.

Question: How do you merge lists by combining their elements into a matrix?
Answer: Use do.call(rbind, c(list1, list2)) to merge and combine into a matrix.

Question: How do you merge lists and apply a function to the combined elements?
Answer: Use lapply() with c() to merge the lists and apply a function, e.g., lapply(c(list1, list2), some_function).

Question: How do you merge lists while keeping track of the origin of each element?
Answer: Use a named list and lapply() to append origin information before merging.

Question: How do you merge lists and avoid creating nested lists?
Answer: Use c() without list() around the elements to prevent nesting.

Question: How do you merge lists and create a summary of the merged elements?
Answer: Use lapply() or sapply() to summarize elements after merging, e.g., sapply(c(list1, list2), summary_function).

Question: How do you merge lists and handle elements that are vectors?
Answer: Use mapply() or Map() to merge lists containing vectors element-wise.

Question: How do you merge lists and remove duplicate elements afterward?
Answer: Use unique() after unlist() on the merged list, e.g., unique_list <- unique(unlist(c(list1, list2))).

Question: How do you merge lists and convert the result to another data structure?
Answer: Use c() to merge and then convert using as.data.frame() or as.matrix().

Question: How do you merge lists based on the length of their elements?
Answer: Use mapply() to merge elements based on their length, ensuring alignment.

Question: How do you merge lists by taking the union of their elements?
Answer: Use union() on the unlisted versions of the lists, e.g., union_list <- union(unlist(list1), unlist(list2)).

Question: How do you merge lists and keep only unique named elements?
Answer: Use unique() on the names of the merged list, e.g., unique_names_list <- list1[unique(names(c(list1, list2)))].

Question: How do you merge lists and compute aggregate statistics on the merged data?
Answer: Use sapply() or lapply() after merging to compute aggregate statistics.

Question: How do you merge lists containing different data types, such as factors and characters?
Answer: Use c() to merge and handle different data types by converting them to a common type if needed.

Question: How do you merge lists that contain elements with different structures?
Answer: Use a custom function within mapply() or Map() to ensure compatibility between different structures during the merge.

Question: How do you merge lists that include lists as elements, without flattening the nested lists?
Answer: Use c() directly without unlist() to keep the nested list structure intact.

List to Vector Conversion

Question: How do you convert a list to a vector in R?
Answer: Use the unlist() function, e.g., vector <- unlist(my_list).

Question: What happens to the different types of elements in a list when it is converted to a vector?
Answer: unlist() coerces all elements to the most flexible common type, usually character if the list contains mixed types.

Question: Can you convert a nested list to a vector?
Answer: Yes, unlist() will flatten a nested list into a single vector.

Question: How do you convert a list of numeric elements to a numeric vector?
Answer: Use unlist() directly, e.g., numeric_vector <- unlist(my_numeric_list).

Question: How do you ensure that a list with mixed data types is converted to a numeric vector?
Answer: Ensure all elements can be coerced to numeric before using unlist(), or manually convert elements.

Question: How do you convert a list to a character vector?
Answer: Use unlist() on the list, e.g., char_vector <- unlist(my_list).

Question: What is the output of unlist() when applied to a list containing NULL elements?
Answer: NULL elements are removed, and the rest of the list is flattened into a vector.

Question: How do you preserve the names of list elements when converting to a vector?
Answer: Use unlist() with use.names = TRUE, e.g., vector <- unlist(my_list, use.names = TRUE).

Question: How do you convert only specific elements of a list to a vector?
Answer: Subset the list before using unlist(), e.g., vector <- unlist(my_list[1:3]).

Question: Can you convert a list of factors to a vector?
Answer: Yes, unlist() will convert the factors to their underlying integer codes, unless you convert them to characters first.

Question: How do you convert a list of logical values to a logical vector?
Answer: Use unlist() on the logical list, e.g., logical_vector <- unlist(my_logical_list).

Question: How do you handle list elements that are vectors when converting to a single vector?
Answer: unlist() will concatenate all elements, including vectors within the list, into a single vector.

Question: How do you convert a list of character vectors to a single character vector?
Answer: Use unlist() to flatten the list into one character vector, e.g., char_vector <- unlist(list_of_char_vectors).

Question: How do you convert a list containing different lengths of elements into a vector?
Answer: unlist() will concatenate all elements regardless of their original length into a single vector.

Question: How do you convert a list of data frames to a vector?
Answer: Use unlist() on the list of data frames, but be aware that this will flatten the entire structure.

Question: How do you convert a list to a named vector?
Answer: Use unlist() with the use.names = TRUE parameter to keep the names, e.g., named_vector <- unlist(my_list, use.names = TRUE).

Question: How do you convert a list with missing values (NA) to a vector?
Answer: unlist() will retain NA values in the resulting vector, e.g., vector_with_na <- unlist(list_with_na).

Question: How do you convert a list of dates to a vector in R?
Answer: Use unlist() to convert the list of dates to a date vector, e.g., date_vector <- unlist(list_of_dates).

Question: How do you convert a list of numeric vectors to a single numeric vector?
Answer: Use unlist() to concatenate all numeric vectors into one, e.g., numeric_vector <- unlist(list_of_numeric_vectors).

Question: How do you handle a list that contains elements of class "matrix" when converting to a vector?
Answer: unlist() will flatten the matrix into a vector, preserving the row-major order.

Question: Can you specify a type for the vector when converting a list in R?
Answer: No, unlist() automatically coerces to the most flexible type, but you can cast the result afterward, e.g., as.numeric(unlist(my_list)).

Question: How do you convert a list with named elements to a vector and extract only the values?
Answer: Use unlist() and ignore the names with use.names = FALSE, e.g., vector <- unlist(my_list, use.names = FALSE).

Question: How do you convert a list of lists to a single vector without losing any information?
Answer: Use unlist() directly; it will flatten all levels of nested lists into a single vector.

Question: How do you convert a list of logical vectors to a single logical vector?
Answer: Use unlist() to combine all logical vectors into one, e.g., logical_vector <- unlist(list_of_logical_vectors).

Question: How do you convert a list of data frame columns to a vector?
Answer: Use unlist() to flatten the list of columns into a single vector.

Question: How do you convert a list of numeric matrices to a numeric vector?
Answer: Use unlist() to flatten the list of matrices into one numeric vector.

Question: How do you ensure that a list of factors is converted to a vector of factor levels as characters?
Answer: Convert factors to characters first using as.character() before applying unlist(), e.g., char_vector <- unlist(lapply(factor_list, as.character)).

Question: How do you convert a list containing complex numbers to a complex vector?
Answer: Use unlist() directly on the list of complex numbers, e.g., complex_vector <- unlist(complex_list).

Question: How do you convert a list of dates to a vector while preserving the date format?
Answer: unlist() will preserve the date format if the list elements are date objects.

Question: How do you convert a list of named lists to a vector and preserve the names?
Answer: Use unlist() with use.names = TRUE, e.g., named_vector <- unlist(named_list, use.names = TRUE).

Question: How do you convert a list with mixed numeric and character elements to a numeric vector?
Answer: Coerce the character elements to numeric first, then use unlist(); non-numeric strings will become NA.

Question: How do you convert a list of integers to a single integer vector?
Answer: Use unlist() directly, e.g., int_vector <- unlist(list_of_integers).

Question: How do you convert a list of data frames to a vector while keeping only specific columns?
Answer: Extract the desired columns first using lapply(), then apply unlist().

Question: How do you handle list elements that cannot be coerced to a common type during conversion to a vector?
Answer: Manually handle type conversion for each element using lapply() before applying unlist().

Question: How do you convert a list with duplicate values to a vector and remove duplicates?
Answer: Use unlist() followed by unique(), e.g., unique_vector <- unique(unlist(my_list)).

Question: How do you convert a list of characters to a vector while removing empty strings?
Answer: Use unlist() combined with Filter(), e.g., char_vector <- Filter(nzchar, unlist(list_of_chars)).

Question: How do you convert a list to a vector while excluding NULL elements?
Answer: Use unlist() with Filter() to exclude NULL, e.g., filtered_vector <- unlist(Filter(Negate(is.null), my_list)).

Question: How do you convert a list of vectors into a concatenated vector in a specific order?
Answer: Use unlist() and order() on the resulting vector, or manually reorder the list before flattening.

Online Resources

Online Practice Paper Link: https://forms.gle/wiYqo2dqrbptuyQq7

QR Code :

YouTube Video Link:
https://www.youtube.com/playlist?list=PLzlh_31VWEFqlE97qh1xOzVC3jSSiuyod

QR Code :

Chapter 6: Matrix

Creating a Matrix

Question: How do you create a matrix in R?
Answer: Use the matrix() function, e.g., matrix(data = 1:9, nrow = 3, ncol = 3).

Question: What arguments are required to create a matrix in R?
Answer: The matrix() function requires data, nrow (number of rows), and ncol (number of columns) as key arguments.

Question: How do you create a matrix by specifying only the number of rows?
Answer: Use the matrix() function with nrow specified, e.g., matrix(1:6, nrow = 2).

Question: How do you create a matrix by specifying only the number of columns?
Answer: Use the matrix() function with ncol specified, e.g., matrix(1:6, ncol = 3).

Question: Can you create a matrix with character data?
Answer: Yes, you can create a matrix with character data, e.g., matrix(letters[1:9], nrow = 3).

Question: How do you create a matrix by filling columns first in R?
Answer: Use the byrow = FALSE argument in matrix(), which is the default behavior, e.g., matrix(1:6, nrow = 2, byrow = FALSE).

Question: How do you create a matrix by filling rows first in R?
Answer: Use the byrow = TRUE argument in matrix(), e.g., matrix(1:6, nrow = 2, byrow = TRUE).

Question: How do you create a matrix from a vector?
Answer: Use the matrix() function and specify the dimensions, e.g., matrix(1:9, nrow = 3, ncol = 3).

Question: How do you create a diagonal matrix in R?
Answer: Use the diag() function, e.g., diag(1:3).

Question: How do you create an identity matrix in R?
Answer: Use diag() with a single argument specifying the dimension, e.g., diag(3).

Question: How do you create a matrix filled with zeros?
Answer: Use matrix(0, nrow = m, ncol = n) where m and n are the desired dimensions.

Question: How do you create a matrix filled with ones?
Answer: Use matrix(1, nrow = m, ncol = n).

Question: How do you create a matrix with random numbers?
Answer: Use matrix(runif(m*n), nrow = m, ncol = n) to create a matrix with random uniform numbers.

Question: How do you create a matrix with normally distributed random numbers?
Answer: Use matrix(rnorm(m*n), nrow = m, ncol = n).

Question: How do you assign names to the rows and columns of a matrix?
Answer: Use dimnames(), e.g., dimnames(mat) <- list(row_names, col_names).

Question: How do you create a block matrix by combining smaller matrices?
Answer: Use rbind() and cbind() to combine matrices, e.g., cbind(mat1, mat2).

Question: How do you create a matrix with factors as elements?
Answer: Convert factors to numeric or characters first, or create directly using matrix().

Question: How do you create a matrix from an existing data frame?
Answer: Use as.matrix(df) to convert a data frame to a matrix.

Question: How do you ensure a matrix has the correct dimensions?
Answer: Use nrow() and ncol() functions to check dimensions after creation.

Question: How do you create a matrix with complex numbers?
Answer: Use matrix(complex(real = 1:3, imaginary = 4:6), nrow = 3).

Question: How do you create a matrix with named dimensions directly?
Answer: Use matrix() and assign names through dimnames().

Question: How do you create a matrix with different data types in R?
Answer: Matrices in R can only contain one data type; mixed types must be coerced to a common type or use a data frame instead.

Question: How do you create a matrix from a list of vectors?
Answer: Use do.call(rbind, list_of_vectors) to combine the vectors into a matrix.

Question: How do you create a matrix with sequential numbering by row?
Answer: Use matrix(1:(m*n), nrow = m, byrow = TRUE).

Question: How do you create a matrix with sequential numbering by column?
Answer: Use matrix(1:(m*n), nrow = m, byrow = FALSE).

Question: How do you create a matrix and fill it with NA values?
Answer: Use matrix(NA, nrow = m, ncol = n).

Question: How do you create a matrix with specific row and column names during creation?
Answer: Use dimnames argument in matrix(), e.g., matrix(1:9, nrow = 3, dimnames = list(c("R1", "R2", "R3"), c("C1", "C2", "C3"))).

Question: How do you replicate a matrix in R?
Answer: Use replicate() or kronecker() for multiple copies, e.g., replicate(3, matrix(1:4, nrow = 2)).

Question: How do you create a matrix by repeating a vector?
Answer: Use matrix(rep(vector, times = n), nrow = m).

Question: How do you create an upper or lower triangular matrix?
Answer: Create a full matrix and use upper.tri() or lower.tri() to set elements to zero accordingly.

Question: How do you create a matrix with row-wise or column-wise means?
Answer: Use rowMeans() or colMeans() on an existing matrix.

Question: How do you create a matrix from existing matrices?
Answer: Use rbind() or cbind() to combine them into a new matrix.

Question: How do you create a matrix with all elements set to a specific value?
Answer: Use matrix(value, nrow = m, ncol = n) where value is the specific value.

Question: How do you create a sparse matrix in R?
Answer: Use the Matrix package and Matrix() function for creating sparse matrices.

Question: How do you create a matrix and assign it to an existing object?
Answer: Create the matrix and assign it directly, e.g., existing_matrix <- matrix(data, nrow, ncol).

Question: How do you create a matrix from an array?
Answer: Convert the array using as.matrix() if it has two dimensions.

Question: How do you initialize a matrix with different values depending on the row and column indices?
Answer: Use nested loops or apply a function to outer() with row and column indices.

Accessing Matrix Elements

Question: How do you access a specific element in a matrix in R?
Answer: Use square brackets with row and column indices, e.g., matrix[row, col].

Question: How do you access all elements in a specific row of a matrix?
Answer: Use indexing with a comma, leaving the column index blank, e.g., matrix[row,].

Question: How do you access all elements in a specific column of a matrix?
Answer: Use indexing with a comma, leaving the row index blank, e.g., matrix[, col].

Question: How do you access multiple rows and columns in a matrix?
Answer: Use vectors for row and column indices, e.g., matrix[c(1, 3), c(2, 4)].

Question: How do you access elements of a matrix using negative indexing?
Answer: Use negative indices to exclude specific rows or columns, e.g., matrix[-1, -2] excludes the first row and second column.

Question: How do you access elements of a matrix conditionally?
Answer: Use logical indexing, e.g., matrix[matrix > 5] to access elements greater than 5.

Question: How do you access elements in the diagonal of a matrix?
Answer: Use the diag() function, e.g., diag(matrix).

Question: How do you access elements in the upper or lower triangle of a matrix?
Answer: Use upper.tri() or lower.tri() in conjunction with logical indexing.

Question: How do you access matrix elements by name if the matrix has row and column names?
Answer: Use named indexing, e.g., matrix["row_name", "col_name"].

Question: How do you access a subset of a matrix and store it in a new matrix?
Answer: Use square brackets for subsetting and assignment, e.g., new_matrix <- matrix[1:2, 1:2].

Question: How do you access the first row and all columns of a matrix?
Answer: Use matrix[1,].

Question: How do you access the last row and all columns of a matrix?
Answer: Use matrix[nrow(matrix),].

Question: How do you access the first column and all rows of a matrix?
Answer: Use matrix[, 1].

Question: How do you access the last column and all rows of a matrix?
Answer: Use matrix[, ncol(matrix)].

Question: How do you access elements of a matrix that satisfy a specific condition?
Answer: Use which() combined with a condition, e.g., which(matrix > 10, arr.ind = TRUE).

Question: How do you access and modify a specific element of a matrix?
Answer: Use indexing for access and assignment, e.g., matrix[1, 1] <- new_value.

Question: How do you access elements of a matrix by excluding specific rows and columns?
Answer: Use negative indexing, e.g., matrix[-c(1, 3), -c(2, 4)].

Question: How do you access elements of a matrix using a logical matrix?
Answer: Use a logical matrix of the same dimensions as the index, e.g., matrix[logical_matrix].

Question: How do you access matrix elements based on the position of another matrix?
Answer: Use a matrix of indices with cbind(), e.g., matrix[cbind(row_indices, col_indices)].

Question: How do you access the entire matrix excluding the diagonal elements?
Answer: Use matrix[!diag(matrix)].

Question: How do you access elements from the middle of a matrix?
Answer: Calculate the middle indices based on dimensions and use them for indexing.

Question: How do you access every other row or column in a matrix?
Answer: Use seq() for row or column indices, e.g., matrix[seq(1, nrow(matrix), 2),].

Question: How do you access and set all elements in a specific column to NA?
Answer: Use matrix[, col] <- NA.

Question: How do you access elements of a matrix using row and column indices stored in vectors?
Answer: Use cbind() with vectors of row and column indices.

Question: How do you access elements of a matrix and replace them with a new value?
Answer: Use indexing for selection and assignment, e.g., matrix[matrix > 10] <- new_value.

Question: How do you access the last n rows of a matrix?
Answer: Use tail(matrix, n) with a custom function to return rows.

Question: How do you access matrix elements that match a specific pattern?
Answer: Use grep() or a similar function to find the pattern, combined with indexing.

Question: How do you access elements of a matrix and store them as a vector?
Answer: Use as.vector(matrix[row_indices, col_indices]).

Question: How do you access non-zero elements of a matrix?
Answer: Use matrix[matrix != 0].

Question: How do you access elements in alternating rows and columns?
Answer: Use seq() with indexing, e.g., matrix[seq(1, nrow(matrix), 2), seq(1, ncol(matrix), 2)].

Question: How do you access elements from a matrix based on a specific function applied to rows or columns?
Answer: Use apply() with indexing, e.g., apply(matrix, 1, function(row) row[row > threshold]).

Question: How do you access elements of a matrix with a custom function?
Answer: Use apply() or lapply() depending on the structure, combined with indexing.

Question: How do you access and remove specific rows and columns from a matrix?
Answer: Use negative indexing to exclude specific rows or columns, e.g., matrix[-rows_to_remove, -cols_to_remove].

Question: How do you access matrix elements to perform vectorized operations?
Answer: Use direct indexing for access and apply vectorized functions directly, e.g., matrix * scalar.

Question: How do you access a matrix by its row and column names?
Answer: Use named indexing, e.g., matrix["row_name", "col_name"].

Question: How do you access matrix elements in a specific order based on custom logic?
Answer: Use order() on the indices and apply them in the desired sequence.

Matrix Arithmetic and Manipulation

Question: How do you perform element-wise addition of two matrices in R?
Answer: Use the + operator, e.g., matrix1 + matrix2.

Question: How do you perform element-wise subtraction of two matrices?
Answer: Use the - operator, e.g., matrix1 - matrix2.

Question: How do you perform element-wise multiplication of two matrices?
Answer: Use the * operator, e.g., matrix1 * matrix2.

Question: How do you perform element-wise division of two matrices?
Answer: Use the / operator, e.g., matrix1 / matrix2.

Question: How do you multiply a matrix by a scalar?
Answer: Use the * operator, e.g., matrix * scalar.

Question: How do you add a scalar to every element of a matrix?
Answer: Use the + operator, e.g., matrix + scalar.

Question: How do you subtract a scalar from every element of a matrix?
Answer: Use the - operator, e.g., matrix - scalar.

Question: How do you raise every element of a matrix to a power?
Answer: Use the ^ operator, e.g., matrix ^ 2.

Question: How do you calculate the sum of all elements in a matrix?
Answer: Use sum(matrix).

Question: How do you calculate the mean of all elements in a matrix?
Answer: Use mean(matrix).

Question: How do you apply a function to each element of a matrix?
Answer: Use apply() with MARGIN = c(1, 2), e.g., apply(matrix, c(1, 2), FUN).

Question: How do you calculate the row sums of a matrix?
Answer: Use rowSums(matrix).

Question: How do you calculate the column sums of a matrix?
Answer: Use colSums(matrix).

Question: How do you calculate the row means of a matrix?
Answer: Use rowMeans(matrix).

Question: How do you calculate the column means of a matrix?
Answer: Use colMeans(matrix).

Question: How do you transpose a matrix in R?
Answer: Use the t() function, e.g., t(matrix).

Question: How do you compute the determinant of a square matrix?
Answer: Use the det() function, e.g., det(matrix).

Question: How do you compute the inverse of a square matrix?
Answer: Use the solve() function, e.g., solve(matrix).

Question: How do you flatten a matrix into a vector?
Answer: Use as.vector(matrix).

Question: How do you replicate a matrix along rows or columns?
Answer: Use kronecker() or replicate(), e.g., kronecker(matrix, matrix(1, 2, 2)).

Question: How do you normalize the elements of a matrix?
Answer: Subtract the mean and divide by the standard deviation, or use a custom normalization function.

Question: How do you rescale the elements of a matrix to a specific range?
Answer: Use the formula (matrix - min(matrix)) / (max(matrix) - min(matrix)) * (new_max - new_min) + new_min.

Question: How do you center the elements of a matrix?
Answer: Subtract the mean from each element, e.g., matrix - mean(matrix).

Question: How do you multiply two matrices (matrix multiplication)?
Answer: Use the %*% operator, e.g., matrix1 %*% matrix2.

Question: How do you perform matrix division in R?
Answer: Use solve(matrix2) %*% matrix1 for solving linear systems.

Question: How do you apply a function to the rows of a matrix?
Answer: Use apply(matrix, 1, FUN).

Question: How do you apply a function to the columns of a matrix?
Answer: Use apply(matrix, 2, FUN).

Question: How do you reshape a matrix into a different dimension?
Answer: Use matrix(matrix, nrow = new_row, ncol = new_col).

Question: How do you remove a specific row from a matrix?
Answer: Use negative indexing, e.g., matrix[-row_index,].

Question: How do you remove a specific column from a matrix?
Answer: Use negative indexing, e.g., matrix[, -col_index].

Question: How do you flip a matrix vertically or horizontally?
Answer: Use matrix[nrow(matrix):1,] for vertical flip and matrix[, ncol(matrix):1] for horizontal flip.

Question: How do you calculate the cumulative sum of elements in a matrix?
Answer: Use apply(matrix, c(1, 2), cumsum) or flatten and apply cumsum().

Question: How do you sort each row or column of a matrix?
Answer: Use apply(matrix, 1, sort) for rows and apply(matrix, 2, sort) for columns.

Question: How do you multiply matrices element-wise and then sum the result?
Answer: Use sum(matrix1 * matrix2).

Question: How do you replace all negative values in a matrix with zeros?
Answer: Use matrix[matrix < 0] <- 0.

Question: How do you find the maximum or minimum element in a matrix?
Answer: Use max(matrix) or min(matrix).

Question: How do you calculate the Euclidean norm of a matrix?
Answer: Use sqrt(sum(matrix^2)).

Question: How do you raise a matrix to a power?
Answer: Use matrix multiplication for powers, e.g., matrix %*% matrix for squaring.

Matrix Operations

Question: How do you perform matrix multiplication in R?
Answer: Use the %*% operator, e.g., matrix1 %*% matrix2.

Question: How do you calculate the cross product of two matrices?
Answer: Use crossprod(matrix1, matrix2).

Question: How do you calculate the dot product of two vectors in R?
Answer: Use sum(vector1 * vector2).

Question: How do you compute the determinant of a matrix?
Answer: Use the det() function, e.g., det(matrix).

Question: How do you compute the inverse of a matrix?
Answer: Use the solve() function, e.g., solve(matrix).

Question: How do you solve a system of linear equations using matrix operations?
Answer: Use solve(A, b) where A is the coefficient matrix and b is the vector of constants.

Question: How do you find the transpose of a matrix?
Answer: Use the t() function, e.g., t(matrix).

Question: How do you compute the eigenvalues of a matrix?
Answer: Use the eigen() function, e.g., eigen(matrix)$values.

Question: How do you compute the eigenvectors of a matrix?
Answer: Use the eigen() function, e.g., eigen(matrix)$vectors.

Question: How do you perform element-wise multiplication of two matrices?
Answer: Use the * operator, e.g., matrix1 * matrix2.

Question: How do you calculate the trace of a matrix (sum of diagonal elements)?
Answer: Use sum(diag(matrix)).

Question: How do you compute the rank of a matrix?
Answer: Use qr(matrix)$rank.

Question: How do you calculate the Frobenius norm of a matrix?
Answer: Use sqrt(sum(matrix^2)).

Question: How do you compute the singular value decomposition (SVD) of a matrix?
Answer: Use svd(matrix).

Question: How do you perform the Cholesky decomposition of a matrix?
Answer: Use chol(matrix).

Question: How do you perform LU decomposition of a matrix?
Answer: Use lu() from the Matrix package.

Question: How do you calculate the Moore-Penrose pseudoinverse of a matrix?
Answer: Use ginv(matrix) from the MASS package.

Question: How do you calculate the projection of a vector onto a matrix?
Answer: Use proj <- A %*% solve(t(A) %*% A) %*% t(A) %*% b.

Question: How do you check if a matrix is positive definite?
Answer: A matrix is positive definite if all its eigenvalues are positive, check with eigen(matrix)$values.

Question: How do you calculate the covariance matrix from a data matrix?
Answer: Use cov(data_matrix).

Question: How do you compute the inverse of a block matrix?
Answer: Compute inverses of submatrices if possible or use the Schur complement.

Question: How do you perform matrix operations in parallel in R?
Answer: Use packages like parallel or foreach to distribute computations across cores.

Question: How do you calculate the outer product of two vectors?
Answer: Use outer(vector1, vector2).

Question: How do you calculate the Hadamard product of two matrices?
Answer: The Hadamard product is the same as element-wise multiplication, e.g., matrix1 * matrix2.

Question: How do you compute the Schur complement of a block matrix?
Answer: Calculate it using the formula: Schur = A - B %*% solve(D) %*% C.

Question: How do you perform matrix factorization in R?
Answer: Use methods like svd() or nmf() for non-negative matrix factorization.

Question: How do you calculate the correlation matrix of a data matrix?
Answer: Use cor(data_matrix).

Question: How do you perform matrix-vector multiplication in R?
Answer: Use %*% between a matrix and a vector, e.g., matrix %*% vector.

Question: How do you calculate the Kronecker product of two matrices?
Answer: Use the kronecker() function, e.g., kronecker(matrix1, matrix2).

Question: How do you perform matrix exponentiation in R?
Answer: Use expm() from the expm package for matrix exponentiation.

Question: How do you compute the logarithm of a matrix?
Answer: Use logm() from the expm package.

Question: How do you apply a custom function to the elements of a matrix?
Answer: Use apply(matrix, c(1, 2), custom_function).

Question: How do you compare two matrices for equality?
Answer: Use all.equal(matrix1, matrix2).

Question: How do you compute the distance matrix between rows of a matrix?
Answer: Use dist(matrix).

Question: How do you calculate the Mahalanobis distance using a covariance matrix?
Answer: Use mahalanobis(x, center, cov) where x is the data vector, center is the mean, and cov is the covariance matrix.

Online Resources

Online Practice Paper Link : https://forms.gle/FArEekdfp6jhbueq8

QR Code:

YouTube Video Link:
https://www.youtube.com/playlist?list=PLzlh_31VWEFqVDlvibcx_BcYaQMRUnplg

QR Code :

Chapter 7: Strings

Strings in R

Question: What is a string in R?
Answer: A string in R is a sequence of characters enclosed in quotes, either single (') or double (").

Question: How do you declare a string in R?
Answer: A string can be declared by assigning text to a variable, e.g., my_string <- "Hello, World!".

Question: What is the difference between single and double quotes in R?
Answer: There is no functional difference between single and double quotes for strings in R; either can be used to define a string.

Question: How do you check the length of a string in R?
Answer: Use the nchar() function, e.g., nchar("Hello") returns 5.

Question: Can strings in R include special characters?
Answer: Yes, strings can include special characters like \n for a new line or \t for a tab.

Question: How do you create a string that spans multiple lines in R?
Answer: Use \n for new lines within a string, e.g., multiline_string <- "Line 1\nLine 2\nLine 3".

Question: How do you include a quotation mark inside a string in R?
Answer: Escape the quotation mark with a backslash, e.g., string_with_quote <- "He said, \"Hello!\"".

Question: How do you convert a number to a string in R?
Answer: Use the as.character() function, e.g., as.character(123).

Question: How do you combine multiple strings into one string?
Answer: Use the paste() or paste0() functions, e.g., paste("Hello", "World").

Question: What is the difference between paste() and paste0()?
Answer:paste() adds a space between the strings by default, while paste0() concatenates them directly without any separator.

Question: How do you split a string into multiple parts in R?
Answer: Use the strsplit() function, e.g., strsplit("Hello World", " ") splits the string into ["Hello", "World"].

Question: How do you extract a substring from a string in R?
Answer: Use the substr() function, e.g., substr("Hello", 2, 4) returns "ell".

Question: How do you replace a part of a string in R?
Answer: Use the sub() or gsub() functions, e.g., sub("World", "R", "Hello World") replaces "World" with "R".

Question: How do you check if a string contains a specific substring?
Answer: Use the grepl() function, e.g., grepl("World", "Hello World") returns TRUE.

Question: How do you compare two strings for equality in R?
Answer: Use the == operator, e.g., "Hello" == "Hello" returns TRUE.

Question: How do you concatenate a string with a number in R?
Answer: Convert the number to a string using as.character() and then use paste() or paste0(), e.g., paste0("Number: ", as.character(123)).

Question: How do you remove leading and trailing spaces from a string?
Answer: Use the trimws() function, e.g., trimws(" Hello ") returns "Hello".

Question: How do you repeat a string multiple times in R?
Answer: Use the strrep() function, e.g., strrep("Hello", 3) returns "HelloHelloHello".

Question: How do you change the case of a string to uppercase in R?
Answer: Use the toupper() function, e.g., toupper("Hello") returns "HELLO".

Question: How do you change the case of a string to lowercase in R?
Answer: Use the tolower() function, e.g., tolower("Hello") returns "hello".

Question: How do you find the position of a substring in a string?
Answer: Use the regexpr() function, e.g., regexpr("World", "Hello World") returns the position of the substring.

Question: How do you determine if a string is empty in R?
Answer: Check if the string has a length of zero using nchar() == 0, or simply use == "".

Question: Can a string in R contain NULL?
Answer: No, NULL is a special object in R and cannot be directly included in a string; you can use NA to represent missing values in strings.

Question: How do you handle NA values in strings?
Answer: Use is.na() to check and na.omit() to remove NA values from string vectors.

Question: How do you format numbers within a string?
Answer: Use the sprintf() function, e.g., sprintf("The value is %.2f", 123.456) formats the number to two decimal places.

Question: How do you detect if a string starts or ends with a specific substring?
Answer: Use the startsWith() and endsWith() functions, e.g., startsWith("Hello World", "Hello") returns TRUE.

Question: How do you create a string vector in R?
Answer: Use the c() function, e.g., string_vector <- c("Hello", "World").

Question: How do you concatenate all elements of a string vector into a single string?
Answer: Use the paste() function with collapse, e.g., paste(string_vector, collapse = " ").

Question: How do you split a string into individual characters?
Answer: Use strsplit() with an empty separator, e.g., strsplit("Hello", "").

Question: How do you escape special characters in a string?
Answer: Use a backslash \ before special characters, e.g., "\\n" to include a newline character.

Question: How do you create a multiline string in R?
Answer: Use paste() with \n to create new lines, or use cat() to print multiline strings.

Question: How do you remove all occurrences of a character in a string?
Answer: Use gsub() to replace the character with an empty string, e.g., gsub("a", "", "banana").

Question: How do you pad a string with leading zeros?
Answer: Use sprintf() or formatC() to format the string with leading zeros, e.g., sprintf("%05d", 42).

Question: How do you count the number of occurrences of a character in a string?
Answer: Use gsub() to remove the character and compare lengths, or use gregexpr() and lengths().

Question: How do you reverse a string in R?
Answer: Use strsplit() to split into characters, then rev() to reverse and paste0() to combine, e.g., paste0(rev(strsplit("Hello", NULL)[[1]]), collapse = "").

Question: How do you interpolate variables into a string in R?
Answer: Use paste() or sprintf() to insert variable values into a string.

Question: How do you encode a string in base64 in R?
Answer: Use the base64enc package with base64encode().

Question: How do you decode a base64 string in R?
Answer: Use the base64enc package with base64decode().

Creating Strings

Question: How do you create a simple string in R?
Answer: Use the assignment operator with text in quotes, e.g., my_string <- "Hello, World!".

Question: How do you create a string containing both single and double quotes?
Answer: Use opposite quotes for enclosing, e.g., string <- 'She said, "Hello!"'.

Question: How do you create a string that includes a newline character?
Answer: Use the newline escape sequence \n, e.g., string <- "Hello\nWorld".

Question: How do you create a string with a tab character?
Answer: Use the tab escape sequence \t, e.g., string <- "Hello\tWorld".

Question: How do you create a string from a numeric value?
Answer: Use the as.character() function, e.g., string <- as.character(123).

Question: How do you create a string by repeating a character multiple times?
Answer: Use the strrep() function, e.g., string <- strrep("-", 10).

Question: How do you create a string by concatenating variables?
Answer: Use the paste() or paste0() functions, e.g., string <- paste("Hello", "World").

Question: How do you create a string by collapsing a vector of strings?
Answer: Use paste() with the collapse argument, e.g., string <- paste(c("Hello", "World"), collapse = " ").

Question: How do you create a string containing the current date?
Answer: Use Sys.Date() combined with as.character(), e.g., date_string <- as.character(Sys.Date()).

Question: How do you create a string from a formatted date?
Answer: Use format() with Sys.Date(), e.g., date_string <- format(Sys.Date(), "%B %d, %Y").

Question: How do you create a string with a number formatted to two decimal places?
Answer: Use sprintf() or formatC(), e.g., string <- sprintf("%.2f", 3.14159).

Question: How do you create a string with dynamic content in R?
Answer: Use paste() or sprintf() to combine variables and text, e.g., paste("The value of x is", x).

Question: How do you create a string from an R object, like a vector or list?
Answer: Use toString() or paste(), e.g., string <- toString(c(1, 2, 3)).

Question: How do you create a multiline string using multiple lines of code?
Answer: Use paste() with \n for new lines, or use a single cat() command.

Question: How do you create a string from user input?
Answer: Use readline() to capture input, e.g., user_input <- readline(prompt = "Enter a string: ").

Question: How do you create a string with leading or trailing spaces?
Answer: Use paste() or sprintf() with padding, e.g., string <- paste(" Hello ").

Question: How do you create a string that contains special symbols like @ or #?
Answer: Simply include the symbols in quotes, e.g., string <- "user@example.com".

Question: How do you create a string containing Unicode characters?
Answer: Use the Unicode escape sequence \u, e.g., string <- "\u00A9".

Question: How do you create a string with non-printable characters, such as a backspace?
Answer: Use appropriate escape sequences, e.g., string <- "Hello\bWorld".

Question: How do you create a string from the contents of a file?
Answer: Use readLines() and collapse into a single string, e.g., string <- paste(readLines("file.txt"), collapse = "\n").

Question: How do you create a string that dynamically includes the result of a calculation?
Answer: Use paste() or sprintf(), e.g., paste("2 + 2 =", 2 + 2).

Question: How do you create a string that repeats a phrase multiple times?
Answer: Use strrep() or rep(), e.g., string <- strrep("Hello ", 3).

Question: How do you create a string from a factor in R?
Answer: Convert the factor to a string using as.character(), e.g., string <- as.character(factor_variable).

Question: How do you create a string with a specific encoding?
Answer: Use iconv() to specify encoding, e.g., string <- iconv("text", from = "UTF-8", to = "ISO-8859-1").

Question: How do you create a string from a formatted number with commas?
Answer: Use formatC() or prettyNum(), e.g., string <- formatC(1000000, format = "d", big.mark = ",").

Question: How do you create a string by converting a logical value?
Answer: Use as.character() on the logical value, e.g., string <- as.character(TRUE).

Question: How do you create a string that includes the name of an R variable?
Answer: Use deparse(substitute(variable_name)), e.g., string <- deparse(substitute(my_var)).

Question: How do you create a string from a list of words?
Answer: Use paste() with collapse, e.g., string <- paste(word_list, collapse = " ").

Question: How do you create a string that mimics the structure of R code?
Answer: Use deparse() on an expression, e.g., string <- deparse(expression(2 + 2)).

Question: How do you create a string by sampling random characters?
Answer: Use paste(sample(letters, 5, replace = TRUE), collapse = "").

Question: How do you create a string from a sequence of numbers?
Answer: Use paste() or toString(), e.g., string <- paste(1:5, collapse = ", ").

Question: How do you create a string with a custom delimiter between elements?
Answer: Use paste() with collapse, e.g., string <- paste(c("A", "B", "C"), collapse = "|").

Question: How do you create a string from an array or matrix in R?
Answer: Use apply() or paste(), e.g., string <- apply(matrix, 1, paste, collapse = ", ").

Question: How do you create a string by converting an entire data frame column?
Answer: Use as.character() on the column, e.g., string_vector <- as.character(df$column).

Question: How do you create a string that is compatible with SQL queries?
Answer: Use shQuote() to safely quote strings for SQL queries, e.g., query <- paste("SELECT * FROM table WHERE column =", shQuote(value)).

Question: How do you create a string by repeating elements of a vector?
Answer: Use rep() and paste(), e.g., string <- paste(rep(c("A", "B"), times = 2), collapse = ", ").

Question: How do you create a string from multiple objects in R?
Answer: Use paste() to combine different objects into a single string, e.g., string <- paste("A =", A, "B =", B).

Basic Strings Operations

Question: How do you find the length of a string in R?
Answer: Use the nchar() function, e.g., nchar("Hello") returns 5.

Question: How do you concatenate two strings in R?
Answer: Use paste() or paste0(), e.g., paste("Hello", "World") or paste0("Hello", "World").

Question: How do you extract a substring from a string in R?
Answer: Use substr() or substring(), e.g., substr("Hello", 2, 4) returns "ell".

Question: How do you replace a substring in a string in R?
Answer: Use sub() or gsub(), e.g., gsub("World", "R", "Hello World") returns "Hello R".

Question: How do you convert a string to uppercase in R?
Answer: Use toupper(), e.g., toupper("hello") returns "HELLO".

Question: How do you convert a string to lowercase in R?
Answer: Use tolower(), e.g., tolower("HELLO") returns "hello".

Question: How do you remove whitespace from the beginning and end of a string?
Answer: Use trimws(), e.g., trimws(" Hello ") returns "Hello".

Question: How do you check if a string contains a specific substring?
Answer: Use grepl(), e.g., grepl("World", "Hello World") returns TRUE.

Question: How do you find the position of a substring within a string?
Answer: Use regexpr() or gregexpr(), e.g., regexpr("World", "Hello World") returns the position 7.

Question: How do you count the number of characters in a string?
Answer: Use nchar(), e.g., nchar("Hello World") returns 11.

Question: How do you split a string into a vector of substrings?
Answer: Use strsplit(), e.g., strsplit("Hello World", " ") returns c("Hello", "World").

Question: How do you combine elements of a vector into a single string?
Answer: Use paste() with collapse, e.g., paste(c("Hello", "World"), collapse = " ").

Question: How do you reverse the characters in a string?
Answer: Use strsplit(), rev(), and paste0(), e.g., paste0(rev(strsplit("Hello", NULL)[[1]]), collapse = "").

Question: How do you repeat a string multiple times?
Answer: Use strrep(), e.g., strrep("Hello", 3) returns "HelloHelloHello".

Question: How do you compare two strings for equality?
Answer: Use == or identical(), e.g., "Hello" == "Hello" returns TRUE.

Question: How do you detect the presence of a pattern in a string?
Answer: Use grepl(), e.g., grepl("l+", "Hello") returns TRUE.

Question: How do you match a regular expression in a string?
Answer: Use regexpr() or gregexpr(), e.g., regexpr("\\d+", "abc123") finds the numeric part.

Question: How do you extract a match from a string using regular expressions?
Answer: Use regmatches() with regexpr() or gregexpr(), e.g., regmatches("abc123", regexpr("\\d+", "abc123")) returns "123".

Question: How do you remove all occurrences of a character from a string?
Answer: Use gsub(), e.g., gsub("a", "", "banana") returns "bnn".

Question: How do you replace the first occurrence of a pattern in a string?
Answer: Use sub(), e.g., sub("a", "o", "banana") returns "bonana".

Question: How do you replace all occurrences of a pattern in a string?
Answer: Use gsub(), e.g., gsub("a", "o", "banana") returns "bonono".

Question: How do you check if a string starts with a specific prefix?
Answer: Use startsWith(), e.g., startsWith("Hello World", "Hello") returns TRUE.

Question: How do you check if a string ends with a specific suffix?
Answer: Use endsWith(), e.g., endsWith("Hello World", "World") returns TRUE.

Question: How do you convert a string to a numeric value?
Answer: Use as.numeric(), e.g., as.numeric("123.45") returns 123.45.

Question: How do you check if a string is numeric?
Answer: Use grepl() with a pattern, or as.numeric() with !is.na(), e.g., !is.na(as.numeric("123.45")).

Question: How do you pad a string with leading zeros?
Answer: Use sprintf() or formatC(), e.g., sprintf("%05d", 42) returns "00042".

Question: How do you remove special characters from a string?
Answer: Use gsub() with a regex pattern, e.g., gsub("[^[:alnum:]]", "", "Hello@World!").

Question: How do you convert a string vector into a data frame column?
Answer: Use data.frame(), e.g., df <- data.frame(strings = c("A", "B", "C")).

Question: How do you concatenate strings with a custom separator?
Answer: Use paste() with the sep argument, e.g., paste("A", "B", sep = "|").

Question: How do you split a string into individual characters?
Answer: Use strsplit() with an empty separator, e.g., strsplit("Hello", "").

Question: How do you handle NA values in string vectors?
Answer: Use is.na() to detect and na.omit() to remove NA values.

Question: How do you encode a string in base64 in R?
Answer: Use the base64enc package, e.g., base64encode("Hello World").

Question: How do you decode a base64 string in R?
Answer: Use the base64enc package, e.g., base64decode("SGVsbG8gV29ybGQ=").

Question: How do you capitalize the first letter of each word in a string?
Answer: Use tools::toTitleCase() or a custom function with strsplit() and toupper().

Question: How do you match multiple patterns in a string?
Answer: Use grepl() with | operator, e.g., grepl("A|B", "ABC").

Advanced String Operations

Question: How do you extract all numeric values from a string?
Answer: Use gregexpr() and regmatches(), e.g., regmatches("a1b23c", gregexpr("\\d+", "a1b23c")) returns c("1", "23").

Question: How do you perform pattern matching with lookahead and lookbehind assertions in R?
Answer: Use perl = TRUE in grepl() or gsub() with lookahead/lookbehind patterns, e.g., grepl("(?<=abc)def", "abcdef", perl = TRUE).

Question: How do you extract only the first occurrence of a pattern in a string?
Answer: Use regexpr() with regmatches(), e.g., regmatches("abc123abc", regexpr("\\d+", "abc123abc")).

Question: How do you extract all matches of a pattern in a string?
Answer: Use gregexpr() with regmatches(), e.g., regmatches("a1b2c3", gregexpr("\\d", "a1b2c3")).

Question: How do you apply a function to each match of a regex pattern in a string?
Answer: Use gsub() with a function, e.g., gsub("\\d+", function(x) as.numeric(x) + 1, "abc123def").

Question: How do you perform case-insensitive pattern matching in R?
Answer: Use ignore.case = TRUE in grep(), gsub(), or grepl() functions, e.g., grepl("hello", "HELLO", ignore.case = TRUE).

Question: How do you extract named groups from a regex match in R?
Answer: Use the stringr package's str_match() function, e.g., str_match("abc123", "(abc)(\\d+)").

Question: How do you find overlapping matches in a string?
Answer: Use a custom function with gregexpr() and regmatches(), or multiple passes with sub().

Question: How do you find and replace text using backreferences in R?
Answer: Use gsub() with perl = TRUE and backreferences, e.g., gsub("(\\w)(\\w)", "\\2\\1", "abc", perl = TRUE).

Question: How do you perform multiline pattern matching in R?
Answer: Use grepl() or gsub() with perl = TRUE and the (?m) modifier, e.g., grepl("^(abc)", "abc\ndef", perl = TRUE).

Question: How do you match patterns across multiple lines in a string?
Answer: Use perl = TRUE with (?s) to enable dot-all mode, e.g., grepl("a.*c", "a\nb\nc", perl = TRUE).

Question: How do you remove HTML tags from a string?
Answer: Use gsub() with a regex pattern, e.g., gsub("<.*?>", "", "<p>Hello</p>").

Question: How do you tokenize a string into words?
Answer: Use strsplit() with a space or regex pattern, e.g., strsplit("This is a sentence", "\\s+").

Question: How do you reverse the words in a string?
Answer: Use strsplit() to split into words, then rev() and paste(), e.g., paste(rev(strsplit("Hello World", " ")[[1]]), collapse = " ").

Question: How do you detect duplicate substrings in a string?
Answer: Use gregexpr() to find matches and check for overlaps or repetitions.

Question: How do you split a string based on multiple delimiters?
Answer: Use strsplit() with a regex pattern, e.g., strsplit("a,b;c d", "[,;\\s]").

Question: How do you perform a global search and replace using regular expressions?
Answer: Use gsub() with the desired pattern and replacement, e.g., gsub("\\d", "#", "abc123def456").

Question: How do you convert a string into a list of substrings based on matches?
Answer: Use strsplit() with gregexpr() and regmatches().

Question: How do you identify and extract repeated sequences in a string?
Answer: Use gregexpr() with a pattern for repetition, e.g., gregexpr("(.)\\1+", "aabbcc").

Question: How do you strip accents and diacritics from a string?
Answer: Use the stringi package's stri_trans_general() function, e.g., stri_trans_general("é", "Latin-ASCII").

Question: How do you validate an email address using regex in R?
Answer: Use a complex regex pattern with grepl(), e.g., grepl("^[\\w\\._%+-]+@[\\w\\.-]+\\.[a-zA-Z]{2,}$", "email@example.com").

Question: How do you extract the domain from an email address in R?
Answer: Use sub() or gsub() with regex, e.g., sub(".*@", "", "email@example.com").

Question: How do you extract text between two delimiters in R?
Answer: Use regmatches() with gregexpr() or sub(), e.g., regmatches("abc[123]def", gregexpr("\\[(.*?)\\]", "abc[123]def")).

Question: How do you generate a string based on a pattern with a variable number of repetitions?
Answer: Use strrep() with paste0() or sprintf(), e.g., paste0("A", strrep("B", 3)) returns "ABBB".

Question: How do you detect and correct common typos in strings?
Answer: Use adist() to calculate string distance and gsub() for replacements.

Question: How do you extract words that follow a specific pattern in R?
Answer: Use regmatches() with a regex capturing group, e.g., regmatches("abc 123 def", gregexpr("\\b\\d+\\b", "abc 123 def")).

Question: How do you match and extract multiple overlapping patterns?
Answer: Use gregexpr() with a lookahead assertion, or multiple passes with gsub().

Question: How do you check if a string matches a specific format, such as a phone number?
Answer: Use grepl() with a regex pattern, e.g., grepl("^\\d{3}-\\d{3}-\\d{4}$", "123-456-7890").

Question: How do you transform a string to be URL-safe in R?
Answer: Use URLencode() from utils package, e.g., URLencode("Hello World!").

Question: How do you extract a substring before a specific character?
Answer: Use sub() or gsub() with regex, e.g., sub("(.*)-.*", "\\1", "abc-def").

Question: How do you extract a substring after a specific character?
Answer: Use sub() with regex, e.g., sub(".*-(.*)", "\\1", "abc-def").

Question: How do you generate a string pattern that matches an IP address?
Answer: Use sprintf() with regex or string manipulation, e.g., sprintf("(%d{1,3}\\.){3}%d{1,3}", "ip").

Question: How do you escape regex metacharacters in a string?
Answer: Use gsub() to add a backslash before each metacharacter, e.g., gsub("([\\^\\$\\.\\|\\?*\\+\\(\\)\\[\\]])", "\\\\\\1", "regex").

Question: How do you convert a string to its ASCII code equivalent?
Answer: Use utf8ToInt(), e.g., utf8ToInt("Hello").

Question: How do you convert an ASCII code back to a string?
Answer: Use intToUtf8(), e.g., intToUtf8(c(72, 101, 108, 108, 111)).

Question: How do you detect and remove invisible characters in a string?
Answer: Use gsub() with a regex pattern, e.g., gsub("[\\p{C}]", "", "string_with_invisibles", perl = TRUE).

Question: How do you standardize case across a string vector in R?
Answer: Use tolower() or toupper() on the entire vector, e.g., tolower(c("A", "B", "C")).

Question: How do you validate and sanitize user input in string form?
Answer: Use a combination of grepl(), gsub(), and custom validation functions to check and clean input.

Question: How do you automatically correct capitalization in a string?
Answer: Use tools::toTitleCase() or a custom function with strsplit() and toupper() for each word.

Question: How do you extract numbers embedded in text from a string?
Answer: Use gregexpr() with regmatches() to extract numeric patterns, e.g., regmatches("abc123def", gregexpr("\\d+", "abc123def")).

String Manipulation Functions

Question: How do you concatenate strings in R?
Answer: Use paste() or paste0(), e.g., paste("Hello", "World").

Question: How do you extract a substring from a string?
Answer: Use substr() or substring(), e.g., substr("Hello", 2, 4).

Question: How do you replace text within a string?
Answer: Use sub() or gsub(), e.g., gsub("World", "R", "Hello World").

Question: How do you convert a string to uppercase?
Answer: Use toupper(), e.g., toupper("hello").

Question: How do you convert a string to lowercase?
Answer: Use tolower(), e.g., tolower("HELLO").

Question: How do you trim leading and trailing spaces from a string?
Answer: Use trimws(), e.g., trimws(" Hello ").

Question: How do you split a string into a vector of substrings?
Answer: Use strsplit(), e.g., strsplit("Hello World", " ").

Question: How do you repeat a string multiple times?
Answer: Use strrep(), e.g., strrep("Hello", 3).

Question: How do you match a regular expression in a string?
Answer: Use regexpr() or gregexpr(), e.g., regexpr("\\d+", "abc123").

Question: How do you extract matched text using regular expressions?
Answer: Use regmatches() with regexpr() or gregexpr(), e.g., regmatches("abc123", regexpr("\\d+", "abc123")).

Question: How do you concatenate elements of a vector into a single string?
Answer: Use paste() with collapse, e.g., paste(c("A", "B", "C"), collapse = "-").

Question: How do you reverse the characters in a string?
Answer: Use strsplit(), rev(), and paste0(), e.g., paste0(rev(strsplit("Hello", NULL)[[1]]), collapse = "").

Question: How do you check if a string starts with a specific prefix?
Answer: Use startsWith(), e.g., startsWith("Hello World", "Hello").

Question: How do you check if a string ends with a specific suffix?
Answer: Use endsWith(), e.g., endsWith("Hello World", "World").

Question: How do you format a string with dynamic content?
Answer: Use sprintf(), e.g., sprintf("Value is %d", 42).

Question: How do you find the position of a substring within a string?
Answer: Use regexpr() or gregexpr(), e.g., regexpr("World", "Hello World").

Question: How do you remove all occurrences of a character in a string?
Answer: Use gsub(), e.g., gsub("a", "", "banana").

Question: How do you remove non-alphanumeric characters from a string?
Answer: Use gsub("[^[:alnum:]]", "", "Hello@World!").

Question: How do you split a string based on multiple delimiters?
Answer: Use strsplit() with a regex pattern, e.g., strsplit("a,b;c", "[,;]").

Question: How do you validate an email address format in R?
Answer: Use grepl() with a regex pattern, e.g., grepl("^[\\w._%+-]+@[\\w.-]+\\.[a-zA-Z]{2,}$", "email@example.com").

Question: How do you escape special characters in a string?
Answer: Use gsub() to escape metacharacters, e.g., gsub("([\\^\\$\\.\\|\\?*\\+\\(\\)\\[\\]])", "\\\\\\1", "regex").

Question: How do you encode a string in base64?
Answer: Use the base64enc package, e.g., base64encode("Hello World").

Question: How do you decode a base64 string?
Answer: Use the base64enc package, e.g., base64decode("SGVsbG8gV29ybGQ=").

Question: How do you capitalize the first letter of each word in a string?
Answer: Use tools::toTitleCase() or a custom function, e.g., gsub("\\b(.)", "\\U\\1", "hello world", perl = TRUE).

Question: How do you remove the last character from a string?
Answer: Use substr() or substring(), e.g., substring("Hello", 1, nchar("Hello") - 1).

Question: How do you repeat a character n times in a string?
Answer: Use strrep(), e.g., strrep("-", 5) returns "-----".

Question: How do you check if a string is numeric in R?
Answer: Use grepl() with a regex pattern or as.numeric() with !is.na(), e.g., !is.na(as.numeric("123.45")).

Question: How do you convert a string to a numeric value?
Answer: Use as.numeric(), e.g., as.numeric("123.45").

Question: How do you find the number of words in a string?
Answer: Use strsplit() and length(), e.g., length(strsplit("Hello World", "\\s+")[[1]]).

Question: How do you extract text between two delimiters?
Answer: Use sub() or gsub() with regex, e.g., sub(".*-(.*)-.*", "\\1", "abc-123-def").

Question: How do you remove duplicate substrings from a string?
Answer: Use gsub() with backreferences, e.g., gsub("(\\b\\w+\\b)(\\s+\\1)+", "\\1", "word word word").

Question: How do you find and replace multiple patterns in a string?
Answer: Use gsub() with | in the pattern, or stringi::stri_replace_all_regex().

Question: How do you count the occurrences of a character in a string?
Answer: Use gsub() to remove the character and compare lengths, or use gregexpr() and lengths().

Question: How do you remove leading zeros from a string?
Answer: Use gsub("^0+", "", "000123").

Question: How do you convert a string to title case (capitalize first letter of each word)?
Answer: Use tools::toTitleCase() or a custom regex function.

Question: How do you split a string into an array of characters?
Answer: Use strsplit() with an empty string, e.g., strsplit("Hello", NULL).

Strings Handling Packages

Question: What is the stringr package in R?
Answer:stringr is a package in R that provides a consistent and simple interface for string operations.

Question: How do you install the stringr package in R?
Answer: Use install.packages("stringr") in the R console.

Question: How do you load the stringr package in R?
Answer: Use library(stringr) to load the package.

Question: What is the difference between stringr and base R string functions?
Answer:stringr functions have a consistent syntax and better handling of edge cases compared to base R string functions.

Question: How do you use str_length() in stringr?
Answer:str_length() returns the length of a string, e.g., str_length("Hello") returns 5.

Question: How do you use str_c() in stringr?
Answer:str_c() concatenates strings, e.g., str_c("Hello", "World").

Question: How do you use str_detect() in stringr?
Answer:str_detect() checks for the presence of a pattern in a string, e.g., str_detect("Hello", "l").

Question: How do you use str_replace() in stringr?
Answer:str_replace() replaces the first occurrence of a pattern, e.g., str_replace("Hello World", "World", "R").

Question: How do you use str_replace_all() in stringr?
Answer:str_replace_all() replaces all occurrences of a pattern, e.g., str_replace_all("Hello World", "l", "L").

Question: How do you use str_split() in stringr?
Answer:str_split() splits a string into a list of substrings, e.g., str_split("Hello World", " ").

Question: How do you use str_sub() in stringr?
Answer:str_sub() extracts substrings based on position, e.g., str_sub("Hello", 2, 4).

Question: How do you use str_trim() in stringr?
Answer:str_trim() removes leading and trailing whitespace, e.g., str_trim(" Hello ").

Question: How do you use str_to_upper() in stringr?
Answer:str_to_upper() converts a string to uppercase, e.g., str_to_upper("hello").

Question: How do you use str_to_lower() in stringr?
Answer:str_to_lower() converts a string to lowercase, e.g., str_to_lower("HELLO").

Question: How do you use str_to_title() in stringr?
Answer:str_to_title() converts a string to title case, e.g., str_to_title("hello world").

Question: How do you use str_view() in stringr?
Answer:str_view() highlights matches of a pattern in a string, useful for visual inspection in RStudio.

Question: How do you use str_match() in stringr?
Answer:str_match() extracts matching groups from a string using regex, e.g., str_match("abc123", "(\\w+)(\\d+)").

Question: How do you use str_count() in stringr?
Answer:str_count() counts the occurrences of a pattern in a string, e.g., str_count("Hello", "l").

Question: What is the stringi package in R?
Answer:stringi is a comprehensive package for string processing in R, offering more advanced functions than stringr.

Question: How do you install the stringi package in R?
Answer: Use install.packages("stringi").

Question: How do you load the stringi package in R?
Answer: Use library(stringi).

Question: How do you use stri_length() in stringi?
Answer:stri_length() returns the length of a string, e.g., stri_length("Hello").

Question: How do you use stri_join() in stringi?
Answer:stri_join() concatenates strings, similar to str_c() in stringr.

Question: How do you use stri_detect() in stringi?
Answer:stri_detect() checks for the presence of a pattern, similar to str_detect().

Question: How do you use stri_replace() in stringi?
Answer:stri_replace() replaces text based on a pattern, similar to str_replace().

Question: How do you use stri_split() in stringi?
Answer:stri_split() splits a string into a list of substrings, similar to str_split().

Question: How do you use stri_sub() in stringi?
Answer:stri_sub() extracts substrings based on position, similar to str_sub().

Question: How do you use stri_trim() in stringi?
Answer:stri_trim() removes leading and trailing whitespace, similar to str_trim().

Question: How do you use stri_trans_tolower() in stringi?
Answer:stri_trans_tolower() converts a string to lowercase, similar to str_to_lower().

Question: How do you use stri_trans_toupper() in stringi?
Answer:stri_trans_toupper() converts a string to uppercase, similar to str_to_upper().

Question: How do you use stri_trans_totitle() in stringi?
Answer:stri_trans_totitle() converts a string to title case, similar to str_to_title().

Question: How do you use stri_view() in stringi?
Answer:stri_view() is similar to str_view() in stringr, used for visual inspection of matches.

Question: How do you use stri_count() in stringi?
Answer:stri_count() counts occurrences of a pattern, similar to str_count().

Question: How do you perform case-folding with stringi?
Answer: Use stri_trans_casefold(), which is a more advanced case conversion function.

Question: How do you convert a string to Unicode normalization form in stringi?
Answer: Use stri_trans_nfc() for NFC normalization.

Question: How do you remove accents or diacritics in stringi?
Answer: Use stri_trans_general("text", "Latin-ASCII") to remove accents.

Question: How do you find the position of a regex match in stringi?
Answer: Use stri_locate() for more advanced position matching.

Question: How do you detect a regex pattern with Unicode support in stringi?
Answer: Use stri_detect_regex() with Unicode properties.

Question: How do you perform collation-aware string comparisons in stringi?
Answer: Use stri_compare(), which is locale-aware.

Question: How do you reverse a string in stringi?
Answer: Use stri_reverse() to reverse the characters in a string.

Question: How do you format strings with custom padding in stringi?
Answer: Use stri_pad() for flexible padding options.

Online Resources

Online Practice Paper Link: https://forms.gle/Qyg128QVsDdSCH6D7

QR Code:

YouTube Video Link: https://www.youtube.com/playlist?list=PLzlh_31VWEFo2g7iaeY2-j-FF3BcUlMZ2

QR Code:

Chapter 8: Arrays

Creating Arrays

Question: How do you create a basic array in R?
Answer: Use the array() function, specifying the data, dimensions, and optional dimnames, e.g., my_array <- array(1:12, dim = c(3, 4)).

Question: How do you create a 3-dimensional array in R?
Answer: Use the array() function with three dimensions, e.g., my_array <- array(1:24, dim = c(3, 4, 2)).

Question: What is the significance of the dim argument in the array() function?
Answer: The dim argument specifies the dimensions of the array, determining its shape and size.

Question: How do you create an array with named dimensions in R?
Answer: Use the dimnames argument in array(), e.g., my_array <- array(1:8, dim = c(2, 2, 2), dimnames = list(c("A1", "A2"), c("B1", "B2"), c("C1", "C2"))).

Question: Can you create an array from a single vector in R?
Answer: Yes, the array() function can convert a vector into an array by specifying appropriate dimensions.

Question: How do you create an empty array in R?
Answer: Use the array() function with NA or NULL, e.g., empty_array <- array(NA, dim = c(3, 3, 3)).

Question: How do you create an array with all elements initialized to zero?
Answer: Use array(0, dim = c(n, m, p)), where n, m, and p are the dimensions of the array.

Question: How do you specify the data type of an array in R?
Answer: Arrays inherit the data type from the input vector; ensure the input vector is of the desired type.

Question: How do you create an array from multiple vectors?
Answer: Combine vectors into one using c() before creating the array, e.g., my_array <- array(c(vec1, vec2), dim = c(3, 3, 2)).

Question: How do you create a multi-dimensional array filled with random numbers?
Answer: Use array(runif(n), dim = c(x, y, z)) where n is the total number of elements and x, y, z are dimensions.

Question: How do you create an array with different lengths for each dimension?
Answer: Specify different values for each dimension in the dim argument, e.g., array(1:24, dim = c(4, 3, 2)).

Question: How do you create a 2D array that acts like a matrix?
Answer: Use array() with two dimensions, e.g., my_matrix_array <- array(1:6, dim = c(2, 3)).

Question: How do you create a 4-dimensional array in R?
Answer: Use array() with four dimensions, e.g., my_array <- array(1:16, dim = c(2, 2, 2, 2)).

Question: How do you create an array where each element is a list?
Answer: Use array(list(), dim = c(x, y, z)), where x, y, z are dimensions.

Question: Can you create an array with a non-numeric data type?
Answer: Yes, arrays can hold any data type, including characters or logical values, e.g., array(letters[1:12], dim = c(3, 4)).

Question: How do you initialize an array with a specific sequence of numbers?
Answer: Use array(seq(start, end), dim = c(x, y, z)), where start and end define the sequence.

Question: How do you create an array from a matrix in R?
Answer: Convert the matrix to an array using as.array(matrix), or directly assign a matrix to an array variable.

Question: How do you create an array with elements distributed normally?
Answer: Use array(rnorm(n), dim = c(x, y, z)) where rnorm(n) generates normally distributed values.

Question: How do you create an array with each element being a factor?
Answer: Convert factors to integers or characters before using array(), e.g., array(as.integer(factor_vector), dim = c(x, y, z)).

Question: How do you create a multi-dimensional array where each dimension has a specific name?
Answer: Use the dimnames argument, e.g., my_array <- array(1:12, dim = c(2, 3, 2), dimnames = list(c("A1", "A2"), c("B1", "B2", "B3"), c("C1", "C2"))).

Question: How do you create an array by combining smaller arrays?
Answer: Use the abind() function from the abind package to combine smaller arrays along a new dimension.

Question: How do you initialize an array where each element is a logical value?
Answer: Use array(TRUE, dim = c(x, y, z)) to initialize with logical values.

Question: How do you create a time-series array in R?
Answer: Use array() to create a 3D array, with one dimension representing time, e.g., time_array <- array(data, dim = c(x, y, t)).

Question: How do you create a 3D array with a custom fill pattern?
Answer: Define a vector with the desired pattern and use array(pattern_vector, dim = c(x, y, z)).

Question: How do you create an array with dimensions based on another array?
Answer: Use dim() to get the dimensions of an existing array and apply them to a new array, e.g., array(new_data, dim =
dim(existing_array)).

Question: How do you create an array with a specific step size between elements?
Answer: Use seq() within array() to generate data with a specific step size, e.g., array(seq(1, 20, by = 2), dim = c(2, 5)).

Question: How do you create an array with repeated elements?
Answer: Use rep() within array(), e.g., array(rep(1:3, each = 4), dim = c(2, 3, 2)).

Question: How do you create an array with data from an external source?
Answer: Import data using appropriate functions like read.csv() and then create an array using array(imported_data, dim = c(x, y, z)).

Question: How do you create a color-coded array for image processing?
Answer: Use array() to create a 3D array representing RGB values, e.g., image_array <- array(runif(300), dim = c(10, 10, 3)).

Question: How do you create an array with each element corresponding to a specific condition?
Answer: Use conditional logic within array(), e.g., array(ifelse(1:24 %% 2 == 0, TRUE, FALSE), dim = c(3, 4, 2)).

Question: How do you create an array and directly assign it to a specific dimension order?
Answer: Use aperm() to permute the dimensions after creation, e.g., my_array <- aperm(array(1:24, dim = c(4, 3, 2)), c(3, 1, 2)).

Question: How do you create a sparse array in R?
Answer: Use the Matrix package's sparseMatrix() function, and then convert it to an array if needed.

Question: How do you create an array using predefined dimensions stored in a variable?
Answer: Pass the dimension variable directly to array(), e.g., dims <- c(3, 4, 2); my_array <- array(1:24, dim = dims).

Question: How do you create an array with a large dataset efficiently?
Answer: Use memory-efficient data structures like bigmemory or ff packages, then convert to an array if needed.

Question: How do you create an array to store complex numbers?
Answer: Use array(complex(real = 1:12, imaginary = 1:12), dim = c(3, 4)).

Question: How do you create an array by reshaping an existing data structure?
Answer: Use array() with the dim argument, e.g., reshaped_array <- array(existing_data, dim = c(3, 4, 2)).

Access Array Elements

Question: How do you access a specific element in a 2D array?
Answer: Use square brackets with row and column indices, e.g., array[row, col].

Question: How do you access a specific element in a 3D array?
Answer: Use square brackets with three indices, e.g., array[row, col, depth].

Question: How do you access all elements in a specific row of a 2D array?
Answer: Use square brackets with a row index and leave the column index blank, e.g., array[row,].

Question: How do you access all elements in a specific column of a 2D array?
Answer: Use square brackets with a column index and leave the row index blank, e.g., array[, col].

Question: How do you access all elements in a specific depth of a 3D array?
Answer: Use square brackets with the depth index, leaving row and column indices blank, e.g., array[,, depth].

Question: How do you access a subarray within a larger array?
Answer: Use square brackets with a range of indices, e.g., subarray <- array[1:2, 1:3, 1].

Question: How do you access elements in an array using negative indexing?
Answer: Use negative indices to exclude specific rows, columns, or depths, e.g., array[-1, -2,] excludes the first row and second column.

Question: How do you access elements conditionally in an array?
Answer: Use logical indexing, e.g., array[array > 5].

Question: How do you access the diagonal elements of a 2D array?
Answer: Use diag(array) for a square 2D array to get the diagonal elements.

Question: How do you access elements in an array using row and column names?
Answer: Use named indices if the array has dimnames, e.g., array["row1", "col1", "depth1"].

Question: How do you access every other element in a specific dimension of an array?
Answer: Use seq() for the indices, e.g., array[seq(1, nrow(array), 2), ,].

Question: How do you access and modify a specific element in an array?
Answer: Use square brackets for access and assignment, e.g., array[1, 2, 3] <- new_value.

Question: How do you access elements of an array by excluding certain dimensions?
Answer: Use negative indexing for the dimensions to be excluded, e.g., array[-c(1, 3),].

Question: How do you access elements of a 3D array across a specific slice?
Answer: Use square brackets with indices for that slice, e.g., array[,, slice].

Question: How do you access the first and last elements in a specific dimension of an array?
Answer: Use indexing with c() for the first and last indices, e.g., array[c(1, nrow(array)), ,].

Question: How do you access elements of an array by their position using a vector of indices?
Answer: Use cbind() with vectors of indices, e.g., array[cbind(row_indices, col_indices, depth_indices)].

Question: How do you access and replace multiple elements in an array at once?
Answer: Use vectorized indexing for selection and assignment, e.g., array[array > 10] <- new_value.

Question: How do you access elements of a multi-dimensional array using a list of indices?
Answer: Use do.call() with [and a list of indices, e.g., do.call([, c(list(array), list_of_indices)).

Question: How do you access the sum of elements along a specific dimension in an array?
Answer: Use apply() with MARGIN specifying the dimension, e.g., apply(array, 1, sum).

Question: How do you access elements of an array based on a condition applied to another array?
Answer: Use logical indexing based on the condition, e.g., array2[array1 > 5].

Question: How do you access the minimum and maximum values in an array?
Answer: Use min(array) and max(array) functions.

Question: How do you access elements in a 3D array using slicing?
Answer: Use array[row_slice, col_slice, depth_slice], where slices are specified by ranges or sequences.

Question: How do you access and extract a specific slice of an array?
Answer: Use square brackets with indices for that slice, e.g., slice <- array[,, slice_index].

Question: How do you access elements in an array that match a specific pattern or condition?
Answer: Use logical conditions within the square brackets, e.g., array[array == specific_value].

Question: How do you access non-zero elements of an array?
Answer: Use logical indexing, e.g., array[array != 0].

Question: How do you access the dimensions of an array?
Answer: Use the dim() function, e.g., dim(array).

Question: How do you access elements of an array in reverse order?
Answer: Use rev() on each dimension, e.g., array[rev(seq_len(dim(array)[1])), ,].

Question: How do you access a diagonal slice in a multi-dimensional array?
Answer: Use a loop or mapply() to access diagonal elements across multiple dimensions.

Question: How do you access and update elements in an array conditionally?
Answer: Use logical indexing for selection and assignment, e.g., array[array > 5] <- new_value.

Question: How do you access elements of an array based on a custom function?
Answer: Use apply() with a custom function, e.g., apply(array, 1, function(x) x[x > threshold]).

Question: How do you access elements of an array by specifying dimensions out of order?
Answer: Use aperm() to rearrange dimensions before accessing elements.

Question: How do you access elements from a specific corner or edge of an array?
Answer: Use square brackets with indices targeting the desired corner or edge, e.g., array[1, 1, 1] for the first corner.

Question: How do you access array elements for visualization or plotting?
Answer: Extract relevant slices or elements using indexing and pass them to visualization functions like image() or plot().

Question: How do you access the unique elements of an array?
Answer: Use the unique() function, e.g., unique(array).

Question: How do you access and aggregate elements of an array along a specific dimension?
Answer: Use apply() with aggregation functions like sum(), mean(), etc., e.g., apply(array, 1, sum).

Array Manipulation

Question: How do you reshape an array in R?
Answer: Use the dim() function to assign new dimensions, e.g., dim(array) <- c(2, 6).

Question: How do you transpose an array in R?
Answer: Use aperm() to permute dimensions, e.g., aperm(array, c(2, 1, 3)).

Question: How do you flatten a multi-dimensional array into a vector?
Answer: Use as.vector(array) to flatten the array.

Question: How do you merge two arrays in R?
Answer: Use abind() from the abind package to combine arrays along a specified dimension.

Question: How do you add a new dimension to an existing array?
Answer: Use array() with the dim argument, or abind() with the new dimension set to 1.

Question: How do you split an array into smaller arrays?
Answer: Use array_split <- lapply(1:dim(array)[3], function(i) array[,, i]) to split along a specific dimension.

Question: How do you reverse the order of elements in a specific dimension of an array?
Answer: Use apply() or rev() on that dimension, e.g., apply(array, 3, rev).

Question: How do you change the order of dimensions in an array?
Answer: Use aperm() with the desired order, e.g., aperm(array, c(3, 1, 2)).

Question: How do you replicate an array multiple times?
Answer: Use replicate() or abind() to duplicate the array along a new dimension.

Question: How do you add or remove specific elements in an array?
Answer: Arrays in R are fixed size, so use array() to create a new array with the desired elements.

Question: How do you modify the values of a specific slice in an array?
Answer: Use indexing to select the slice and assign new values, e.g., array[,, 1] <- new_values.

Question: How do you convert an array to a data frame?
Answer: Use as.data.frame.table(array) to convert the array.

Question: How do you modify elements in an array based on a condition?
Answer: Use logical indexing for selection and assignment, e.g., array[array > 10] <- 0.

Question: How do you concatenate two arrays along a new dimension?
Answer: Use abind() with a new dimension, e.g., abind(array1, array2, along = 4).

Question: How do you rotate an array by 90 degrees?
Answer: Use aperm() and indexing to rotate, e.g., aperm(array[,, 1], c(2, 1)).

Question: How do you delete a specific dimension from an array?
Answer: Arrays cannot have dimensions removed directly, but you can reshape the array without the dimension using dim().

Question: How do you normalize the elements of an array?
Answer: Subtract the mean and divide by the standard deviation, e.g., (array - mean(array)) / sd(array).

Question: How do you create a subset of an array with specific elements?
Answer: Use indexing with conditions, e.g., subset_array <- array[array > threshold].

Question: How do you update multiple elements in an array simultaneously?
Answer: Use vectorized assignment, e.g., array[indices] <- new_values.

Question: How do you perform element-wise operations between two arrays?
Answer: Use standard arithmetic operators like +, -, *, / on arrays of the same dimensions.

Question: How do you round all elements in an array to the nearest integer?
Answer: Use round() on the array, e.g., round(array).

Question: How do you convert a logical array to a numeric array?
Answer: Use as.numeric() on the logical array, e.g., as.numeric(logical_array).

Question: How do you shift elements in an array along a specific dimension?
Answer: Use apply() with a custom function to shift elements, e.g., apply(array, 1, function(x) c(tail(x, -1), head(x, 1))).

Question: How do you scale an array's elements to a specific range?
Answer: Use min-max normalization, e.g., (array - min(array)) / (max(array) - min(array)) * (new_max - new_min) + new_min.

Question: How do you swap two dimensions in an array?
Answer: Use aperm() with the dimensions to be swapped, e.g., aperm(array, c(2, 1, 3)).

Question: How do you convert a 2D slice of an array to a matrix?
Answer: Use array[,, slice] and as.matrix() to convert the slice to a matrix.

Question: How do you duplicate specific rows or columns in an array?
Answer: Use rep() or cbind()/rbind() to duplicate rows or columns.

Question: How do you compute cumulative sums along a dimension of an array?
Answer: Use apply() with cumsum(), e.g., apply(array, 1, cumsum).

Question: How do you sort the elements of an array?
Answer: Use apply() with sort() for each dimension, e.g., apply(array, 1, sort).

Question: How do you add noise to elements in an array?
Answer: Use array + rnorm(length(array), mean = 0, sd = noise_level).

Question: How do you invert the values of an array (e.g., 1/x)?
Answer: Use 1 / array for element-wise inversion.

Question: How do you apply a function across a specific dimension of an array?
Answer: Use apply() with the desired dimension, e.g., apply(array, 1, FUN).

Question: How do you replicate a slice of an array multiple times?
Answer: Use replicate() or abind() to replicate the slice, e.g., abind(replicate(n, array[,, slice], simplify = FALSE), along = 3).

Question: How do you convert an array to a factor array?
Answer: Convert the array to a vector of factors using as.factor(), then reshape it back to an array.

Question: How do you remove NA values from an array?
Answer: Use is.na() with logical indexing to remove NA values, e.g., array[!is.na(array)].

Array Operations

Question: How do you perform element-wise addition of two arrays?
Answer: Use the + operator, e.g., result_array <- array1 + array2.

Question: How do you perform element-wise subtraction of two arrays?
Answer: Use the - operator, e.g., result_array <- array1 - array2.

Question: How do you perform element-wise multiplication of two arrays?
Answer: Use the * operator, e.g., result_array <- array1 * array2.

Question: How do you perform element-wise division of two arrays?
Answer: Use the / operator, e.g., result_array <- array1 / array2.

Question: How do you calculate the sum of all elements in an array?
Answer: Use the sum() function, e.g., total_sum <- sum(array).

Question: How do you calculate the mean of all elements in an array?
Answer: Use the mean() function, e.g., mean_value <- mean(array).

Question: How do you apply a function to each element of an array?
Answer: Use apply() with MARGIN = c(1, 2, ...), e.g., apply(array, c(1, 2), FUN).

Question: How do you perform matrix multiplication on a 2D slice of an array?
Answer: Use %*% on the 2D slice, e.g., result <- array[,, slice] %*% matrix.

Question: How do you calculate the cumulative sum of elements in an array?
Answer: Use apply() with cumsum(), e.g., apply(array, 1, cumsum).

Question: How do you perform element-wise power operations on an array?
Answer: Use the ^ operator, e.g., result_array <- array^2.

Question: How do you calculate the row sums of a 2D slice of an array?
Answer: Use rowSums(), e.g., row_sums <- rowSums(array[,, slice]).

Question: How do you calculate the column sums of a 2D slice of an array?
Answer: Use colSums(), e.g., col_sums <- colSums(array[,, slice]).

Question: How do you calculate the row means of a 2D slice of an array?
Answer: Use rowMeans(), e.g., row_means <- rowMeans(array[,, slice]).

Question: How do you calculate the column means of a 2D slice of an array?
Answer: Use colMeans(), e.g., col_means <- colMeans(array[,, slice]).

Question: How do you compute the determinant of a 2D slice of an array?
Answer: Use the det() function, e.g., det_value <- det(array[,, slice]).

Question: How do you compute the inverse of a 2D slice of an array?
Answer: Use the solve() function, e.g., inverse <- solve(array[,, slice]).

Question: How do you perform element-wise logical operations on an array?
Answer: Use logical operators like &, |, !, e.g., result <- array1 & array2.

Question: How do you compute the cross product of two arrays?
Answer: Use crossprod() for the cross product of 2D slices, e.g., result <- crossprod(array1[,, slice1], array2[,, slice2]).

Question: How do you compute the dot product of two vectors from an array?
Answer: Use sum(vector1 * vector2) for dot products of 1D slices.

Question: How do you transpose a 2D slice of an array?
Answer: Use the t() function, e.g., transposed <- t(array[,, slice]).

Question: How do you compute the trace of a 2D slice of an array?
Answer: Use sum(diag(array[,, slice])) to compute the trace.

Question: How do you perform scalar multiplication on an array?
Answer: Use the * operator with a scalar, e.g., result_array <- array * scalar.

Question: How do you calculate the Euclidean norm of an array?
Answer: Use sqrt(sum(array^2)) for the Euclidean norm.

Question: How do you perform vectorized operations on an array?
Answer: Apply vectorized functions like +, -, *, etc., directly to the array.

Question: How do you calculate the maximum or minimum element in an array?
Answer: Use max(array) or min(array).

Question: How do you compute the eigenvalues of a 2D slice of an array?
Answer: Use eigen(array[,, slice])$values.

Question: How do you compute the singular value decomposition (SVD) of a 2D slice of an array?
Answer: Use svd(array[,, slice]).

Question: How do you compute the rank of a 2D slice of an array?
Answer: Use qr(array[,, slice])$rank.

Question: How do you compute the Frobenius norm of an array?
Answer: Use sqrt(sum(array^2)).

Question: How do you perform matrix exponentiation on a 2D slice of an array?
Answer: Use expm() from the expm package, e.g., expm(array[,, slice]).

Question: How do you calculate the outer product of two vectors from an array?
Answer: Use outer(vector1, vector2).

Question: How do you perform element-wise comparison between two arrays?
Answer: Use comparison operators like ==, !=, <, >, e.g., array1 == array2.

Question: How do you compute the Mahalanobis distance using an array?
Answer: Use mahalanobis(x, center, cov) where x is a vector from the array.

Question: How do you calculate the correlation matrix of a 2D slice of an array?
Answer: Use cor(array[,, slice]).

Question: How do you calculate the covariance matrix from a 2D slice of an array?
Answer: Use cov(array[,, slice]).

Question: How do you perform element-wise modulo operation on an array?
Answer: Use the %% operator, e.g., result_array <- array1 %% array2.

Question: How do you compute the Schur complement of a block matrix in an array?
Answer: Calculate it using the formula: Schur = A - B %*% solve(D) %*% C, where A, B, C, D are slices of the array.

Array Functions

Question: How do you apply a function to each element in an array?
Answer: Use apply() or lapply(), e.g., apply(array, 1, FUN).

Question: How do you use the apply() function with arrays in R?
Answer: Use apply() with MARGIN to specify the dimensions, e.g., apply(array, c(1, 2), sum).

Question: How do you calculate the sum of elements along a specific dimension of an array?
Answer: Use apply(array, MARGIN, sum) where MARGIN specifies the dimension.

Question: How do you find the mean along a specific dimension in an array?
Answer: Use apply(array, MARGIN, mean) where MARGIN specifies the dimension.

Question: How do you use lapply() with an array?
Answer: Convert the array to a list and apply lapply(), e.g., lapply(as.list(array), FUN).

Question: How do you use sapply() with an array?
Answer: Convert the array to a list and apply sapply(), e.g., sapply(as.list(array), FUN).

Question: How do you use tapply() to apply a function over subsets of an array?
Answer: Use tapply() with a factor and a function, e.g., tapply(array, INDEX, FUN).

Question: How do you compute cumulative products along a dimension in an array?
Answer: Use apply(array, MARGIN, cumprod).

Question: How do you calculate the cumulative maximum along a dimension in an array?
Answer: Use apply(array, MARGIN, cummax).

Question: How do you calculate the cumulative minimum along a dimension in an array?
Answer: Use apply(array, MARGIN, cummin).

Question: How do you apply a custom function across multiple dimensions of an array?
Answer: Use apply(array, c(1, 2), custom_function).

Question: How do you apply a rolling function to an array?
Answer: Use the zoo package with rollapply(), e.g., rollapply(array, width = 3, FUN).

Question: How do you calculate the median along a specific dimension of an array?
Answer: Use apply(array, MARGIN, median).

Question: How do you apply a function to a specific slice of an array?
Answer: Use apply() with indexing, e.g., apply(array[,, slice], 1, FUN).

Question: How do you perform group-wise operations on an array?
Answer: Use tapply() or aggregate() after reshaping the array into a data frame.

Question: How do you use mapply() to apply a function to multiple arrays?
Answer: Use mapply() with the function and arrays, e.g., mapply(FUN, array1, array2).

Question: How do you calculate the geometric mean along a dimension in an array?
Answer: Use apply(array, MARGIN, function(x) exp(mean(log(x)))).

Question: How do you calculate the harmonic mean along a dimension in an array?
Answer: Use apply(array, MARGIN, function(x) length(x) / sum(1/x)).

Question: How do you compute the variance along a specific dimension of an array?
Answer: Use apply(array, MARGIN, var).

Question: How do you calculate the standard deviation along a dimension in an array?
Answer: Use apply(array, MARGIN, sd).

Question: How do you calculate the skewness along a specific dimension in an array?
Answer: Use apply(array, MARGIN, function(x) mean((x - mean(x))^3) / sd(x)^3).

Question: How do you calculate the kurtosis along a specific dimension in an array?
Answer: Use apply(array, MARGIN, function(x) mean((x - mean(x))^4) / sd(x)^4).

Question: How do you calculate the root mean square (RMS) along a specific dimension in an array?
Answer: Use apply(array, MARGIN, function(x) sqrt(mean(x^2))).

Question: How do you apply a function that returns multiple values to an array?
Answer: Use apply() with a custom function that returns a list, then reshape the output if needed.

Question: How do you use outer() to apply a function to all pairs of elements from two arrays?
Answer: Use outer(array1, array2, FUN).

Question: How do you use Vectorize() to vectorize a function for array operations?
Answer: Use Vectorize() on the custom function, then apply it to the array.

Question: How do you perform element-wise cumulative operations on an array?
Answer: Use apply() with cumsum(), cumprod(), etc., e.g., apply(array, 1, cumsum).

Question: How do you reshape an array after applying a function?
Answer: Use array() with the new dimensions on the result.

Question: How do you apply a function to each slice of an array separately?
Answer: Use apply(array, MARGIN, FUN) where MARGIN represents the dimensions excluding the slice.

Question: How do you normalize an array using a custom function?
Answer: Use apply(array, MARGIN, custom_normalization_function).

Question: How do you apply a function only to non-NA elements in an array?
Answer: Use apply(array, MARGIN, function(x) FUN(na.omit(x))).

Question: How do you calculate the weighted sum along a dimension in an array?
Answer: Use apply(array, MARGIN, function(x) sum(x * weights)).

Question: How do you generate an array by applying a function to a vectorized version of another array?
Answer: Use apply() on the vectorized array, then reshape the result.

Array Applications

Question: How are arrays used in image processing?
Answer: Arrays are used to represent images as multi-dimensional data structures, where each element corresponds to a pixel value (e.g., RGB channels).

Question: How are arrays used in time series analysis?
Answer: Arrays can store multiple time series data across dimensions like time, variables, and groups for simultaneous analysis.

Question: How are arrays applied in machine learning?
Answer: Arrays are used to store data inputs, weights, and outputs in models, particularly in neural networks where data is multi-dimensional.

Question: How do arrays support financial modeling?
Answer: Arrays store multiple scenarios of financial data, allowing for simulations, risk analysis, and portfolio optimization.

Question: How are arrays used in scientific computing?
Answer: Arrays represent multi-dimensional data in simulations, numerical methods, and solving differential equations.

Question: How are arrays used in genetic data analysis?
Answer: Arrays store genetic information, such as DNA sequences, and allow for analysis of gene expression across conditions.

Question: How do arrays facilitate meteorological data analysis?
Answer: Arrays store data from various sensors over time, allowing for analysis of temperature, pressure, and other climate variables.

Question: How are arrays applied in image recognition tasks?
Answer: Arrays store image pixel data used as input for machine learning models in tasks like object detection and classification.

Question: How are arrays used in signal processing?
Answer: Arrays store sampled signals, enabling operations like Fourier transforms, filtering, and convolution.

Question: How are arrays used in spatial data analysis?
Answer: Arrays store spatial data as grids, allowing for geographic information system (GIS) operations like interpolation and spatial statistics.

Question: How are arrays utilized in audio processing?
Answer: Arrays represent audio signals, allowing for processing tasks such as noise reduction, feature extraction, and synthesis.

Question: How are arrays used in game development?
Answer: Arrays store game states, including positions, scores, and levels, enabling game logic and rendering operations.

Question: How are arrays applied in robotics?
Answer: Arrays store sensor data and control signals, enabling real-time decision-making and movement in robots.

Question: How are arrays used in network data analysis?
Answer: Arrays represent adjacency matrices in network graphs, enabling analysis of connectivity, clustering, and flow.

Question: How are arrays used in quantum computing simulations?
Answer: Arrays represent quantum states and operators, allowing for the simulation of quantum algorithms and systems.

Question: How are arrays used in optimization problems?
Answer: Arrays store candidate solutions, objective function values, and constraints, facilitating iterative optimization methods.

Question: How are arrays used in bioinformatics?
Answer: Arrays store biological data like protein sequences and gene expressions, enabling pattern recognition and functional analysis.

Question: How are arrays utilized in computer graphics?
Answer: Arrays store vertex and texture data, enabling 3D rendering and transformations in computer graphics.

Question: How are arrays used in multi-dimensional statistical analysis?
Answer: Arrays store data for methods like ANOVA, MANOVA, and multivariate regression, allowing analysis across multiple dimensions.

Question: How are arrays used in economic modeling?
Answer: Arrays store multi-dimensional economic data for modeling consumption, production, and market behavior.

Question: How are arrays used in weather prediction models?
Answer: Arrays store and process multi-dimensional atmospheric data, facilitating numerical weather prediction models.

Question: How are arrays used in computer vision?
Answer: Arrays store image and video data, enabling tasks like object detection, tracking, and facial recognition.

Question: How are arrays used in neural network training?
Answer: Arrays store inputs, weights, biases, and activations, enabling forward and backward propagation in neural network training.

Question: How are arrays used in reservoir simulation?
Answer: Arrays model fluid flow and pressure in reservoirs, enabling predictions of resource extraction and management.

Question: How are arrays used in chemical reaction modeling?
Answer: Arrays store concentration and temperature data over time, enabling simulation and analysis of chemical reactions.

Question: How are arrays used in radar signal processing?
Answer: Arrays store radar return signals, enabling tasks like target detection, range estimation, and Doppler shift analysis.

Question: How are arrays used in text processing?
Answer: Arrays represent text data as sequences of characters or tokens, enabling natural language processing tasks.

Question: How are arrays used in geophysical data analysis?
Answer: Arrays store seismic and other geophysical data, enabling analysis of earth structures and resource exploration.

Question: How are arrays used in multi-agent simulations?
Answer: Arrays store agent states and actions, enabling simulation of interactions and emergent behavior in multi-agent systems.

Question: How are arrays used in medical image analysis?
Answer: Arrays store MRI, CT, and other medical image data, enabling tasks like segmentation, registration, and diagnosis.

Question: How are arrays used in aerospace engineering simulations?
Answer: Arrays store aerodynamic and structural data, enabling simulation of aircraft and spacecraft performance.

Question: How are arrays used in pharmacokinetic modeling?
Answer: Arrays store drug concentration data over time, enabling modeling of drug absorption, distribution, metabolism, and excretion.

Question: How are arrays used in traffic flow simulation?
Answer: Arrays store vehicle positions and speeds, enabling simulation and analysis of traffic dynamics and congestion.

Question: How are arrays used in cryptographic algorithms?
Answer: Arrays store data for encryption and decryption processes, enabling secure communication and data protection.

Question: How are arrays used in econometrics?
Answer: Arrays store economic data for statistical analysis, enabling econometric modeling and hypothesis testing.

Question: How are arrays used in marine biology simulations?
Answer: Arrays store environmental and biological data, enabling simulation of marine ecosystems and species behavior.

Question: How are arrays used in fluid dynamics simulations?
Answer: Arrays store velocity, pressure, and temperature fields, enabling computational fluid dynamics (CFD) simulations.

Question: How are arrays used in space exploration data analysis?
Answer: Arrays store data from space missions, enabling analysis of planetary surfaces, atmospheres, and celestial phenomena.

Online Resources

Online Practice Paper Link: https://forms.gle/7zLsPWJ91nbHeupY6

QR Code:

YouTube Video Link:
https://www.youtube.com/playlist?list=PLzlh_31VWEFpDkrVHJ7xOa5vo-cLgi6nO

QR Code:

Chapter 9: Factors

Creating Factors

Question: How do you create a basic factor in R?
Answer: Use the factor() function, e.g., factor(c("red", "blue", "green")).

Question: What is the purpose of creating a factor in R?
Answer: Factors are used to handle categorical data by storing the unique levels and representing the data as integers internally.

Question: How do you specify levels when creating a factor in R?
Answer: Use the levels argument in factor(), e.g., factor(c("low", "medium", "high"), levels = c("low", "medium", "high")).

Question: How do you create an ordered factor in R?
Answer: Use ordered = TRUE in the factor() function, e.g., factor(c("low", "medium", "high"), ordered = TRUE).

Question: What happens if you create a factor without specifying levels?
Answer: R will automatically determine the levels based on the unique values in the data.

Question: How do you create a factor with specific labels?
Answer: Use the labels argument in factor(), e.g., factor(c("M", "F"), levels = c("M", "F"), labels = c("Male", "Female")).

Question: How do you create a factor from numeric data?
Answer: Simply pass numeric data to factor(), e.g., factor(c(1, 2, 3)).

Question: How do you create a factor from a character vector with specific levels?
Answer: Use factor() with the levels argument to specify the order of levels, e.g., factor(c("apple", "banana"), levels = c("banana", "apple")).

Question: How do you handle missing values when creating a factor?
Answer: Use NA in the input vector, which will automatically be handled as a missing level, e.g., factor(c("apple", NA, "banana")).

Question: How do you create a factor with levels that are not present in the data?
Answer: Specify extra levels in the levels argument, e.g., factor(c("apple", "banana"), levels = c("apple", "banana", "orange")).

Question: How do you create a factor with an integer sequence?
Answer: Use factor() with a sequence, e.g., factor(1:5).

Question: Can you create a factor with repeated levels?
Answer: Yes, factors can have repeated levels, e.g., factor(c("low", "medium", "low", "high")).

Question: How do you create a factor where the levels are in alphabetical order?
Answer: Use factor() without specifying levels, as R orders them alphabetically by default.

Question: How do you create a factor with numeric levels but treat them as categories?
Answer: Use factor() with numeric data, e.g., factor(c(1, 2, 3)).

Question: How do you create a factor from a logical vector?
Answer: Use factor() with logical data, e.g., factor(c(TRUE, FALSE, TRUE)).

Question: How do you create a factor with custom level order that is not alphabetical?
Answer: Specify the levels explicitly, e.g., factor(c("medium", "low", "high"), levels = c("low", "medium", "high")).

Question: How do you create an empty factor with predefined levels?
Answer: Use factor() with an empty vector and the levels argument, e.g., factor(character(0), levels = c("A", "B", "C")).

Question: How do you create a factor with levels that include special characters?
Answer: Use factor() with a vector containing special characters, e.g., factor(c("A$", "B%", "C#")).

Question: How do you create a factor from a data frame column?
Answer: Use factor() on the column, e.g., factor(df$column_name).

Question: How do you create a factor that distinguishes between upper and lower case?
Answer: Use factor() on a vector with mixed case, e.g., factor(c("a", "A", "b", "B")).

Question: How do you create a factor with predefined levels that are not present in the data?
Answer: Use the levels argument with additional levels, e.g., factor(c("cat", "dog"), levels = c("cat", "dog", "bird")).

Question: How do you create a factor from a numeric sequence with specific levels?
Answer: Specify the sequence and levels in factor(), e.g., factor(1:3, levels = c(3, 2, 1)).

Question: How do you create a factor with an ordering that reflects a natural sequence?
Answer: Use ordered = TRUE with levels specifying the natural order, e.g., factor(c("first", "second", "third"), ordered = TRUE).

Question: How do you create a factor with duplicate levels?
Answer: Use factor() with repeated levels in the vector, e.g., factor(c("A", "B", "A", "B", "A")).

Question: How do you create a factor with levels that include numbers and text?
Answer: Use factor() with a mixed vector, e.g., factor(c("1-High", "2-Medium", "3-Low")).

Question: How do you create a factor with levels sorted in reverse order?
Answer: Use factor() with levels specified in reverse order, e.g., factor(c("low", "medium", "high"), levels = c("high", "medium",
"low")).

Question: How do you create a factor with levels that represent ranges?
Answer: Use cut() to create factors from numeric ranges, e.g., cut(c(1, 2, 3), breaks = c(0, 1.5, 2.5, 3.5), labels = c("low", "medium", "high")).

Question: How do you create a factor from an already existing factor?
Answer: Use factor() on the existing factor, optionally with new levels, e.g., factor(old_factor, levels = c("new_level1", "new_level2")).

Question: How do you create a factor with default levels for a character vector?
Answer: Use factor() on the vector without specifying levels, e.g., factor(c("apple", "banana", "apple")).

Question: How do you create a factor that will be used in a statistical model?
Answer: Use factor() with meaningful levels representing categories relevant to the model.

Question: How do you create a factor with a large number of levels efficiently?
Answer: Use unique() to first get the levels, then create the factor, e.g., factor(vector, levels = unique(vector)).

Question: How do you create a factor with levels that include whitespace?
Answer: Use factor() on a vector that includes whitespace, e.g., factor(c(" low", " medium", " high")).

Question: How do you create a factor that represents a hierarchical category?
Answer: Use interaction() to combine factors, or manually create levels that reflect the hierarchy.

Question: How do you create a factor with levels that should be treated as equal?
Answer: Use factor() and combine levels using levels(factor) <- list(new_level = c("level1", "level2")).

Question: How do you create a factor from a numeric vector with non-integer values?
Answer: Use factor() directly on the numeric vector, e.g., factor(c(1.1, 2.2, 3.3)).

Question: How do you create a factor for data that will be used in a plot?
Answer: Use factor() with levels ordered as desired for the plot.

Question: How do you create a factor with user-defined labels?
Answer: Use the labels argument in factor(), e.g., factor(c("M", "F"), labels = c("Male", "Female")).

Question: How do you create a factor that ignores specific values?
Answer: Use factor() with a subset of values or use droplevels() after creation.

Accessing Factors

Question: How do you access the levels of a factor in R?
Answer: Use the levels() function, e.g., levels(factor_variable).

Question: How do you access a specific element in a factor?
Answer: Use indexing, e.g., factor_variable[1] to access the first element.

Question: How do you check the number of levels in a factor?
Answer: Use the nlevels() function, e.g., nlevels(factor_variable).

Question: How do you access all elements of a specific level in a factor?
Answer: Use logical indexing, e.g., factor_variable[factor_variable == "level_name"].

Question: How do you access the underlying integer codes of a factor?
Answer: Use the as.integer() function, e.g., as.integer(factor_variable).

Question: How do you access factor elements that match a condition?
Answer: Use logical conditions for indexing, e.g., factor_variable[factor_variable != "exclude_level"].

Question: How do you access and change the levels of a factor?
Answer: Use levels(factor_variable) <- new_levels.

Question: How do you access the levels of a factor in a specific order?
Answer: Use factor_variable[order(factor_variable)].

Question: How do you access the levels of a factor after subsetting it?
Answer: Use levels() after subsetting, e.g., levels(factor_variable[1:10]).

Question: How do you access elements of a factor based on their position?
Answer: Use indexing with which(), e.g., factor_variable[which(factor_variable == "level_name")].

Question: How do you access a summary of a factor in R?
Answer: Use the summary() function, e.g., summary(factor_variable).

Question: How do you access the frequency of each level in a factor?
Answer: Use table(factor_variable) to see the count of each level.

Question: How do you access the first element of each level in a factor?
Answer: Use tapply() with factor_variable and unique(), e.g., tapply(factor_variable, factor_variable, function(x) x[1]).

Question: How do you access a factor's levels and check if they are ordered?
Answer: Use is.ordered(factor_variable).

Question: How do you access the last element of a factor?
Answer: Use factor_variable[length(factor_variable)].

Question: How do you access factor elements and convert them to a different data type?
Answer: Use as.character() or as.numeric() on the factor, e.g., as.character(factor_variable).

Question: How do you access elements of a factor based on their level names?
Answer: Use which(levels(factor_variable) == "level_name").

Question: How do you access factor elements that are missing (NA)?
Answer: Use is.na() to find and access missing elements, e.g., factor_variable[is.na(factor_variable)].

Question: How do you access elements of a factor that match multiple levels?
Answer: Use %in% for matching, e.g., factor_variable[factor_variable %in% c("level1", "level2")].

Question: How do you access and reorder the levels of a factor?
Answer: Use factor_variable <- factor(factor_variable, levels = new_order).

Question: How do you access the length of a factor?
Answer: Use the length() function, e.g., length(factor_variable).

Question: How do you access the unique elements in a factor?
Answer: Use unique(factor_variable).

Question: How do you access the mode of a factor?
Answer: Use table(factor_variable) and find the most frequent level.

Question: How do you access and drop unused levels in a factor?
Answer: Use droplevels(factor_variable).

Question: How do you access elements of a factor in reverse order?
Answer: Use rev(factor_variable).

Question: How do you access factor elements and convert them into a data frame?
Answer: Use as.data.frame(factor_variable).

Question: How do you access the cumulative frequency of a factor?
Answer: Use cumsum(table(factor_variable)).

Question: How do you access and replace specific elements in a factor?
Answer: Use indexing for access and assignment, e.g., factor_variable[1] <- "new_level".

Question: How do you access elements of a factor that are within a specific range?
Answer: Use indexing with a range, e.g., factor_variable[1:10].

Question: How do you access and convert a factor into an ordered factor?
Answer: Use factor_variable <- ordered(factor_variable).

Question: How do you access factor elements as part of a conditional operation?
Answer: Use ifelse() with the factor, e.g., ifelse(factor_variable == "level", "yes", "no").

Question: How do you access factor elements and convert them to a numeric variable?
Answer: Use as.numeric(levels(factor_variable))[factor_variable].

Question: How do you access elements of a factor and perform an operation on them?
Answer: Use lapply() or sapply() on the factor, e.g., lapply(factor_variable, FUN).

Question: How do you access factor elements to create a logical vector?
Answer: Use factor_variable == "level_name" to create a logical vector.

Question: How do you access the first occurrence of a level in a factor?
Answer: Use which(factor_variable == "level_name")[1].

Question: How do you access factor elements to create a matrix?
Answer: Use matrix(as.integer(factor_variable), nrow, ncol) to create a matrix from the factor.

Question: How do you access elements of a factor to create a summary statistic?
Answer: Use summary() or table() to generate summary statistics.

Question: How do you access a factor with a specific sorting order?
Answer: Use sort(factor_variable).

Factor Operations

Question: How do you change the levels of a factor?
Answer: Use levels(factor_variable) <- new_levels.

Question: How do you combine two factors in R?
Answer: Use factor(c(as.character(factor1), as.character(factor2))).

Question: How do you reorder the levels of a factor?
Answer: Use factor_variable <- factor(factor_variable, levels = new_order).

Question: How do you concatenate two factors?
Answer: Convert them to characters, concatenate, and then convert back to a factor, e.g., factor(c(as.character(factor1),
as.character(factor2))).

Question: How do you add new levels to an existing factor?
Answer: Use levels(factor_variable) <- c(levels(factor_variable), "new_level").

Question: How do you drop unused levels from a factor?
Answer: Use droplevels(factor_variable).

Question: How do you reorder a factor based on the frequency of levels?
Answer: Use factor_variable <- factor(factor_variable, levels = names(sort(table(factor_variable), decreasing = TRUE))).

Question: How do you merge two factors with different levels?
Answer: Convert both to characters, merge, and then convert back to a factor, ensuring all levels are included.

Question: How do you reverse the levels of a factor?
Answer: Use factor_variable <- factor(factor_variable, levels = rev(levels(factor_variable))).

Question: How do you rename levels in a factor?
Answer: Use levels(factor_variable) <- c("new_name1", "new_name2").

Question: How do you compare two factors?
Answer: Use all.equal(factor1, factor2) or identical(factor1, factor2).

Question: How do you subset a factor?
Answer: Use logical or index-based subsetting, e.g., factor_variable[1:5].

Question: How do you split a factor into a list based on levels?
Answer: Use split(factor_variable, factor_variable).

Question: How do you calculate the length of a factor?
Answer: Use the length() function, e.g., length(factor_variable).

Question: How do you check if a factor contains a specific level?
Answer: Use %in%, e.g., "level" %in% levels(factor_variable).

Question: How do you apply a function to each level of a factor?
Answer: Use tapply() or by() on the factor.

Question: How do you remove specific levels from a factor?
Answer: Use factor_variable <- factor(factor_variable, levels = setdiff(levels(factor_variable), "level_to_remove")).

Question: How do you convert a factor to a character vector?
Answer: Use as.character(factor_variable).

Question: How do you perform mathematical operations on factors?
Answer: Convert the factor to numeric or integer first, e.g., as.numeric(factor_variable).

Question: How do you handle NA values in a factor?
Answer: Use is.na() to detect and handle NA values, e.g., factor_variable[!is.na(factor_variable)].

Question: How do you aggregate data by factor levels?
Answer: Use aggregate() or tapply() with the factor.

Question: How do you create a factor interaction between two factors?
Answer: Use interaction(factor1, factor2).

Question: How do you convert an ordered factor to an unordered factor?
Answer: Use factor(factor_variable, ordered = FALSE).

Question: How do you calculate the mode of a factor?
Answer: Use table(factor_variable) and extract the most frequent level.

Question: How do you perform cross-tabulation with factors?
Answer: Use table(factor1, factor2).

Question: How do you recode factor levels?
Answer: Use recode() from the car package or manually use levels().

Question: How do you sort a factor by the levels?
Answer: Use factor_variable <- factor(factor_variable, levels = sort(levels(factor_variable))).

Question: How do you check if two factors are equal?
Answer: Use identical(factor1, factor2).

Question: How do you find the index of a specific level in a factor?
Answer: Use which(levels(factor_variable) == "level_name").

Question: How do you combine multiple factors into a single factor?
Answer: Use interaction(factor1, factor2, factor3).

Question: How do you apply a transformation to each level of a factor?
Answer: Use levels(factor_variable) <- lapply(levels(factor_variable), FUN).

Question: How do you group factor levels into a single level?
Answer: Use levels(factor_variable) <- list("new_level" = c("old_level1", "old_level2")).

Question: How do you check for duplicated levels in a factor?
Answer: Use duplicated(levels(factor_variable)).

Question: How do you convert a factor to a numeric variable?
Answer: Use as.numeric(levels(factor_variable))[factor_variable].

Question: How do you invert the levels of a factor?
Answer: Use levels(factor_variable) <- rev(levels(factor_variable)).

Question: How do you split a factor into its constituent levels?
Answer: Use split(as.character(factor_variable), factor_variable).

Question: How do you check for the presence of a level in a factor?
Answer: Use any(factor_variable == "level_name").

Question: How do you merge similar levels in a factor?
Answer: Use levels(factor_variable) <- list("merged_level" = c("level1", "level2")).

Factors in Data Frames

Question: How do you create a data frame with a factor column?
Answer: Use data.frame() with a factor, e.g., data.frame(id = 1:3, category = factor(c("A", "B", "A"))).

Question: How do you convert a data frame column to a factor?
Answer: Use factor() on the column, e.g., df$column <- factor(df$column).

Question: How do you add a factor column to an existing data frame?
Answer: Assign a factor to a new column, e.g., df$new_factor <- factor(c("A", "B", "C")).

Question: How do you check if a column in a data frame is a factor?
Answer: Use is.factor(df$column).

Question: How do you reorder the levels of a factor in a data frame?
Answer: Use df$column <- factor(df$column, levels = new_order).

Question: How do you summarize a factor column in a data frame?
Answer: Use summary(df$factor_column).

Question: How do you drop unused factor levels in a data frame?
Answer: Use df$factor_column <- droplevels(df$factor_column).

Question: How do you create an interaction between two factor columns in a data frame?
Answer: Use interaction(df$factor1, df$factor2).

Question: How do you merge two data frames by a factor column?
Answer: Use merge(df1, df2, by = "factor_column").

Question: How do you subset a data frame based on a factor column?
Answer: Use subset(df, factor_column == "level_name").

Question: How do you group a data frame by a factor column?
Answer: Use split(df, df$factor_column) or group_by() from dplyr.

Question: How do you convert a factor column to numeric in a data frame?
Answer: Use df$factor_column <- as.numeric(levels(df$factor_column))[df$factor_column].

Question: How do you check the levels of a factor column in a data frame?
Answer: Use levels(df$factor_column).

Question: How do you aggregate data in a data frame by factor levels?
Answer: Use aggregate(value ~ factor_column, df, FUN).

Question: How do you convert all character columns in a data frame to factors?
Answer: Use df[] <- lapply(df, function(x) if(is.character(x)) factor(x) else x).

Question: How do you apply a function to a factor column in a data frame?
Answer: Use lapply(df$factor_column, FUN).

Question: How do you drop a factor column from a data frame?
Answer: Use df$factor_column <- NULL.

Question: How do you combine two factor columns into one in a data frame?
Answer: Use df$new_factor <- interaction(df$factor1, df$factor2).

Question: How do you sort a data frame by a factor column?
Answer: Use df <- df[order(df$factor_column),].

Question: How do you rename factor levels in a data frame?
Answer: Use levels(df$factor_column) <- c("new_name1", "new_name2").

Question: How do you calculate the mode of a factor column in a data frame?
Answer: Use table(df$factor_column) and find the most frequent level.

Question: How do you create dummy variables from a factor column in a data frame?
Answer: Use model.matrix(~ factor_column - 1, data = df).

Question: How do you handle NA values in a factor column in a data frame?
Answer: Use is.na() to detect and handle NA values, e.g., df <- df[!is.na(df$factor_column),].

Question: How do you apply a transformation to a factor column in a data frame?
Answer: Use df$factor_column <- lapply(df$factor_column, FUN).

Question: How do you summarize multiple factor columns in a data frame?
Answer: Use summary(df[, sapply(df, is.factor)]).

Question: How do you convert a factor column in a data frame back to character?
Answer: Use df$factor_column <- as.character(df$factor_column).

Question: How do you filter a data frame based on multiple factor columns?
Answer: Use logical conditions, e.g., df <- df[df$factor1 == "A" & df$factor2 == "B",].

Question: How do you plot a factor column in a data frame?
Answer: Use plot(df$factor_column) or ggplot(df, aes(x = factor_column)) + geom_bar().

Question: How do you merge data frames with factor columns that have different levels?
Answer: Ensure levels are consistent before merging or use as.character() to avoid issues.

Question: How do you compare factor columns across data frames?
Answer: Use identical(df1$factor_column, df2$factor_column) or all.equal().

Question: How do you save a data frame with factor columns to a file?
Answer: Use write.csv(df, "filename.csv") or saveRDS(df, "filename.rds").

Question: How do you find the levels of all factor columns in a data frame?
Answer: Use sapply(df, levels) on factor columns.

Question: How do you create a pivot table from a factor column in a data frame?
Answer: Use xtabs() or table() with factor columns.

Question: How do you reorder factor levels in a data frame based on another column?
Answer: Use df$factor_column <- factor(df$factor_column, levels = df$other_column).

Question: How do you visualize the distribution of a factor column in a data frame?
Answer: Use ggplot() with geom_bar() or plot().

Question: How do you impute missing values in a factor column in a data frame?
Answer: Use df$factor_column[is.na(df$factor_column)] <- "ImputedValue".

Factors Manipulations

Question: How do you change the levels of a factor in R?
Answer: Use levels(factor_variable) <- new_levels.

Question: How do you add new levels to a factor?
Answer: Use levels(factor_variable) <- c(levels(factor_variable), "new_level").

Question: How do you drop unused levels in a factor?
Answer: Use droplevels(factor_variable).

Question: How do you reorder levels in a factor?
Answer: Use factor(factor_variable, levels = new_order).

Question: How do you merge multiple levels in a factor?
Answer: Use levels(factor_variable) <- list("new_level" = c("level1", "level2")).

Question: How do you split a factor into multiple factors?
Answer: Use split(factor_variable, factor_variable) or interaction() with other factors.

Question: How do you convert a factor to an ordered factor?
Answer: Use ordered(factor_variable).

Question: How do you convert an ordered factor back to an unordered factor?
Answer: Use factor(factor_variable, ordered = FALSE).

Question: How do you check if a factor is ordered?
Answer: Use is.ordered(factor_variable).

Question: How do you rename levels in a factor?
Answer: Use levels(factor_variable) <- c("new_name1", "new_name2").

Question: How do you find the frequency of levels in a factor?
Answer: Use table(factor_variable).

Question: How do you recode levels in a factor?
Answer: Use recode() from the car package or manually with levels().

Question: How do you convert a factor to a numeric vector?
Answer: Use as.numeric(levels(factor_variable))[factor_variable].

Question: How do you combine two factors into one?
Answer: Use interaction(factor1, factor2).

Question: How do you subset a factor?
Answer: Use indexing or subset(), e.g., factor_variable[1:5].

Question: How do you remove specific levels from a factor?
Answer: Use factor(factor_variable, levels = setdiff(levels(factor_variable), "level_to_remove")).

Question: How do you reorder a factor based on another variable?
Answer: Use factor(factor_variable, levels = unique(other_variable)).

Question: How do you check the number of levels in a factor?
Answer: Use nlevels(factor_variable).

Question: How do you convert a factor to a character vector?
Answer: Use as.character(factor_variable).

Question: How do you reverse the levels of a factor?
Answer: Use factor(factor_variable, levels = rev(levels(factor_variable))).

Question: How do you create a factor with custom labels?
Answer: Use factor(variable, labels = c("Label1", "Label2")).

Question: How do you change the order of levels in a factor based on frequency?
Answer: Use factor(factor_variable, levels = names(sort(table(factor_variable), decreasing = TRUE))).

Question: How do you create dummy variables from a factor?
Answer: Use model.matrix(~ factor_variable - 1).

Question: How do you handle NA values in a factor?
Answer: Use is.na() and replace or omit as needed.

Question: How do you apply a function to each level of a factor?
Answer: Use tapply() or by() with the factor.

Question: How do you create a factor from a numeric variable?
Answer: Use factor() on the numeric vector.

Question: How do you perform mathematical operations on factors?
Answer: Convert the factor to numeric first.

Question: How do you combine factors with different levels?
Answer: Convert to characters, combine, then convert back to a factor.

Question: How do you find the index of a specific level in a factor?
Answer: Use which(levels(factor_variable) == "level_name").

Question: How do you check for duplicated levels in a factor?
Answer: Use duplicated(levels(factor_variable)).

Question: How do you check if a factor contains a specific level?
Answer: Use %in%, e.g., "level_name" %in% levels(factor_variable).

Question: How do you invert the levels of a factor?
Answer: Use factor(factor_variable, levels = rev(levels(factor_variable))).

Question: How do you convert a factor to a logical vector?
Answer: Use factor_variable == "level_name".

Question: How do you concatenate two factors?
Answer: Convert to characters, concatenate, then convert back to a factor.

Question: How do you compute the length of a factor?
Answer: Use length(factor_variable).

Question: How do you extract the levels of a factor?
Answer: Use levels(factor_variable).

Question: How do you compute the mode of a factor?
Answer: Use table(factor_variable) and extract the most frequent level.

Question: How do you plot the levels of a factor?
Answer: Use plot(factor_variable) or ggplot().

Question: How do you save a factor as part of a data frame?
Answer: Use write.csv(df, "filename.csv").

Factors Applications

Question: How are factors used in statistical modeling in R?
Answer: Factors are used to represent categorical variables in statistical models, ensuring that categorical data is handled correctly.

Question: How are factors applied in data visualization?
Answer: Factors are used to map categorical data to visual elements such as colors, shapes, or axes in plots.

Question: How are factors used in machine learning in R?
Answer: Factors are used to represent categorical features in machine learning models, ensuring proper encoding and interpretation.

Question: How are factors used in regression analysis?
Answer: Factors are used to include categorical variables in regression models, allowing for the estimation of different effects for each level.

Question: How are factors applied in ANOVA (Analysis of Variance)?
Answer: Factors represent the categorical groups being compared in ANOVA, allowing for the analysis of variance between groups.

Question: How are factors used in clustering analysis?
Answer: Factors can represent categorical variables that help in the interpretation of clusters, especially when analyzing group characteristics.

Question: How are factors used in time series analysis?
Answer: Factors are used to represent categorical variables such as seasons, holidays, or events that might affect the time series.

Question: How are factors used in survey data analysis?
Answer: Factors represent categorical survey responses, allowing for the analysis of response distributions and cross-tabulations.

Question: How are factors used in hypothesis testing?
Answer: Factors are used to define the groups or categories for which hypotheses are tested, such as comparing means across different groups.

Question: How are factors applied in experimental design?
Answer: Factors represent the different treatments or conditions in an experiment, allowing for the analysis of their effects on the outcome.

Question: How are factors used in ecological studies?
Answer: Factors represent categorical environmental variables or species classifications, facilitating the analysis of ecological data.

Question: How are factors used in genetics research?
Answer: Factors represent different genetic groups or conditions, allowing for the analysis of their effects on phenotypic traits.

Question: How are factors applied in marketing analysis?
Answer: Factors represent categorical variables like customer segments, regions, or product types, enabling targeted analysis.

Question: How are factors used in social science research?
Answer: Factors represent demographic variables such as gender, age group, or education level, facilitating the analysis of social patterns.

Question: How are factors used in public health studies?
Answer: Factors represent categorical variables like disease status, treatment groups, or demographic characteristics, enabling analysis of health outcomes.

Question: How are factors used in finance and economics?
Answer: Factors represent categories like industry sectors, credit ratings, or economic regions, allowing for segmented financial analysis.

Question: How are factors used in customer segmentation?
Answer: Factors represent categorical customer attributes, enabling the analysis and visualization of customer segments.

Question: How are factors used in sports analytics?
Answer: Factors represent categorical variables like team, position, or game outcome, facilitating the analysis of sports data.

Question: How are factors used in HR analytics?
Answer: Factors represent categorical employee attributes like department, role, or performance rating, enabling analysis of workforce data.

Question: How are factors used in operations research?
Answer: Factors represent categorical decision variables or constraints, facilitating optimization and decision-making processes.

Question: How are factors applied in product development?
Answer: Factors represent categorical variables like product features, customer preferences, or market segments, enabling targeted product development.

Question: How are factors used in environmental science?
Answer: Factors represent categorical variables like land use, pollution levels, or habitat types, enabling the analysis of environmental data.

Question: How are factors used in education research?
Answer: Factors represent categorical variables like grade level, subject area, or teaching method, facilitating the analysis of educational outcomes.

Question: How are factors used in political science?
Answer: Factors represent categorical variables like party affiliation, voting behavior, or policy support, enabling political analysis.

Question: How are factors used in consumer behavior studies?
Answer: Factors represent categorical variables like purchase frequency, brand loyalty, or shopping channel, enabling the analysis of consumer behavior.

Question: How are factors used in media and communication research?
Answer: Factors represent categorical variables like media type, audience segment, or content genre, facilitating the analysis of media data.

Question: How are factors used in clinical trials?
Answer: Factors represent categorical variables like treatment group, dosage, or patient demographics, enabling the analysis of clinical trial data.

Question: How are factors used in transportation studies?
Answer: Factors represent categorical variables like mode of transport, route, or travel purpose, facilitating transportation analysis.

Question: How are factors used in criminology research?
Answer: Factors represent categorical variables like crime type, offender profile, or geographic location, enabling criminological analysis.

Question: How are factors used in real estate analysis?
Answer: Factors represent categorical variables like property type, location, or market segment, enabling the analysis of real estate data.

Question: How are factors used in agriculture studies?
Answer: Factors represent categorical variables like crop type, farming method, or soil quality, facilitating agricultural analysis.

Question: How are factors used in cultural studies?
Answer: Factors represent categorical variables like cultural practices, language, or religious affiliation, enabling cultural analysis.

Question: How are factors used in retail analytics?
Answer: Factors represent categorical variables like product category, store type, or promotion, facilitating retail data analysis.

Question: How are factors used in energy and utilities research?
Answer: Factors represent categorical variables like energy source, usage type, or geographic region, enabling analysis in the energy sector.

Question: How are factors used in supply chain management?
Answer: Factors represent categorical variables like supplier, transportation method, or inventory type, facilitating supply chain analysis.

Question: How are factors used in disaster management studies?
Answer: Factors represent categorical variables like disaster type, response level, or affected region, enabling disaster management analysis.

Question: How are factors used in military and defense studies?
Answer: Factors represent categorical variables like unit type, mission category, or threat level, facilitating military analysis.

Question: How are factors used in psychology research?
Answer: Factors represent categorical variables like personality type, treatment group, or behavioral response, enabling psychological analysis.

Online Resources

Online Practice Paper Link: https://forms.gle/MQgpnQ7su6Cp3K688

QR Code:

YouTube Video Link:
https://www.youtube.com/playlist?list=PLzlh_31VWEFosbvQhW4P3GQJzVKdSskgX

QR Code:

Chapter 10: Data Frames

Creating Data Frames

Question: How do you create a data frame in R?
Answer: Use the data.frame() function to create a data frame, passing named vectors as arguments.

Question: How can you create a data frame from a list in R?
Answer: Use the as.data.frame() function on a list to convert it into a data frame.

Question: How do you create a data frame with specific column types?
Answer: Use the data.frame() function with the stringsAsFactors = FALSE argument and explicitly define each column's data type using functions like as.numeric(), as.character(), etc.

Question: How can you create a data frame with row names in R?
Answer: Use the row.names argument in data.frame() to assign row names.

Question: How do you create a data frame with factors?
Answer: Define a column as a factor using the factor() function when passing it to data.frame().

Question: How do you initialize an empty data frame with predefined column names?
Answer: Use data.frame() with ncol and nrow set to 0 and specify the colnames().

Question: How do you create a data frame from existing vectors?
Answer: Pass the vectors as arguments to the data.frame() function, ensuring they have the same length.

Question: How do you ensure a column in a data frame is treated as a factor?
Answer: Use the factor() function on the column when creating the data frame.

Question: How do you create a data frame from an existing matrix?
Answer: Use the as.data.frame() function to convert a matrix to a data frame.

Question: How do you create a data frame from a CSV file in R?
Answer: Use read.csv() to read the CSV file and create a data frame.

Question: How do you create a data frame with missing values?
Answer: Introduce NA values within the vectors when passing them to data.frame().

Question: How do you create a data frame from multiple lists?
Answer: Combine the lists using data.frame(list1, list2, ...) ensuring they have the same length.

Question: How do you specify column names when creating a data frame?
Answer: Use the names() function to set or modify column names after creating the data frame.

Question: How do you ensure numeric columns are not converted to factors?
Answer: Set stringsAsFactors = FALSE in data.frame() and use as.numeric() where necessary.

Question: How do you create a data frame with column names derived from a character vector?
Answer: Create the data frame and then use colnames(df) <- c("col1", "col2", ...) to assign names.

Question: How do you create a data frame by combining other data frames?
Answer: Use cbind() or rbind() to combine data frames by columns or rows, respectively.

Question: How do you create a data frame with default values?
Answer: Use the rep() function to fill columns with default values when creating the data frame.

Question: How do you create a data frame with row numbers as a column?
Answer: Use the row.names argument or create a column with 1:nrow(df).

Question: How do you create a data frame from a JSON file?
Answer: Use the fromJSON() function from the jsonlite package to read the JSON file and convert it into a data frame.

Question: How do you create a data frame from scratch with manually specified columns and rows?
Answer: Use the data.frame() function, passing each column as a named argument and ensuring all columns have the same number of rows.

Question: How do you create a data frame from a SQL query result in R?
Answer: Use dbGetQuery() from the DBI package to execute the query and return the results as a data frame.

Question: How do you create a data frame from an existing data frame but with selected columns?
Answer: Use indexing, e.g., new_df <- old_df[, c("col1", "col2")].

Question: How do you create a data frame with column data coming from different sources?
Answer: Use data.frame() by passing columns created from different sources like vectors, lists, or other data frames.

Question: How do you create a data frame with specific data types for each column?
Answer: Use the data.frame() function and convert each column to the desired data type using as.numeric(), as.character(), etc.

Question: How do you create a data frame with mixed data types?
Answer: Use data.frame() and ensure each vector is correctly typed before passing it to the function.

Question: How do you create a data frame from a table?
Answer: Use as.data.frame() on a table object to convert it to a data frame.

Question: How do you create a data frame with column names that include spaces or special characters?
Answer: Enclose the column names in backticks () or use make.names()` to create valid column names.

Question: How do you create a data frame where some columns are lists?
Answer: Use I() to treat lists as a column when creating the data frame, e.g., data.frame(col1 = I(list1)).

Question: How do you create a data frame from a time series object?
Answer: Use data.frame() in conjunction with time() and coredata() functions to convert the time series to a data frame.

Question: How do you create a data frame with factors having predefined levels?
Answer: Use the factor() function with the levels argument when creating the column.

Question: How do you create a data frame from an Excel file?
Answer: Use read_excel() from the readxl package to read the Excel file into a data frame.

Question: How do you create a data frame from scratch with specific row names?
Answer: Use the row.names argument in data.frame() to specify row names when creating the data frame.

Question: How do you create a data frame from a SQL database table in R?
Answer: Use dbReadTable() to read the table from the database into a data frame.

Question: How do you create a data frame from a hierarchical data structure like a nested list?
Answer: Use custom logic to flatten the structure and then convert it to a data frame.

Question: How do you create a data frame with logical vectors?
Answer: Use data.frame(logical_col = c(TRUE, FALSE)) to include logical vectors as columns.

Question: How do you create a data frame from an API response in R?
Answer: Use fromJSON() to parse the JSON response and convert it to a data frame.

Question: How do you create a data frame from a CSV file without converting strings to factors?
Answer: Use read.csv(stringsAsFactors = FALSE) to read the CSV file into a data frame.

Question: How do you create a data frame with columns in a specific order?
Answer: Arrange the vectors in the desired order when passing them to data.frame() or reorder them afterward using indexing.

Question: How do you create a data frame from a named vector?
Answer: Use data.frame() by passing the named vector and using names() to set column names.

General Operations on Data Frames

Question: How do you select specific columns from a data frame?
Answer: Use indexing, e.g., df[, c("col1", "col2")] or the select() function from dplyr.

Question: How do you filter rows in a data frame based on a condition?
Answer: Use subset() or dplyr::filter() to select rows that meet a condition.

Question: How do you rename columns in a data frame?
Answer: Use names(df) <- c("new_name1", "new_name2") or rename() from dplyr.

Question: How do you sort a data frame by a specific column?
Answer: Use order() inside the indexing, e.g., df[order(df$col),].

Question: How do you add a new column to a data frame?
Answer: Use $ or mutate() to create a new column, e.g., df$new_col <- values.

Question: How do you remove columns from a data frame?
Answer: Use df <- df[, -which(names(df) %in% c("col1", "col2"))] or select() with a negative sign in dplyr.

Question: How do you find the number of rows and columns in a data frame?
Answer: Use nrow(df) for rows and ncol(df) for columns, or dim(df) for both.

Question: How do you check for missing values in a data frame?
Answer: Use is.na(df) to identify missing values.

Question: How do you replace missing values in a data frame?
Answer: Use df[is.na(df)] <- value to replace NA values.

Question: How do you calculate summary statistics for each column in a data frame?
Answer: Use summary(df) or sapply(df, summary).

Question: How do you merge two data frames by a common column?
Answer: Use merge(df1, df2, by = "common_col") or dplyr::inner_join().

Question: How do you remove duplicate rows from a data frame?
Answer: Use df <- df[!duplicated(df),].

Question: How do you aggregate data in a data frame by a grouping variable?
Answer: Use aggregate() or dplyr::group_by() followed by summarise().

Question: How do you convert a data frame column to a different data type?
Answer: Use as.numeric(), as.character(), etc., on the specific column.

Question: How do you subset a data frame by multiple conditions?
Answer: Use logical operators inside subset(), e.g., subset(df, col1 > 5 & col2 < 10).

Question: How do you randomly sample rows from a data frame?
Answer: Use sample() with row indexing, e.g., df[sample(nrow(df), 10),].

Question: How do you reorder the rows of a data frame?
Answer: Use df <- df[order(df$col1, df$col2),].

Question: How do you concatenate data frames by rows or columns?
Answer: Use rbind() to concatenate by rows and cbind() to concatenate by columns.

Question: How do you calculate the correlation between columns in a data frame?
Answer: Use cor(df) to calculate the correlation matrix.

Question: How do you export a data frame to a CSV file?
Answer: Use write.csv(df, "filename.csv").

Question: How do you create a data frame with a specified subset of columns?
Answer: Use df_subset <- df[, c("col1", "col2")] to create a new data frame with selected columns.

Question: How do you group data by one or more columns in a data frame?
Answer: Use dplyr::group_by() or aggregate().

Question: How do you perform a left join between two data frames?
Answer: Use merge(df1, df2, by = "common_col", all.x = TRUE) or dplyr::left_join().

Question: How do you create a new column that is a function of existing columns?
Answer: Use df$new_col <- df$col1 + df$col2 or mutate() from dplyr.

Question: How do you reshape a data frame from wide to long format?
Answer: Use reshape() or gather() from tidyr.

Question: How do you reshape a data frame from long to wide format?
Answer: Use spread() from tidyr or reshape().

Question: How do you create a data frame by filtering out rows with missing values?
Answer: Use df <- df[complete.cases(df),].

Question: How do you normalize a column in a data frame?
Answer: Use df$col <- (df$col - min(df$col)) / (max(df$col) - min(df$col)).

Question: How do you calculate the mean of a column, ignoring NA values?
Answer: Use mean(df$col, na.rm = TRUE).

Question: How do you calculate the sum of a column, ignoring NA values?
Answer: Use sum(df$col, na.rm = TRUE).

Question: How do you create a pivot table from a data frame?
Answer: Use dcast() from the reshape2 package or spread() from tidyr.

Question: How do you remove rows with NA values from specific columns in a data frame?
Answer: Use df <- df[!is.na(df$col),] for specific columns.

Question: How do you add a column to a data frame with a sequence of numbers?
Answer: Use df$new_col <- seq(1, nrow(df)).

Question: How do you remove all rows with any NA values from a data frame?
Answer: Use df <- df[complete.cases(df),].

Question: How do you combine multiple data frames into one by columns?
Answer: Use cbind(df1, df2, ...).

Question: How do you apply a function to every column in a data frame?
Answer: Use lapply(df, function) or sapply(df, function).

Expanding a Data Frame

Question: How do you add a new column to an existing data frame?
Answer: Use df$new_col <- values or mutate() from dplyr.

Question: How do you add multiple columns to a data frame at once?
Answer: Use cbind() to bind new columns to the data frame or use mutate().

Question: How do you append rows to a data frame?
Answer: Use rbind() to add new rows to an existing data frame.

Question: How do you expand a data frame by adding new rows with specific values?
Answer: Create a new data frame with the desired rows and use rbind() to add them.

Question: How do you insert a column into a specific position in a data frame?
Answer: Use cbind(df[, 1:pos-1], new_col, df[, pos:ncol(df)]) to insert at position pos.

Question: How do you concatenate multiple data frames by rows?
Answer: Use rbind(df1, df2, ...) to combine data frames by rows.

Question: How do you expand a data frame with data from another data frame?
Answer: Use merge() or rbind() depending on whether you are adding rows or columns.

Question: How do you add a new column based on the values of existing columns?
Answer: Use df$new_col <- df$col1 + df$col2 or a custom function.

Question: How do you add a row of means for each column to a data frame?
Answer: Use rbind(df, colMeans(df, na.rm = TRUE)).

Question: How do you combine data frames with different column names?
Answer: Use rbind.fill() from the plyr package to handle different column names.

Question: How do you expand a data frame by adding a calculated column?
Answer: Use df$new_col <- df$col1 * df$col2.

Question: How do you add a new factor level to a column in a data frame?
Answer: Use factor(df$col, levels = c(levels(df$col), "new_level")).

Question: How do you add rows from another data frame to an existing one?
Answer: Use rbind(df1, df2) to add rows from df2 to df1.

Question: How do you insert NA values into a column to expand a data frame?
Answer: Use df$col[c(positions)] <- NA to insert NA at specific positions.

Question: How do you add a cumulative sum column to a data frame?
Answer: Use df$cumsum_col <- cumsum(df$col).

Question: How do you add columns with values based on conditions from other columns?
Answer: Use df$new_col <- ifelse(df$col1 > df$col2, value1, value2).

Question: How do you expand a data frame by replicating rows?
Answer: Use df[rep(1:nrow(df), times),] to replicate rows.

Question: How do you add a column with row indices to a data frame?
Answer: Use df$row_index <- 1:nrow(df).

Question: How do you add a column that is a lagged version of another column?
Answer: Use df$lagged_col <- c(NA, df$col[-nrow(df)]).

Question: How do you add a new column as a factor with predefined levels?
Answer: Use df$new_col <- factor(values, levels = c("level1", "level2")).

Question: How do you append rows from a list to a data frame?
Answer: Convert the list to a data frame with as.data.frame() and then use rbind().

Question: How do you add a summary row to a data frame?
Answer: Use rbind(df, summary_row) where summary_row contains the summary statistics.

Question: How do you expand a data frame by adding columns from a matrix?
Answer: Use cbind(df, matrix_data) to add columns from a matrix.

Question: How do you add a column with cumulative product values?
Answer: Use df$cumprod_col <- cumprod(df$col).

Question: How do you add rows with interpolated values to a data frame?
Answer: Use a combination of approx() and rbind() to interpolate and add rows.

Question: How do you add a running total column to a data frame?
Answer: Use df$running_total <- cumsum(df$col).

Question: How do you add rows to a data frame with missing columns?
Answer: Use rbind.fill() from the plyr package to handle missing columns.

Question: How do you add a new column by applying a function to each row?
Answer: Use df$new_col <- apply(df, 1, function(row) custom_function(row)).

Question: How do you append a data frame with rows from a CSV file?
Answer: Read the CSV file into a data frame and use rbind() to append the rows.

Question: How do you add a column with exponentially weighted moving average values?
Answer: Use df$ewma_col <- zoo::rollapply(df$col, width, mean, align = "right", fill = NA).

Question: How do you add columns from a nested list to a data frame?
Answer: Use df <- cbind(df, as.data.frame(do.call(rbind, nested_list))).

Question: How do you expand a data frame with cross-joined rows from another data frame?
Answer: Use merge(df1, df2, by = NULL) to perform a cross join and expand the data frame.

Question: How do you add a column with running maximum values to a data frame?
Answer: Use df$run_max <- cummax(df$col).

Question: How do you add a new column that is a function of the current and previous row values?
Answer: Use df$new_col <- c(NA, diff(df$col)) for differences or custom logic for other functions.

Applying Functions to Data Frames

Question: How do you apply a function to every element in a data frame?
Answer: Use apply(df, c(1, 2), function) to apply the function across all elements.

Question: How do you apply a function to each column of a data frame?
Answer: Use lapply(df, function) or sapply(df, function) to apply the function to each column.

Question: How do you apply a function to each row of a data frame?
Answer: Use apply(df, 1, function) to apply the function row-wise.

Question: How do you use dplyr::mutate() to apply a function to create a new column?
Answer: Use mutate(df, new_col = function(col1, col2)) to apply the function and create a new column.

Question: How do you use dplyr::summarise() to apply a function and return summary statistics?
Answer: Use summarise(df, new_col = function(col)) to apply the function and return summary statistics.

Question: How do you apply a function conditionally to elements in a data frame?
Answer: Use df <- ifelse(condition, function(df), df) or mutate() with ifelse() for conditional operations.

Question: How do you apply a function to specific columns of a data frame?
Answer: Use mutate_at(vars(col1, col2), function) from dplyr to apply the function to specific columns.

Question: How do you apply a function to each group in a grouped data frame?
Answer: Use group_by() followed by summarise() or mutate() to apply the function within groups.

Question: How do you apply a function to a sliding window of rows in a data frame?
Answer: Use zoo::rollapply(df$col, width, function, align = "right", fill = NA).

Question: How do you apply a function that returns multiple outputs to each row?
Answer: Use apply(df, 1, function(row) c(output1, output2)) and convert the result back into a data frame.

Question: How do you apply a custom function to a data frame and return a modified data frame?
Answer: Use df <- custom_function(df) where custom_function modifies and returns the data frame.

Question: How do you apply a function to every element in a data frame with purrr::map()?
Answer: Use map(df, function) to apply the function across all elements in the data frame.

Question: How do you apply a function to each column with a condition based on column names?
Answer: Use mutate_if(is.numeric, function) to apply the function only to numeric columns.

Question: How do you apply a function to multiple columns at once in dplyr?
Answer: Use mutate(across(c(col1, col2), function)) to apply the function across multiple columns.

Question: How do you apply a function with additional arguments to columns in a data frame?
Answer: Use lapply(df, function(x) custom_function(x, arg1, arg2)).

Question: How do you apply a function that modifies a data frame in place?
Answer: Use df <- within(df, {new_col <- function(col)}) to apply the function and modify the data frame.

Question: How do you apply a function to create a new column based on the current and previous row?
Answer: Use df$new_col <- c(NA, diff(df$col)) or custom logic for more complex operations.

Question: How do you apply a function to a nested data frame in tidyverse?
Answer: Use nest() to create a nested data frame, then map() to apply the function within the nested structure.

Question: How do you apply a function to a data frame that returns a data frame as output?
Answer: Use df <- do.call(rbind, lapply(df, function)) to combine the resulting data frames.

Question: How do you apply a function to calculate a rolling mean in a data frame?
Answer: Use zoo::rollapply(df$col, width, mean, align = "right", fill = NA).

Question: How do you apply a function to each element of a data frame and return a data frame?
Answer: Use apply(df, c(1, 2), function) and then convert the result back to a data frame with as.data.frame().

Question: How do you apply a function that requires multiple columns as input?
Answer: Use mutate(df, new_col = function(col1, col2)) or apply(df, 1, function(row)
custom_function(row["col1"], row["col2"])).

Question: How do you apply a function to rows in parallel using future.apply?
Answer: Use future_apply(df, 1, function) to apply the function to each row in parallel.

Question: How do you apply a function and save the result in a new data frame?
Answer: Use new_df <- lapply(df, function) and then convert it to a data frame with as.data.frame().

Question: How do you apply a function to each cell in a data frame and replace the values?
Answer: Use df[] <- lapply(df, function) to apply the function and replace the values in the original data frame.

Question: How do you apply a function that returns a data frame for each group in a data frame?
Answer: Use group_by() followed by do() or nest() and map() to apply the function and return a data frame.

Question: How do you apply a function to create multiple new columns in a data frame?
Answer: Use mutate() or mutate_at() with a custom function that returns a list of new columns.

Question: How do you apply a function to the last n rows of a data frame?
Answer: Use apply(tail(df, n), 1, function) to apply the function to the last n rows.

Question: How do you apply a function with different arguments to each column?
Answer: Use mapply(function, df$col1, df$col2, MoreArgs = list(arg1 = value1, arg2 = value2)).

Question: How do you apply a function to remove specific patterns in a column of a data frame?
Answer: Use mutate(df, col = gsub("pattern", "replacement", df$col)).

Question: How do you apply a function to compute cumulative operations on data frame columns?
Answer: Use mutate(df, cum_sum = cumsum(df$col)) or similar cumulative functions.

Question: How do you apply a function to transform data frame columns into a matrix?
Answer: Use as.matrix() after applying the function, e.g., as.matrix(df), or within apply().

Question: How do you apply a function to each level of a factor column in a data frame?
Answer: Use lapply(levels(df$factor_col), function(level) { custom_function(subset(df, factor_col == level)) }).

Question: How do you apply a function across multiple data frames at once?
Answer: Use Map(function, df1, df2) or mapply(function, df1, df2) to apply the function across multiple data frames.

Question: How do you apply a function that requires the previous and next row as input?
Answer: Use df$new_col <- c(NA, function(df$col[-1], df$col[-nrow(df)]), NA) or use zoo::rollapply().

Question: How do you apply a function to calculate row-wise statistics in a data frame?
Answer: Use apply(df, 1, function(row) custom_statistic(row)).

Question: How do you apply a function to pivot data from wide to long format?
Answer: Use pivot_longer() from tidyr after applying the necessary transformations.

Question: How do you apply a function conditionally to data frame elements based on their value?
Answer: Use mutate(df, new_col = ifelse(col > threshold, function(col), col)).

Data Type Conversion

Question: How do you convert a column to numeric in a data frame?
Answer: Use df$col <- as.numeric(df$col) to convert a column to numeric.

Question: How do you convert a factor to a character in a data frame?
Answer: Use df$col <- as.character(df$col) to convert a factor to a character.

Question: How do you convert a character column to a date in a data frame?
Answer: Use df$col <- as.Date(df$col, format = "%Y-%m-%d") to convert a character to a date.

Question: How do you convert a numeric column to a factor in a data frame?
Answer: Use df$col <- as.factor(df$col) to convert a numeric column to a factor.

Question: How do you convert a list column to a vector in a data frame?
Answer: Use df$col <- unlist(df$col) to convert a list column to a vector.

Question: How do you convert a data frame to a matrix in R?
Answer: Use as.matrix(df) to convert a data frame to a matrix.

Question: How do you convert a date column to POSIXct in a data frame?
Answer: Use df$col <- as.POSIXct(df$col, format = "%Y-%m-%d %H:%M:%S") for conversion.

Question: How do you convert a logical column to numeric in a data frame?
Answer: Use df$col <- as.numeric(df$col) to convert a logical column to numeric.

Question: How do you convert a column of numbers stored as characters to numeric?
Answer: Use df$col <- as.numeric(as.character(df$col)).

Question: How do you handle NA values when converting a factor to numeric?
Answer: Use df$col <- as.numeric(as.character(df$col)) to handle factors with NA values.

Question: How do you convert a data frame with mixed data types to a list?
Answer: Use as.list(df) to convert a data frame with mixed types to a list.

Question: How do you convert a matrix back to a data frame in R?
Answer: Use as.data.frame(matrix) to convert a matrix back to a data frame.

Question: How do you convert a factor with numeric levels to numeric directly?
Answer: Use df$col <- as.numeric(levels(df$col))[df$col].

Question: How do you convert a character vector to factors with custom levels?
Answer: Use df$col <- factor(df$col, levels = c("level1", "level2")).

Question: How do you convert a character column with currency symbols to numeric?
Answer: Use df$col <- as.numeric(gsub("[$,]", "", df$col)).

Question: How do you convert a data frame of factors to a data frame of characters?
Answer: Use df[] <- lapply(df, as.character) to convert all factors to characters.

Question: How do you convert a date column to a character column in R?
Answer: Use df$col <- as.character(df$col) to convert a date column to a character.

Question: How do you convert a data frame to a table object in R?
Answer: Use as.table(as.matrix(df)) to convert a data frame to a table object.

Question: How do you convert a data frame to a tibble in R?
Answer: Use as_tibble(df) from the tibble package.

Question: How do you convert a data frame column with logical values to character?
Answer: Use df$col <- as.character(df$col) to convert logical values to character strings.

Question: How do you convert a character column with percentage values to numeric?
Answer: Use df$col <- as.numeric(gsub("%", "", df$col))/100.

Question: How do you convert a data frame column with dates to a numeric epoch time?
Answer: Use df$col <- as.numeric(as.POSIXct(df$col)).

Question: How do you convert a numeric column to an ordered factor?
Answer: Use df$col <- factor(df$col, ordered = TRUE) to convert a numeric column to an ordered factor.

Question: How do you convert a data frame with multiple date columns to POSIXct?
Answer: Use df <- lapply(df, function(x) if(is.character(x)) as.POSIXct(x) else x).

Question: How do you convert a time series object to a data frame?
Answer: Use df <- as.data.frame(time_series_object).

Question: How do you convert a data frame with string representations of numbers to numeric?
Answer: Use df[] <- lapply(df, function(x) as.numeric(as.character(x))).

Question: How do you convert a factor column with levels to numeric based on the order of levels?
Answer: Use df$col <- as.numeric(df$col) to convert based on the order of levels.

Question: How do you convert a list of vectors to a data frame in R?
Answer: Use df <- as.data.frame(do.call(cbind, list_of_vectors)).

Question: How do you convert a data frame with text representations of dates to Date objects?
Answer: Use df[] <- lapply(df, function(x) as.Date(x, format = "%Y-%m-%d")).

Question: How do you convert a numeric column with categorical data to a factor?
Answer: Use df$col <- factor(df$col, labels = c("label1", "label2")).

Question: How do you convert a data frame with characters and numerics to all characters?
Answer: Use df[] <- lapply(df, as.character).

Question: How do you convert a POSIXct column to Date in a data frame?
Answer: Use df$col <- as.Date(df$col) to convert a POSIXct column to Date.

Question: How do you convert a data frame with lists as elements to a flat data frame?
Answer: Use df <- do.call(data.frame, df) or tidyr::unnest() to flatten the data frame.

Question: How do you convert a tibble back to a data frame in R?
Answer: Use df <- as.data.frame(tibble).

Question: How do you convert a data frame with missing values to a matrix?
Answer: Use as.matrix(df) after handling missing values, if necessary.

Question: How do you convert a list of data frames to a single data frame?
Answer: Use df <- do.call(rbind, list_of_dataframes).

Question: How do you convert a character column with special symbols to numeric?
Answer: Use df$col <- as.numeric(gsub("[^0-9.-]", "", df$col)).

Question: How do you convert a data frame with boolean values to numeric (0/1)?
Answer: Use df$col <- as.numeric(df$col) to convert boolean values to numeric.

Online Resources

Online Practice Paper Link: https://forms.gle/XibWCUhdhpuVxzPYA

QR Code:

YouTube Video Link:
https://www.youtube.com/playlist?list=PLzlh_31VWEFqLuHlOTONvuYlGX1u9uffb

QR Code:

Chapter 11: Graphs

Introduction to Graphs

Question: What are the main differences between base R graphics and ggplot2?
Answer: Base R graphics offer quick, simple plots with functions like plot(), hist(), and boxplot(). ggplot2, on the other hand, is more powerful and flexible, built on the grammar of graphics, allowing for more complex and customizable plots.

Question: What is the purpose of the par() function in base R graphics?
Answer: The par() function is used to set or query graphical parameters in base R, such as margins, layout, and axis options, which affect the appearance of plots.

Question: How does ggplot2 implement the concept of the grammar of graphics?
Answer:ggplot2 uses a layered approach to building plots, where users start with a data frame and map aesthetics using aes(), then add geometric objects like points or lines with geom_*, and customize the plot with scales, themes, and facets.

Question: What is the purpose of the aes() function in ggplot2?
Answer: The aes() function in ggplot2 defines the mapping of variables in your data to aesthetic properties of the plot, such as position, color, size, and shape.

Question: How do you change the plotting area size in base R?
Answer: Use the par(mar = c(bottom, left, top, right)) function to set the size of the margins around the plotting area, which indirectly changes the plotting area size.

Question: What is the role of the theme() function in ggplot2?
Answer: The theme() function in ggplot2 allows you to customize non-data elements of a plot, such as text, background, gridlines, and legends, providing fine control over the plot's appearance.

Question: How do you add a title and axis labels to a plot in base R?
Answer: Use the main, xlab, and ylab arguments in the plot() function to add a title and axis labels.

Question: How do you create a plot with multiple lines or points using base R graphics?
Answer: Use the plot() function to create the initial plot, then use lines() or points() to add additional lines or points.

Question: What is the difference between geom_point() and geom_line() in ggplot2?
Answer:geom_point() adds points to the plot, while geom_line() connects the data points with lines. Both are used to represent data in different ways.

Question: How do you create a scatter plot matrix in base R?
Answer: Use the pairs() function to create a scatter plot matrix, which displays bivariate relationships between all pairs of variables in a data frame.

Question: How can you combine multiple plots in one display in base R?
Answer: Use par(mfrow = c(nrows, ncols)) to arrange multiple plots in a grid format or layout() for more complex arrangements.

Question: How do you overlay multiple plots in ggplot2?
Answer: Add multiple geom_* layers to a ggplot object using the + operator to overlay different plots.

Question: What are some common geometric objects (geoms) used in ggplot2?
Answer: Common geoms include geom_point() for scatter plots, geom_line() for line plots, geom_bar() for bar plots, and geom_histogram() for histograms.

Question: How do you set up a basic plot with custom axis limits in base R?
Answer: Use the xlim and ylim arguments in the plot() function to set custom axis limits.

Question: How do you customize the color of points in a ggplot2 plot?
Answer: Use the aes(color = variable) inside ggplot() or geom_* to map colors to a variable, or use scale_color_manual() to specify custom colors.
Question: What are the advantages of using ggplot2 over base R graphics?
Answer:ggplot2 provides a more consistent and coherent system for creating plots, allowing for complex and layered visualizations, better customization options, and easier integration with modern data science workflows.

Question: How do you adjust the size of points or lines in base R?
Answer: Use the cex argument for points and lwd for line width in plotting functions like plot() and lines().

Question: How do you create a faceted plot in ggplot2?
Answer: Use facet_wrap(~ variable) or facet_grid(rows ~ cols) to create a faceted plot that splits the data into multiple panels based on the levels of a factor.

Question: How do you create a logarithmic plot in base R?
Answer: Use the log argument in plot(), such as plot(x, y, log = "xy"), to create a logarithmic plot on the x and/or y axis.

Question: How do you add a legend to a base R plot?
Answer: Use the legend() function to add a legend to a plot, specifying the position, labels, and colors.

Question: How do you control the appearance of the plot grid in ggplot2?
Answer: Use theme(panel.grid.major = element_line(), panel.grid.minor = element_line()) to customize the major and minor gridlines.

Question: What is a graphical device in R?
Answer: A graphical device in R is an environment where plots are rendered. Examples include windows on the screen, files like PNG or PDF, and external devices like printers.

Question: How do you create a plot with a custom background color in base R?
Answer: Use par(bg = "color") to set a custom background color before creating the plot.

Question: How do you save a plot to a file using ggplot2?
Answer: Use the ggsave("filename.png") function to save the last plot created by ggplot2 to a file.

Question: How do you add text annotations to a plot in base R?
Answer: Use the text(x, y, labels) function to add text annotations at specified coordinates.

Question: How do you create a multi-page PDF with multiple plots in base R?
Answer: Use pdf("filename.pdf") to open the PDF device, create multiple plots, and close with dev.off().

Question: How do you handle missing data in plots using ggplot2?
Answer: By default, ggplot2 ignores NA values in plots. You can also use na.rm = TRUE in geom_* functions to remove missing data.

Question: How do you adjust the aspect ratio of a plot in ggplot2?
Answer: Use coord_fixed(ratio = 1) to set a fixed aspect ratio.

Question: How do you create a plot with a logarithmic scale in ggplot2?
Answer: Use scale_x_log10() or scale_y_log10() to create a plot with a logarithmic scale on the x or y axis.

Question: How do you create a 3D plot in R?
Answer: Use functions like persp() in base R, scatterplot3d() from the scatterplot3d package, or plot3d() from the rgl package for interactive 3D plots.

Question: What is the purpose of theme_minimal() in ggplot2?
Answer:theme_minimal() provides a clean, minimalist appearance for the plot, removing background elements and simplifying gridlines.

Question: How do you customize axis ticks in base R?
Answer: Use the axis() function to manually add and customize axis ticks after suppressing the default axis with xaxt = "n" or yaxt = "n" in plot().

Question: How do you create a plot with custom line types in base R?
Answer: Use the lty argument in functions like plot() and lines() to specify custom line types.

Question: How do you export a plot to a PowerPoint presentation in R?
Answer: Use the officer package, specifically read_pptx() and ph_with() functions, to export a plot to a PowerPoint slide.

Question: How do you create a plot with subplots in base R?
Answer: Use par(mfrow = c(nrows, ncols)) to create a layout for subplots in a single plotting window.

Question: How do you apply custom themes in ggplot2?
Answer: Use theme() with specific elements like element_text(), element_line(), and element_rect() to create a custom theme.

Question: How do you overlay different types of plots in a single base R plot?
Answer: Use functions like points(), lines(), and abline() after the initial plot() to overlay different types of plots.

Question: How do you include mathematical notation in plot labels in base R?
Answer: Use the expression() function to include mathematical notation in plot labels, axis titles, and text annotations.

Creating Graphs

Question: How do you create a basic scatter plot in base R?
Answer: Use the plot(x, y) function where x and y are vectors representing the data points.

Question: How do you create a line plot in ggplot2?
Answer: Use ggplot(data, aes(x = x_var, y = y_var)) + geom_line() to create a line plot.

Question: How do you create a bar plot in base R?
Answer: Use the barplot(height) function, where height is a vector or matrix of bar heights.

Question: How do you create a histogram in ggplot2?
Answer: Use ggplot(data, aes(x = variable)) + geom_histogram(binwidth = value) to create a histogram.

Question: How do you customize the color of points in a scatter plot in base R?
Answer: Use the col argument in the plot() function, e.g., plot(x, y, col = "blue").

Question: How do you add a title to a plot in ggplot2?
Answer: Use ggtitle("Your Title Here") to add a title to the plot.

Question: How do you create a box plot in base R?
Answer: Use the boxplot(data) function, where data is a vector or formula indicating the data to plot.

Question: How do you create a scatter plot with different colors for each group in ggplot2?
Answer: Use aes(color = factor(group_var)) within ggplot() and geom_point() to map colors to groups.

Question: How do you add labels to the x and y axes in base R?
Answer: Use the xlab and ylab arguments in the plot() function to add axis labels.

Question: How do you create a stacked bar plot in ggplot2?
Answer: Use geom_bar(aes(fill = factor(group_var)), position = "stack") to create a stacked bar plot.

Question: How do you create a pie chart in base R?
Answer: Use the pie(x) function, where x is a vector of numeric values representing the pie slices.

Question: How do you create a histogram with custom bin widths in base R?
Answer: Use the hist(x, breaks = seq(min(x), max(x), by = bin_width)) function to set custom bin widths.

Question: How do you create a density plot in ggplot2?
Answer: Use ggplot(data, aes(x = variable)) + geom_density() to create a density plot.

Question: How do you create a dot plot in base R?
Answer: Use the dotchart(x) function, where x is a numeric vector.

Question: How do you create a bar plot with multiple groups in ggplot2?
Answer: Use geom_bar(aes(fill = factor(group_var)), position = "dodge") to create a grouped bar plot.

Question: How do you create a plot with logarithmic scales in base R?
Answer: Use the log argument in the plot() function, e.g., plot(x, y, log = "xy").

Question: How do you add a regression line to a scatter plot in ggplot2?
Answer: Use geom_smooth(method = "lm") to add a linear regression line to a scatter plot.

Question: How do you create a heatmap in base R?
Answer: Use the heatmap(matrix) function, where matrix is a numeric matrix representing the data.

Question: How do you create a violin plot in ggplot2?
Answer: Use ggplot(data, aes(x = factor_var, y = value_var)) + geom_violin() to create a violin plot.

Question: How do you create a line plot with multiple lines in base R?
Answer: Use plot(x, y1, type = "l") to create the first line, and then use lines(x, y2) to add additional lines.

Question: How do you create a scatter plot with jitter in ggplot2?
Answer: Use geom_jitter() to add jitter to a scatter plot, which helps in visualizing overlapping points.

Question: How do you create a histogram with density overlay in ggplot2?
Answer: Use ggplot(data, aes(x = variable)) + geom_histogram(aes(y = ..density..)) + geom_density() to overlay a density plot on a histogram.

Question: How do you create a bar plot with error bars in base R?
Answer: Use barplot(height) to create the bars, and arrows() or segments() to add error bars.

Question: How do you create a plot with custom axis limits in ggplot2?
Answer: Use scale_x_continuous(limits = c(min, max)) or scale_y_continuous(limits = c(min, max)) to set custom axis limits.

Question: How do you create a plot with facets in ggplot2?
Answer: Use facet_wrap(~ factor_var) to create multiple panels (facets) based on the levels of a factor.

Question: How do you create a line plot with shaded confidence intervals in ggplot2?
Answer: Use geom_ribbon(aes(ymin = lower, ymax = upper), alpha = 0.2) to add shaded areas representing confidence intervals.

Question: How do you create a 3D scatter plot in base R?
Answer: Use the scatterplot3d() function from the scatterplot3d package to create a 3D scatter plot.

Question: How do you customize the line type in a line plot in ggplot2?
Answer: Use aes(linetype = factor_var) inside geom_line() to customize line types based on a factor.

Question: How do you create a plot with dual y-axes in base R?
Answer: Create the first plot using plot(), then use par(new = TRUE) to overlay a second plot with a different y-axis using axis(side = 4).

Question: How do you create a bar plot with labels inside the bars in ggplot2?
Answer: Use geom_text(aes(label = value), position = position_stack(vjust = 0.5)) to add labels inside the bars.

Question: How do you create a plot with custom markers in base R?
Answer: Use the pch argument in plot() to specify custom markers for points.

Question: How do you create a dot plot with custom dot sizes in ggplot2?
Answer: Use aes(size = value) inside geom_dotplot() to customize the size of dots.

Question: How do you add annotations to a plot in base R?
Answer: Use the text(x, y, labels) function to add annotations at specific points on the plot.

Question: How do you create a heatmap with customized color gradients in ggplot2?
Answer: Use scale_fill_gradient(low = "color1", high = "color2") inside geom_tile() to customize the color gradient.

Question: How do you create a plot with transparent points in base R?
Answer: Use the rgb() function with an alpha value in the col argument of plot() to set transparency.

Question: How do you create a scatter plot matrix in ggplot2?
Answer: Use the ggpairs() function from the GGally package to create a scatter plot matrix.

Question: How do you create a plot with custom line colors in base R?
Answer: Use the col argument in the plot() or lines() function to specify custom line colors.

Question: How do you create a pie chart with percentage labels in base R?
Answer: Calculate percentages and use the labels argument in pie() to display percentage labels

Histograms and Density Plots

Question: How do you create a basic histogram in base R?
Answer: Use the hist(x) function, where x is a numeric vector, to create a basic histogram.

Question: How do you create a histogram in ggplot2?
Answer: Use ggplot(data, aes(x = variable)) + geom_histogram() to create a histogram, where variable is the numeric data.

Question: How do you adjust the number of bins in a histogram in base R?
Answer: Use the breaks argument in hist(x, breaks = number_of_bins) to specify the number of bins.

Question: How do you adjust bin width in a ggplot2 histogram?
Answer: Use the binwidth argument in geom_histogram(binwidth = value) to adjust the width of the bins.

Question: How do you overlay a density plot on a histogram in ggplot2?
Answer: Use ggplot(data, aes(x = variable)) + geom_histogram(aes(y = ..density..)) + geom_density() to overlay a density plot.

Question: How do you create a density plot in base R?
Answer: Use the plot(density(x)) function, where x is a numeric vector, to create a density plot.

Question: How do you customize the color of a histogram in base R?
Answer: Use the col argument in hist(x, col = "color") to set the color of the bars.

Question: How do you fill a ggplot2 histogram with different colors?
Answer: Use aes(fill = factor_variable) within geom_histogram() to color the bars based on a factor.

Question: How do you create a histogram with normalized counts (density) in base R?
Answer: Set probability = TRUE in the hist() function to create a histogram with normalized counts.

Question: How do you create a histogram with custom breaks in ggplot2?
Answer: Use geom_histogram(breaks = seq(min, max, by = binwidth)) to define custom breaks.

Question: How do you smooth a density plot in base R?
Answer: Adjust the bw (bandwidth) parameter in density(x, bw = value) to smooth the density plot.

Question: How do you add a rug plot to a density plot in ggplot2?
Answer: Use geom_rug() to add a rug plot, which displays individual data points along the axis.

Question: How do you create a cumulative histogram in base R?
Answer: Use the cumulative = TRUE argument in the hist() function to create a cumulative histogram.

Question: How do you create a density plot with filled areas in ggplot2?
Answer: Use geom_density(fill = "color", alpha = 0.5) to fill the area under the density curve with color.

Question: How do you create a log-transformed histogram in base R?
Answer: Use the log = "x" argument in hist(x, log = "x") to create a histogram with a log-transformed x-axis.

Question: How do you create a histogram with different colors for each bin in ggplot2?
Answer: Use aes(fill = ..count..) + scale_fill_gradient() within geom_histogram() to color each bin differently based on count.

Question: How do you plot multiple density plots on the same graph in base R?
Answer: Use lines(density(x1)), lines(density(x2)), etc., to overlay multiple density plots on the same graph.

Question: How do you create a histogram with transparency in ggplot2?
Answer: Use geom_histogram(alpha = 0.5) to add transparency to the bars of the histogram.

Question: How do you create a histogram with a normal distribution curve overlay in base R?
Answer: Use curve(dnorm(x, mean = mean(data), sd = sd(data)), add = TRUE) to overlay a normal distribution curve on a histogram.

Question: How do you create a density plot with a custom bandwidth in ggplot2?
Answer: Use geom_density(adjust = value) to control the smoothness of the density plot by adjusting the bandwidth.

Question: How do you create a stacked histogram in base R?
Answer: Base R does not directly support stacked histograms; you can use barplot() with table() instead or rely on ggplot2 for this functionality.

Question: How do you create a histogram with customized axis labels in ggplot2?
Answer: Use xlab("X-axis Label") and ylab("Y-axis Label") to customize axis labels.

Question: How do you add a legend to a histogram with multiple variables in ggplot2?
Answer: Use aes(fill = variable) within geom_histogram() and labs(fill = "Legend Title") to add a legend.

Question: How do you customize the color of a density plot in base R?
Answer: Use the col argument in plot(density(x), col = "color") to set the color of the density curve.

Question: How do you create a density plot with a different kernel in base R?
Answer: Use the kernel argument in density(x, kernel = "kernel_type") to specify the type of kernel.

Question: How do you create a faceted histogram in ggplot2?
Answer: Use facet_wrap(~ variable) to create multiple histograms based on the levels of a factor variable.

Question: How do you create a density plot with custom y-axis limits in ggplot2?
Answer: Use ylim(min, max) within geom_density() or coord_cartesian(ylim = c(min, max)) to set custom y-axis limits.

Question: How do you create a histogram with vertical lines in base R?
Answer: Use abline(v = value) to add vertical lines to a histogram, often to mark specific data points like the mean.

Question: How do you create a histogram with a density curve in base R?
Answer: Use hist(x, probability = TRUE) to create the histogram, then add lines(density(x)) to overlay the density curve.

Question: How do you customize the fill color of a histogram in ggplot2?
Answer: Use geom_histogram(fill = "color") to set the fill color of the bars.

Question: How do you create a density plot with a custom x-axis scale in ggplot2?
Answer: Use scale_x_continuous(limits = c(min, max)) to customize the x-axis scale.

Question: How do you create a horizontal density plot in base R?
Answer: Use the density() function to create the density object, then plot it with plot(density_obj, horiz = TRUE).

Question: How do you create a density plot with different line types for different groups in ggplot2?
Answer: Use aes(linetype = factor_variable) within geom_density() to create different line types.

Question: How do you create a histogram with custom text annotations in base R?
Answer: Use the text() function to add annotations at specific positions on the histogram.

Question: How do you create a density plot with confidence intervals in ggplot2?
Answer: Use geom_ribbon(aes(ymin = lower_bound, ymax = upper_bound), fill = "color", alpha = 0.2) to add confidence intervals.

Question: How do you create a cumulative density plot in base R?
Answer: Use the ecdf() function to create an empirical cumulative density function and plot it with plot().

Question: How do you create a histogram with facet grids in ggplot2?
Answer: Use facet_grid(rows ~ cols) with geom_histogram() to create a grid of histograms.

Dot Plots

Question: How do you create a simple dot plot in base R?
Answer: Use the dotchart(x) function, where x is a numeric vector, to create a basic dot plot.

Question: How do you create a dot plot in ggplot2?
Answer: Use ggplot(data, aes(x = variable)) + geom_dotplot() to create a dot plot, where variable is the data you want to plot.

Question: How do you customize the color of dots in a dot plot in base R?
Answer: Use the col argument in dotchart(x, col = "color") to set the color of the dots.

Question: How do you adjust the dot density in a ggplot2 dot plot?
Answer: Use binwidth inside geom_dotplot(binwidth = value) to adjust the density of the dots.

Question: How do you create a horizontal dot plot in base R?
Answer: The default dotchart() function in base R creates horizontal dot plots.

Question: How do you create a stacked dot plot in ggplot2?
Answer: Use geom_dotplot(binaxis = "y", stackdir = "center") to create a stacked dot plot.

Question: How do you create a dot plot with labels in base R?
Answer: Use the labels argument in dotchart(x, labels = names_vector) to add labels to the dots.

Question: How do you customize dot size in a ggplot2 dot plot?
Answer: Use the dotsize argument in geom_dotplot(dotsize = value) to adjust the size of the dots.

Question: How do you create a dot plot with jitter in base R?
Answer: Use dotchart(jitter(x)) to add a jitter effect to the dots, preventing overlap.

Question: How do you color dots based on a factor in ggplot2?
Answer: Use aes(fill = factor_variable) inside geom_dotplot() to color the dots based on a factor variable.

Question: How do you create a dot plot with multiple groups in base R?
Answer: Use dotchart(x, groups = group_variable) to create a dot plot grouped by a factor.

Question: How do you add a legend to a dot plot in ggplot2?
Answer: Use labs(fill = "Legend Title") and ensure aes(fill = factor_variable) is used to create a legend.

Question: How do you create a dot plot with variable dot sizes in ggplot2?
Answer: Use aes(size = value_variable) within geom_dotplot() to vary the size of dots based on a variable.

Question: How do you adjust the space between dots in a base R dot plot?
Answer: Use the space argument in dotchart(x, space = value) to adjust the space between dots.

Question: How do you create a dot plot with custom axis labels in ggplot2?
Answer: Use xlab("X-axis Label") and ylab("Y-axis Label") to customize axis labels in a ggplot2 dot plot.

Question: How do you create a grouped dot plot in base R?
Answer: Use dotchart(x, groups = group_variable, color = "color") to create a grouped dot plot with specific colors.

Question: How do you create a dot plot with different shapes for dots in ggplot2?
Answer: Use aes(shape = factor_variable) within geom_dotplot() to change the shape of the dots based on a factor.

Question: How do you rotate axis labels in a ggplot2 dot plot?
Answer: Use theme(axis.text.x = element_text(angle = 90, hjust = 1)) to rotate x-axis labels in a dot plot.

Question: How do you create a dot plot with a specific bin position in ggplot2?
Answer: Use geom_dotplot(binpositions = "all") to control the bin position of dots.

Question: How do you create a dot plot with a custom color palette in ggplot2?
Answer: Use scale_fill_manual(values = c("color1", "color2", ...)) to apply a custom color palette to the dots.

Question: How do you add a title to a dot plot in base R?
Answer: Use the main argument in dotchart(x, main = "Your Title Here") to add a title.

Question: How do you create a dot plot with different point styles in base R?
Answer: Use the pch argument in dotchart(x, pch = value) to specify different point styles.

Question: How do you create a dot plot with faceting in ggplot2?
Answer: Use facet_wrap(~ variable) within ggplot() and geom_dotplot() to create faceted dot plots.

Question: How do you create a dot plot with cumulative values in base R?
Answer: Base R does not directly support cumulative dot plots, but you can manually calculate cumulative values and
plot them.

Question: How do you create a dot plot with custom grid lines in ggplot2?
Answer: Use theme(panel.grid.major = element_line(), panel.grid.minor = element_line()) to customize grid lines.

Question: How do you add a background color to a dot plot in base R?
Answer: Use the bg argument within par(bg = "color") before calling dotchart().

Question: How do you create a dot plot with overlapping dots in ggplot2?
Answer: Use geom_dotplot(stackdir = "centerwhole") to allow dots to overlap in a central stacking direction.

Question: How do you create a dot plot with vertical orientation in base R?
Answer: Base R's dotchart() function only supports horizontal dot plots. Use ggplot2 with coord_flip() for vertical orientation.

Question: How do you create a dot plot with log-scaled axes in ggplot2?
Answer: Use scale_x_log10() or scale_y_log10() with geom_dotplot() to create a dot plot with log-scaled axes.

Question: How do you add text labels to dots in a dot plot in base R?
Answer: Use the text() function to add text labels near specific dots after creating the dot plot.

Question: How do you create a dot plot with a rug plot overlay in ggplot2?
Answer: Use geom_rug() in combination with geom_dotplot() to add a rug plot to your dot plot.

Question: How do you create a dot plot with transparency in ggplot2?
Answer: Use aes(alpha = value) within geom_dotplot() to adjust the transparency of dots.

Question: How do you plot multiple dot plots in the same figure in base R?
Answer: Use par(mfrow = c(nrows, ncols)) to set up a plotting area for multiple dot plots.

Question: How do you create a dot plot with highlighted specific points in ggplot2?
Answer: Use aes(color = ifelse(condition, "highlight_color", "default_color")) to highlight specific points in geom_dotplot().

Question: How do you create a dot plot with interactive elements in R?
Answer: Use the plotly package by converting ggplot2 objects with ggplotly() to create interactive dot plots.

Question: How do you add horizontal lines to a dot plot in base R?
Answer: Use abline(h = value) to add horizontal lines to the dot plot, marking specific values.

Question: How do you create a dot plot with custom spacing in ggplot2?
Answer: Use geom_dotplot(binwidth = value, binaxis = "y") and adjust the binwidth to control dot spacing.

Bar Plots

Question: How do you create a basic bar plot in base R?
Answer: Use the barplot(height) function, where height is a vector or matrix of bar heights.

Question: How do you create a bar plot in ggplot2?
Answer: Use ggplot(data, aes(x = factor_variable, y = numeric_variable)) + geom_bar(stat = "identity") to create a bar plot.

Question: How do you create a horizontal bar plot in base R?
Answer: Use barplot(height, horiz = TRUE) to create a horizontal bar plot.

Question: How do you create a grouped bar plot in ggplot2?
Answer: Use geom_bar(position = "dodge", aes(fill = factor_variable)) to create a grouped bar plot.

Question: How do you add labels to bars in a base R bar plot?
Answer: Use the text() function to add labels to the bars after plotting, e.g., text(x, y, labels).

Question: How do you add labels to bars in a ggplot2 bar plot?
Answer: Use geom_text(aes(label = numeric_variable), vjust = -0.5) to add labels above the bars.

Question: How do you create a stacked bar plot in base R?
Answer: Use barplot(height, beside = FALSE) to create a stacked bar plot.

Question: How do you create a stacked bar plot in ggplot2?
Answer: Use geom_bar(position = "stack", aes(fill = factor_variable)) to create a stacked bar plot.

Question: How do you customize bar colors in a base R bar plot?
Answer: Use the col argument in barplot(height, col = "color") to customize the color of the bars.

Question: How do you customize bar colors in a ggplot2 bar plot?
Answer: Use aes(fill = factor_variable) and customize colors with scale_fill_manual(values = c("color1", "color2")).

Question: How do you adjust bar widths in a base R bar plot?
Answer: Use the width argument in barplot(height, width = value) to adjust the bar widths.

Question: How do you adjust bar widths in a ggplot2 bar plot?
Answer: Use the width argument in geom_bar(width = value) to adjust the width of the bars.

Question: How do you create a bar plot with log-transformed y-axis in base R?
Answer: Use the log = "y" argument in barplot(height, log = "y") to create a bar plot with a log-transformed y-axis.

Question: How do you create a bar plot with custom axis labels in base R?
Answer: Use the names.arg argument in barplot(height, names.arg = c("Label1", "Label2")) to set custom axis labels.

Question: How do you create a bar plot with custom axis labels in ggplot2?
Answer: Use xlab("X-axis Label") and ylab("Y-axis Label") to set custom axis labels.

Question: How do you add a legend to a grouped or stacked bar plot in base R?
Answer: Use the legend() function after creating the bar plot, specifying the position, labels, and colors.

Question: How do you add a legend to a grouped or stacked bar plot in ggplot2?
Answer: Use labs(fill = "Legend Title") and ensure aes(fill = factor_variable) is used to create the legend.

Question: How do you create a bar plot with error bars in base R?
Answer: Use arrows() or segments() after barplot() to manually add error bars to the bars.

Question: How do you create a bar plot with error bars in ggplot2?
Answer: Use geom_errorbar(aes(ymin = lower_bound, ymax = upper_bound)) to add error bars to the bar plot.

Question: How do you create a dodged bar plot in ggplot2?
Answer: Use geom_bar(position = "dodge", aes(fill = factor_variable)) to create a dodged bar plot.

Question: How do you create a bar plot with specific colors for each bar in base R?
Answer: Provide a vector of colors to the col argument in barplot(height, col = c("color1", "color2")).

Question: How do you create a bar plot with specific colors for each bar in ggplot2?
Answer: Use scale_fill_manual(values = c("color1", "color2")) to manually set the colors for each bar.

Question: How do you create a cumulative bar plot in base R?
Answer: Manually calculate cumulative sums and plot them using barplot(), or use cumsum() before plotting.

Question: How do you create a cumulative bar plot in ggplot2?
Answer: Calculate cumulative values in your data frame and then plot them using geom_bar().

Question: How do you add a title to a bar plot in base R?
Answer: Use the main argument in barplot(height, main = "Your Title Here") to add a title.

Question: How do you add a title to a bar plot in ggplot2?
Answer: Use ggtitle("Your Title Here") to add a title to the bar plot.

Question: How do you rotate x-axis labels in a base R bar plot?
Answer: Use the las argument in par(las = 2) before plotting to rotate x-axis labels.

Question: How do you rotate x-axis labels in a ggplot2 bar plot?
Answer: Use theme(axis.text.x = element_text(angle = 90, hjust = 1)) to rotate x-axis labels.

Question: How do you create a bar plot with patterned fills in base R?
Answer: Base R does not support patterned fills directly, but you can use external packages or custom plotting functions.

Question: How do you create a bar plot with patterned fills in ggplot2?
Answer: Use the ggpattern package to add patterned fills to bars.

Question: How do you customize the axis limits in a base R bar plot?
Answer: Use the ylim argument in barplot(height, ylim = c(min, max)) to set custom y-axis limits.

Question: How do you customize the axis limits in a ggplot2 bar plot?
Answer: Use scale_y_continuous(limits = c(min, max)) to set custom y-axis limits.

Question: How do you create a bar plot with a custom color gradient in ggplot2?
Answer: Use scale_fill_gradient(low = "color1", high = "color2") to apply a color gradient to the bars.

Question: How do you create a bar plot with custom bar spacing in base R?
Answer: Use the space argument in barplot(height, space = value) to adjust the spacing between bars.

Question: How do you create a faceted bar plot in ggplot2?
Answer: Use facet_wrap(~ factor_variable) to create faceted bar plots for different levels of a factor.

Question: How do you add custom text annotations to a bar plot in base R?
Answer: Use the text() function to add annotations at specific positions after plotting the bars.

Question: How do you add custom text annotations to a bar plot in ggplot2?
Answer: Use geom_text(aes(label = value)) to add text annotations to the bars.

Question: How do you create a bar plot with transparent bars in ggplot2?
Answer: Use aes(alpha = value) within geom_bar() to adjust the transparency of the bars.

Question: How do you save a bar plot to a file in base R?
Answer: Use png("filename.png") to open the device, barplot() to create the plot, and dev.off() to save the file.

Question: How do you save a bar plot to a file in ggplot2?
Answer: Use ggsave("filename.png", plot = last_plot()) to save the last ggplot2 plot to a file.

Line Charts

Question: How do you create a basic line chart in base R?
Answer: Use the plot(x, y, type = "l") function, where x and y are numeric vectors representing the data points, and type = "l" specifies that a line chart should be drawn.

Question: How do you create a line chart in ggplot2?
Answer: Use ggplot(data, aes(x = x_var, y = y_var)) + geom_line() to create a line chart, where x_var and y_var are the variables representing the data points.

Question: How do you add points to a line chart in base R?
Answer: Use the points(x, y) function after the plot() function to add points to the line chart.

Question: How do you create a line chart with multiple lines in ggplot2?
Answer: Use aes(color = group_var) within ggplot() and geom_line() to differentiate multiple lines by color, where group_var is the grouping variable.

Question: How do you customize the line type in a base R line chart?
Answer: Use the lty argument in plot() or lines() to customize the line type, such as lty = 2 for dashed lines.

Question: How do you customize the line color in a ggplot2 line chart?
Answer: Use aes(color = group_var) within geom_line() to map line colors to a variable, or use scale_color_manual() to set specific colors.

Question: How do you add a legend to a line chart in base R?
Answer: Use the legend() function to add a legend, specifying the position, labels, and colors corresponding to the lines.

Question: How do you add a legend to a line chart in ggplot2?
Answer: Use labs(color = "Legend Title") and ensure aes(color = group_var) is included to generate a legend.

Question: How do you create a line chart with log-scaled axes in base R?
Answer: Use plot(x, y, type = "l", log = "xy") to create a line chart with logarithmic scales on both axes.

Question: How do you create a line chart with smoothed lines in ggplot2?
Answer: Use geom_smooth() in combination with geom_line() to add a smoothed line to the chart.

Question: How do you create a line chart with customized axis labels in base R?
Answer: Use the xlab and ylab arguments in plot() to customize the axis labels.

Question: How do you create a line chart with customized axis labels in ggplot2?
Answer: Use xlab("X-axis Label") and ylab("Y-axis Label") to set custom axis labels in ggplot2.

Question: How do you create a line chart with a secondary y-axis in base R?
Answer: Plot the first line using plot(), then use par(new = TRUE) and axis(side = 4) to add a secondary y-axis and plot the second line.

Question: How do you create a line chart with a secondary y-axis in ggplot2?
Answer:ggplot2 does not natively support secondary y-axes; you can manually create one by overlaying two plots using gridExtra or cowplot.

Question: How do you add custom text annotations to a line chart in base R?
Answer: Use the text(x, y, labels) function to add custom text annotations at specific data points.

Question: How do you add custom text annotations to a line chart in ggplot2?
Answer: Use geom_text(aes(label = label_var)) or annotate() to add text annotations to the line chart.

Question: How do you create a line chart with customized line widths in base R?
Answer: Use the lwd argument in plot() or lines() to set the line width.

Question: How do you customize line widths in a ggplot2 line chart?
Answer: Use geom_line(size = value) to set the line width in ggplot2.

Question: How do you create a line chart with a shaded area in base R?
Answer: Use the polygon() function after plot() to create a shaded area under the line.

Question: How do you create a line chart with a shaded area in ggplot2?
Answer: Use geom_ribbon(aes(ymin = lower_bound, ymax = upper_bound), fill = "color", alpha = 0.2) to add a shaded area.

Question: How do you create a cumulative line chart in base R?
Answer: Use cumsum() on the y-values before plotting, e.g., plot(x, cumsum(y), type = "l").

Question: How do you create a cumulative line chart in ggplot2?
Answer: Use geom_line(aes(y = cumsum(y_var))) to plot cumulative values.

Question: How do you create a line chart with faceting in ggplot2?
Answer: Use facet_wrap(~ factor_var) to create multiple line charts, one for each level of the factor.

Question: How do you create a line chart with different line styles for each group in base R?
Answer: Use the lty argument inside plot() and lines() with different values for each group.

Question: How do you create a line chart with different line styles for each group in ggplot2?
Answer: Use aes(linetype = factor_var) inside geom_line() to vary line styles by group.

Question: How do you add a title to a line chart in base R?
Answer: Use the main argument in plot() to add a title, e.g., plot(x, y, type = "l", main = "Your Title Here").

Question: How do you add a title to a line chart in ggplot2?
Answer: Use ggtitle("Your Title Here") to add a title to the line chart.

Question: How do you create a line chart with custom markers in base R?
Answer: Use pch inside plot() or points() to specify custom markers for data points.

Question: How do you create a line chart with custom markers in ggplot2?
Answer: Use geom_point(aes(shape = factor_var)) to add custom markers to the line chart.

Question: How do you add a grid to a line chart in base R?
Answer: Use the grid() function after plot() to add grid lines to the chart.

Question: How do you customize grid lines in a ggplot2 line chart?
Answer: Use theme(panel.grid.major = element_line(), panel.grid.minor = element_line()) to customize grid lines.

Question: How do you create an interactive line chart in R?
Answer: Use the plotly package to convert a ggplot2 line chart into an interactive chart with ggplotly().

Question: How do you create a line chart with confidence intervals in ggplot2?
Answer: Use geom_ribbon(aes(ymin = lower_bound, ymax = upper_bound), alpha = 0.2) to add confidence intervals to the line chart.

Question: How do you create a line chart with date-time axes in base R?
Answer: Use as.POSIXct() or as.Date() to convert your date-time data, and then use plot() with type = "l" to create the line chart.

Question: How do you create a line chart with date-time axes in ggplot2?
Answer: Use scale_x_datetime() or scale_x_date() with geom_line() to create a line chart with date-time axes.

Question: How do you save a line chart to a file in base R?
Answer: Use png("filename.png") to open the device, plot() to create the line chart, and dev.off() to save the file.

Question: How do you save a line chart to a file in ggplot2?
Answer: Use ggsave("filename.png", plot = last_plot()) to save the last ggplot2 plot to a file.

Question: How do you create a line chart with missing data points in base R?
Answer: Base R will automatically skip NA values, creating breaks in the line. Alternatively, you can use approx() for interpolation.

Question: How do you handle missing data points in a ggplot2 line chart?
Answer: Use geom_line(na.rm = TRUE) to automatically remove missing data points, or geom_point() to highlight them.

Pie Chart

Question: How do you create a basic pie chart in base R?
Answer: Use the pie(x) function, where x is a numeric vector representing the sizes of the pie slices.

Question: How do you create a pie chart in ggplot2?
Answer: Use ggplot(data, aes(x = "", y = value, fill = factor_variable)) + geom_bar(width = 1, stat = "identity") + coord_polar(theta = "y") to create a pie chart.

Question: How do you customize the colors of slices in a pie chart in base R?
Answer: Use the col argument in pie(x, col = c("color1", "color2", ...)) to customize the slice colors.

Question: How do you add labels to slices in a pie chart in base R?
Answer: Use the labels argument in pie(x, labels = c("Label1", "Label2", ...)) to add labels to the slices.

Question: How do you create a 3D pie chart in R?
Answer: Use the pie3D() function from the plotrix package to create a 3D pie chart.

Question: How do you add percentage labels to a pie chart in base R?
Answer: Calculate percentages and use them in the labels argument, e.g., labels = paste0(round(100 * x / sum(x), 1), "%").

Question: How do you create a pie chart with exploded slices in base R?
Answer: Use the radius argument in pie(x, radius = 1.2) to create an exploded pie chart with slices slightly separated.

Question: How do you rotate the starting angle of a pie chart in base R?
Answer: Use the init.angle argument in pie(x, init.angle = 90) to rotate the pie chart.

Question: How do you create a donut chart in ggplot2?
Answer: Use coord_polar(theta = "y") with a ggplot2 bar plot and set geom_bar(width = 1) and xlim(c(0.5, 2)) to create a donut chart.

Question: How do you add a title to a pie chart in base R?
Answer: Use the main argument in pie(x, main = "Your Title Here") to add a title to the pie chart.

Question: How do you add a legend to a pie chart in base R?
Answer: Use the legend() function after creating the pie chart to add a legend, specifying the position, labels, and colors.

Question: How do you create a pie chart with specific slice ordering in base R?
Answer: Reorder the x vector according to your desired slice order before calling the pie() function.

Question: How do you create a pie chart with a custom color palette in ggplot2?
Answer: Use scale_fill_manual(values = c("color1", "color2", ...)) to apply a custom color palette to the pie chart slices.

Question: How do you save a pie chart to a file in base R?
Answer: Use png("filename.png") to open the device, pie(x) to create the pie chart, and dev.off() to save the file.

Question: How do you save a pie chart to a file in ggplot2?
Answer: Use ggsave("filename.png", plot = last_plot()) to save the last ggplot2 plot to a file.

Question: How do you create a pie chart with transparent slices in base R?
Answer: Use the rgb() function with an alpha value in the col argument of pie(x, col = rgb(1, 0, 0, 0.5)) to set transparency.

Question: How do you create a pie chart with patterned fills in ggplot2?
Answer: Use the ggpattern package to add patterned fills to the slices of the pie chart.

Question: How do you create a pie chart with custom labels outside the slices in base R?
Answer: Use the text() function to manually place custom labels outside the slices after creating the pie chart.

Question: How do you create a pie chart with a legend that includes percentages in base R?
Answer: Calculate percentages, then use legend() with labels = paste(labels, ": ", round(100 * x / sum(x), 1), "%", sep = "") to include percentages in the legend.

Question: How do you create a pie chart with slices ordered by size in base R?
Answer: Sort the x vector in descending order before passing it to pie() to order slices by size.

Question: How do you create a pie chart with a specific starting slice in ggplot2?
Answer: Use the xlim() function in combination with coord_polar() to start the pie chart at a specific angle.

Question: How do you create a pie chart with interactive elements in R?
Answer: Use the plotly package to convert a ggplot2 pie chart into an interactive chart with ggplotly().

Question: How do you create a pie chart with a custom radius in base R?
Answer: Use the radius argument in pie(x, radius = 1.5) to adjust the size of the pie chart.

Question: How do you create a pie chart with custom text annotations in base R?
Answer: Use the text() function to add custom annotations to the pie chart after it is created.

Question: How do you create a pie chart with grouped data in ggplot2?
Answer: Use facet_wrap(~ group_var) in combination with geom_bar() and coord_polar() to create pie charts for each group.

Question: How do you customize the line width of the pie slices in ggplot2?
Answer: Use geom_bar(color = "color", size = value) within the ggplot2 setup to adjust the line width of the slices.

Question: How do you create a pie chart with different slice angles in base R?
Answer: The pie() function automatically calculates slice angles based on the proportion of each value in x.

Question: How do you create a pie chart with slices representing percentages in base R?
Answer: Calculate the percentages before calling pie() and use them directly, or label them as percentages.

Question: How do you create a pie chart with custom slice borders in base R?
Answer: Use the border argument in pie(x, border = "color") to set custom borders for the slices.

Question: How do you adjust the spacing between slices in a 3D pie chart in R?
Answer: Use the explode argument in the pie3D() function from the plotrix package to adjust the spacing.

Question: How do you create a pie chart with custom font sizes in ggplot2?
Answer: Use theme(text = element_text(size = value)) to adjust the font size of labels and legends in the pie chart.

Question: How do you create a pie chart with a log scale in base R?
Answer: Pie charts do not typically support log scales due to their circular nature; consider using a bar chart for log-scaled data.

Question: How do you create a pie chart with a shadow effect in base R?
Answer: Base R does not support shadow effects directly; consider using the plotrix package's floating.pie() for similar visual effects.

Question: How do you create a pie chart with specific slice labels in ggplot2?
Answer: Use geom_text(aes(label = paste0(value, "%")), position = position_stack(vjust = 0.5)) to label each slice with specific text.

Box Plots

Question: How do you create a basic box plot in base R?
Answer: Use the boxplot(x) function, where x is a numeric vector or a formula indicating the data to plot.

Question: How do you create a box plot in ggplot2?
Answer: Use ggplot(data, aes(x = factor_var, y = numeric_var)) + geom_boxplot() to create a box plot, where factor_var is the grouping variable, and numeric_var is the data to be plotted.

Question: How do you add notches to a box plot in base R?
Answer: Use the notch = TRUE argument in boxplot(x, notch = TRUE) to add notches, which indicate the confidence interval around the median.

Question: How do you create a horizontal box plot in ggplot2?
Answer: Use coord_flip() after geom_boxplot() to flip the coordinates, creating a horizontal box plot.

Question: How do you customize the color of boxes in a base R box plot?
Answer: Use the col argument in boxplot(x, col = "color") to customize the fill color of the boxes.

Question: How do you customize the color of boxes in a ggplot2 box plot?
Answer: Use aes(fill = factor_var) inside geom_boxplot() to color the boxes based on a factor, or use scale_fill_manual(values = c("color1", "color2")) for custom colors.

Question: How do you add labels to a box plot in base R?
Answer: Use the names argument in boxplot(x, names = c("Label1", "Label2")) to label each box.

Question: How do you add labels to a box plot in ggplot2?
Answer: Use xlab("X-axis Label") and ylab("Y-axis Label") to add axis labels, and labs(title = "Title") for the plot title.

Question: How do you create a grouped box plot in base R?
Answer: Use the formula method, e.g., boxplot(y ~ group_var) to create a grouped box plot where group_var is a factor that defines the groups.

Question: How do you create a grouped box plot in ggplot2?
Answer: Use aes(group = group_var) inside geom_boxplot() to group the data by a factor.

Question: How do you add points representing individual data to a box plot in base R?
Answer: Use the points() function after boxplot() to add individual data points.

Question: How do you add points representing individual data to a ggplot2 box plot?
Answer: Use geom_jitter() in combination with geom_boxplot() to add jittered points, representing individual observations.

Question: How do you create a box plot with customized whisker lengths in base R?
Answer: Use the range argument in boxplot(x, range = value) to adjust the whisker length.

Question: How do you customize the width of boxes in a ggplot2 box plot?
Answer: Use geom_boxplot(width = value) to set the width of the boxes.

Question: How do you add a legend to a box plot in ggplot2?
Answer: Use labs(fill = "Legend Title") and ensure that aes(fill = factor_var) is included to generate a legend.

Question: How do you create a box plot with log-scaled y-axis in base R?
Answer: Use the log = "y" argument in boxplot(x, log = "y") to create a box plot with a log-scaled y-axis.

Question: How do you create a box plot with log-scaled y-axis in ggplot2?
Answer: Use scale_y_log10() in combination with geom_boxplot() to apply a logarithmic scale to the y-axis.

Question: How do you create a box plot with multiple groups in base R?
Answer: Use the formula interface, e.g., boxplot(y ~ factor1 + factor2) to create a box plot grouped by two factors.

Question: How do you create a box plot with multiple groups in ggplot2?
Answer: Use interaction(factor1, factor2) within aes(x = interaction(factor1, factor2), y = numeric_var) in geom_boxplot().

Question: How do you add text annotations to a box plot in base R?
Answer: Use the text() function to add text annotations at specific points on the box plot.

Question: How do you add text annotations to a box plot in ggplot2?
Answer: Use geom_text(aes(label = label_var)) to add text annotations to the boxes.

Question: How do you create a faceted box plot in ggplot2?
Answer: Use facet_wrap(~ factor_var) to create separate box plots for each level of a factor.

Question: How do you create a violin plot overlay on a box plot in ggplot2?
Answer: Use geom_violin() followed by geom_boxplot(width = 0.1) to create a violin plot with a box plot overlay.

Question: How do you create a box plot with custom axis labels in base R?
Answer: Use the xlab and ylab arguments in boxplot() to set custom axis labels.

Question: How do you rotate x-axis labels in a ggplot2 box plot?
Answer: Use theme(axis.text.x = element_text(angle = 90, hjust = 1)) to rotate the x-axis labels.

Question: How do you add notches to a box plot in ggplot2?
Answer: Use geom_boxplot(notch = TRUE) to add notches, which indicate the confidence interval around the median.

Question: How do you create a box plot with customized whisker lengths in ggplot2?
Answer: Use geom_boxplot(coef = value) to adjust the whisker length (where coef controls the extension of the whiskers).

Question: How do you create a box plot with outliers highlighted in a different color in base R?
Answer: Use the outcol argument in boxplot(x, outcol = "color") to change the color of the outliers.

Question: How do you create a box plot with outliers highlighted in a different color in ggplot2?
Answer: Use geom_boxplot(outlier.colour = "color") to change the color of the outliers.

Question: How do you save a box plot to a file in base R?
Answer: Use png("filename.png") to open the device, boxplot(x) to create the plot, and dev.off() to save the file.

Question: How do you save a box plot to a file in ggplot2?
Answer: Use ggsave("filename.png", plot = last_plot()) to save the last ggplot2 plot to a file.

Question: How do you add grid lines to a box plot in base R?
Answer: Use the grid() function after boxplot() to add grid lines to the plot.

Question: How do you customize grid lines in a ggplot2 box plot?
Answer: Use theme(panel.grid.major = element_line(), panel.grid.minor = element_line()) to customize grid lines.

Question: How do you create a box plot with custom colors for each group in base R?
Answer: Provide a vector of colors to the col argument in boxplot(x, col = c("color1", "color2")) to customize the colors.

Question: How do you create a box plot with custom colors for each group in ggplot2?
Answer: Use scale_fill_manual(values = c("color1", "color2")) to set specific colors for each group.

Question: How do you create a box plot with variable widths in base R?
Answer: Use the varwidth = TRUE argument in boxplot(x, varwidth = TRUE) to create a box plot where the width of each box is proportional to the square root of the sample size.

Question: How do you create a box plot with variable widths in ggplot2?
Answer: Use geom_boxplot(varwidth = TRUE) to create a box plot with variable widths in ggplot2.

Question: How do you overlay multiple box plots in the same figure in base R?
Answer: Use the par(mfrow = c(n, m)) function to set up a grid layout, then call boxplot() multiple times to overlay different box plots.

Question: How do you overlay multiple box plots in ggplot2?
Answer: Use facet_wrap(~ factor_var) to overlay multiple box plots for different levels of a factor in the same figure.

Scatter Plots

Question: How do you create a basic scatter plot in base R?
Answer: Use the plot(x, y) function, where x and y are numeric vectors representing the data points.

Question: How do you create a scatter plot in ggplot2?
Answer: Use ggplot(data, aes(x = x_var, y = y_var)) + geom_point() to create a scatter plot, where x_var and y_var are the variables representing the data points.

Question: How do you add a title to a scatter plot in base R?
Answer: Use the main argument in plot(x, y, main = "Your Title Here") to add a title to the scatter plot.

Question: How do you add a title to a scatter plot in ggplot2?
Answer: Use ggtitle("Your Title Here") to add a title to the scatter plot.

Question: How do you customize point colors in a base R scatter plot?
Answer: Use the col argument in plot(x, y, col = "color") to customize the color of the points.

Question: How do you customize point colors in a ggplot2 scatter plot?
Answer: Use aes(color = factor_var) within geom_point() to color the points based on a factor variable, or use scale_color_manual(values = c("color1", "color2")) for custom colors.

Question: How do you adjust the size of points in a base R scatter plot?
Answer: Use the cex argument in plot(x, y, cex = value) to adjust the size of the points.

Question: How do you adjust the size of points in a ggplot2 scatter plot?
Answer: Use aes(size = value_var) within geom_point() to adjust point sizes based on a variable, or directly set size = value for uniform point sizes.

Question: How do you add labels to points in a scatter plot in base R?
Answer: Use the text(x, y, labels) function to add text labels near specific points.

Question: How do you add labels to points in a ggplot2 scatter plot?
Answer: Use geom_text(aes(label = label_var)) to add text labels to points.

Question: How do you add a regression line to a scatter plot in base R?
Answer: Use abline(lm(y ~ x)) to add a regression line to the scatter plot.

Question: How do you add a regression line to a scatter plot in ggplot2?
Answer: Use geom_smooth(method = "lm") to add a linear regression line to the scatter plot.

Question: How do you create a scatter plot matrix in base R?
Answer: Use the pairs(data_frame) function to create a scatter plot matrix displaying pairwise relationships between variables in the data frame.

Question: How do you create a scatter plot matrix in ggplot2?
Answer: Use the ggpairs() function from the GGally package to create a scatter plot matrix.

Question: How do you add a smoothing line to a scatter plot in base R?
Answer: Use the lowess(x, y) function to add a locally weighted scatterplot smoothing line.

Question: How do you add a smoothing line to a scatter plot in ggplot2?
Answer: Use geom_smooth() to add a smoothing line to the scatter plot.

Question: How do you create a scatter plot with log-scaled axes in base R?
Answer: Use plot(x, y, log = "xy") to create a scatter plot with logarithmic scales on both axes.

Question: How do you create a scatter plot with log-scaled axes in ggplot2?
Answer: Use scale_x_log10() and/or scale_y_log10() in combination with geom_point() to apply logarithmic scales.

Question: How do you create a 3D scatter plot in R?
Answer: Use the scatterplot3d() function from the scatterplot3d package to create a 3D scatter plot.

Question: How do you add jitter to a scatter plot in base R?
Answer: Use the jitter(x) and jitter(y) functions to add random noise to the data points before plotting.

Question: How do you add jitter to a scatter plot in ggplot2?
Answer: Use geom_jitter() to add jitter to the points, which helps to visualize overlapping data points.

Question: How do you create a scatter plot with different shapes for points in base R?
Answer: Use the pch argument in plot(x, y, pch = shape_value) to specify different point shapes.

Question: How do you create a scatter plot with different shapes for points in ggplot2?
Answer: Use aes(shape = factor_var) within geom_point() to assign different shapes to points based on a factor variable.

Question: How do you create a scatter plot with a color gradient in ggplot2?
Answer: Use aes(color = continuous_var) within geom_point() and apply scale_color_gradient() or scale_color_gradientn() for a color gradient.

Question: How do you add a secondary y-axis to a scatter plot in base R?
Answer: After creating the first plot with plot(), use par(new = TRUE) to overlay a second plot with a different y-axis, and use axis(side = 4) for the secondary y-axis.

Question: How do you create a scatter plot with facets in ggplot2?
Answer: Use facet_wrap(~ factor_var) or facet_grid(rows ~ cols) in combination with geom_point() to create multiple scatter plots, each representing a different level of a factor.

Question: How do you create a scatter plot with custom axis labels in base R?
Answer: Use the xlab and ylab arguments in plot(x, y, xlab = "X-axis Label", ylab = "Y-axis Label") to set custom axis labels.

Question: How do you create a scatter plot with custom axis labels in ggplot2?
Answer: Use xlab("X-axis Label") and ylab("Y-axis Label") to customize the axis labels in ggplot2.

Question: How do you create a scatter plot with customized point transparency in base R?
Answer: Use the rgb() function with an alpha value in the col argument of plot(x, y, col = rgb(1, 0, 0, 0.5)) to adjust transparency.

Question: How do you create a scatter plot with customized point transparency in ggplot2?
Answer: Use aes(alpha = value_var) within geom_point() to set point transparency based on a variable.

Question: How do you create a scatter plot with marginal histograms in ggplot2?
Answer: Use the ggMarginal() function from the ggExtra package to add marginal histograms or density plots to a scatter plot.

Question: How do you add a legend to a scatter plot in base R?
Answer: Use the legend() function to add a legend to the scatter plot, specifying the position, labels, and colors.

Question: How do you add a legend to a scatter plot in ggplot2?
Answer: Use labs(color = "Legend Title", shape = "Legend Title") to create a legend based on color and shape mappings.

Question: How do you create a scatter plot with specific axis limits in base R?
Answer: Use the xlim and ylim arguments in plot(x, y, xlim = c(min, max), ylim = c(min, max)) to set axis limits.

Question: How do you create a scatter plot with specific axis limits in ggplot2?
Answer: Use scale_x_continuous(limits = c(min, max)) and scale_y_continuous(limits = c(min, max)) to set custom axis limits in ggplot2.

Question: How do you create a scatter plot with multiple groups in base R?
Answer: Use plot() for the first group, then add the other groups using points() with different colors or shapes.

Question: How do you create a scatter plot with multiple groups in ggplot2?
Answer: Use aes(color = group_var) and/or aes(shape = group_var) within geom_point() to differentiate multiple groups.

Saving Graphs to a File in R Programming

Question: How do you save a plot to a PDF file in base R?
Answer: Use the pdf("filename.pdf") function to start the device, followed by your plotting commands, and then close with dev.off().

Question: How do you save a plot to a PNG file using ggplot2?
Answer: Use the ggsave("filename.png", plot = last_plot()) function to save the last ggplot2 plot to a PNG file.

Question: How do you save a high-resolution plot in PNG format in base R?
Answer: Use png("filename.png", res = 300) to set the resolution, followed by your plotting commands, and close with dev.off().

Question: How do you save multiple plots to a single PDF file in base R?
Answer: Use pdf("filename.pdf") to open the PDF device, plot multiple graphs, and then close with dev.off().

Question: How do you save a plot to a JPEG file in R?
Answer: Use jpeg("filename.jpg"), followed by your plotting commands, and close with dev.off().

Question: How do you adjust the width and height of a saved plot in ggplot2?
Answer: Use ggsave("filename.png", width = 6, height = 4) to specify the width and height in inches.

Question: How do you save a plot to a TIFF file in R?
Answer: Use tiff("filename.tiff"), followed by your plotting commands, and close with dev.off().

Question: How do you save a plot with a transparent background in PNG format?
Answer: Use png("filename.png", bg = "transparent") to save the plot with a transparent background.

Question: How do you save a plot to a bitmap format in base R?
Answer: Use bmp("filename.bmp"), followed by your plotting commands, and close with dev.off().

Question: How do you specify the DPI (dots per inch) when saving a plot in ggplot2?
Answer: Use ggsave("filename.png", dpi = 300) to set the resolution.

Question: How do you save a plot with custom margins in base R?
Answer: Adjust the mar parameter with par(mar = c(bottom, left, top, right)) before saving.

Question: How do you save a plot to a PDF file with custom page size?
Answer: Use pdf("filename.pdf", width = 8, height = 6) to specify the page size in inches.

Question: How do you save a plot as a vector image in SVG format?
Answer: Use svg("filename.svg"), followed by your plotting commands, and close with dev.off().

Question: How do you save a plot to a PostScript file in base R?
Answer: Use postscript("filename.ps"), followed by your plotting commands, and close with dev.off().

Question: How do you export a plot to PowerPoint using the officer package?
Answer: Use read_pptx(), add a slide with add_slide(), and then use ph_with() to insert the plot.

Question: How do you save a plot to a file without displaying it in base R?
Answer: Open a device (e.g., pdf()), execute your plotting commands, and close the device with dev.off() without displaying it.

Question: How do you save a plot with a specific aspect ratio in ggplot2?
Answer: Use ggsave("filename.png", aspect.ratio = 1.5) to maintain a specific aspect ratio.

Question: How do you save multiple plots to a multi-page PDF in base R?
Answer: Use pdf("filename.pdf"), create each plot on a new page, and close with dev.off().

Question: How do you embed fonts in a PDF file when saving a plot?
Answer: Use pdf("filename.pdf", family = "font_name"), and ensure the font is embedded in the PDF.

Question: How do you save a plot to an EPS (Encapsulated PostScript) file in base R?
Answer: Use postscript("filename.eps"), followed by your plotting commands, and close with dev.off().

Question: How do you save a ggplot2 plot with customized text size?
Answer: Use ggsave("filename.png", dpi = 300, height = 4, width = 6) with theme(text = element_text(size = 14)).

Question: How do you save a base R plot with specific dimensions?
Answer: Use pdf("filename.pdf", width = 7, height = 5) to set specific dimensions.

Question: How do you save a plot to a PNG file in a loop in R?
Answer: Use png() inside the loop, followed by the plot code, and close with dev.off() at each iteration.

Question: How do you save a ggplot2 plot with the correct color profile for printing?
Answer: Use ggsave("filename.png", color_profile = "CMYK") if the device supports it, or convert colors manually before saving.

Question: How do you save a plot to a file using a dynamic filename in base R?
Answer: Use paste() to dynamically generate the filename, e.g., png(paste0("plot_", i, ".png")).

Question: How do you include a timestamp in the filename when saving a plot?
Answer: Use format(Sys.time(), "%Y%m%d_%H%M%S") to append a timestamp to the filename.

Question: How do you save a plot with custom line widths in base R?
Answer: Use the lwd parameter in plot() before saving.

Question: How do you save a high-resolution plot for publication in ggplot2?
Answer: Use ggsave("filename.png", dpi = 600) to save a high-resolution plot suitable for publication.

Question: How do you export a plot to Excel using the openxlsx package?
Answer: Save the plot to a file (e.g., PNG) and then insert it into Excel using insertImage() from openxlsx.

Question: How do you save a plot with customized axis labels in base R?
Answer: Use xlab and ylab in plot() before saving.

Question: How do you save a plot in ggplot2 with a custom filename based on variable values?
Answer: Use ggsave(paste0("plot_", var_name, ".png")) to create a custom filename.

Question: How do you save a plot with transparency in ggplot2?
Answer: Use ggsave("filename.png", bg = "transparent") for a transparent background.

Question: How do you automate saving multiple plots in different formats in base R?
Answer: Use a loop with different devices (pdf(), png(), etc.) and save the plot with dev.off() for each format.

Question: How do you save a plot with custom tick marks in base R?
Answer: Customize tick marks with axis() and then save the plot.

Question: How do you save a plot with custom text annotations in ggplot2?
Answer: Use geom_text() or annotate() before saving the plot with ggsave().

Question: How do you save a plot to both PDF and PNG formats simultaneously in base R?
Answer: Open both devices (pdf() and png()), execute the plot code, and close with dev.off() for both.

Question: How do you save a plot with embedded images or logos in ggplot2?
Answer: Use annotation_custom() to embed images before saving with ggsave().

Question: How do you save a plot with custom gridlines in ggplot2?
Answer: Customize gridlines with theme(panel.grid.major = element_line()) before saving.

Creating Three-Dimensional Plots Exercises in R Programming

Question: How do you create a basic 3D scatter plot in R?
Answer: Use the scatterplot3d() function from the scatterplot3d package, where x, y, and z are numeric vectors representing the data points.

Question: How do you create a 3D surface plot in base R?
Answer: Use the persp() function, where x and y are vectors, and z is a matrix representing the surface heights.

Question: How do you create an interactive 3D plot using the rgl package?
Answer: Use plot3d(x, y, z) from the rgl package to create an interactive 3D scatter plot.

Question: How do you customize the perspective of a 3D plot in base R?
Answer: Use the theta and phi arguments in persp() to adjust the viewing angles (azimuthal and colatitude angles).

Question: How do you add color to a 3D scatter plot in scatterplot3d?
Answer: Use the color argument in scatterplot3d() to specify colors for the points.

Question: How do you create a 3D wireframe plot in R?
Answer: Use the wireframe() function from the lattice package, where z ~ x * y represents the surface to plot.

Question: How do you add a regression plane to a 3D scatter plot in scatterplot3d?
Answer: Use the plane3d() function to fit and draw a regression plane in the scatterplot3d() plot.

Question: How do you create a 3D bar plot in base R?
Answer: Use the bar3d() function from the plot3D package, where x, y, and z represent the bar heights.

Question: How do you rotate a 3D plot in the rgl package?
Answer: Use the play3d(spin3d()) function to animate and rotate the 3D plot interactively.

Question: How do you save a 3D plot created with the rgl package?
Answer: Use rgl.snapshot("filename.png") to save a snapshot of the 3D plot as an image file.

Question: How do you create a 3D contour plot in R?
Answer: Use the contour3d() function from the misc3d package, where f(x, y, z) represents the function to contour.

Question: How do you create a 3D histogram in base R?
Answer: Use the hist3D() function from the plot3D package, where x, y, and z represent the frequency counts.

Question: How do you create a 3D density plot in R?
Answer: Use the kde3d() function from the MASS package to estimate the density, then plot it using persp() or rgl functions.

Question: How do you add axes labels to a 3D plot in scatterplot3d?
Answer: Use the xlab, ylab, and zlab arguments in scatterplot3d() to add labels to the axes.

Question: How do you customize the tick marks in a 3D plot created with persp()?
Answer: Use the ticktype = "detailed" argument in persp() to add detailed tick marks on the axes.

Question: How do you overlay a 3D plot on a 2D plot in R?
Answer: Create the 2D plot first, then use par(new = TRUE) to overlay the 3D plot using scatterplot3d() or persp().

Question: How do you create a 3D plot with grouped data in scatterplot3d?
Answer: Use different colors or symbols for each group and specify them in the color or pch arguments within scatterplot3d().

Question: How do you create a 3D surface plot with color gradients in base R?
Answer: Use the col argument in persp() to specify a color ramp, e.g., col = terrain.colors(100).

Question: How do you create an interactive 3D plot with labels in rgl?
Answer: Use text3d(x, y, z, texts = labels) in combination with plot3d() to add interactive labels to the plot.

Question: How do you adjust the lighting in a 3D plot created with rgl?
Answer: Use the rgl.light() function to add or customize lighting in the 3D plot.

Question: How do you save a 3D plot as a web page using rgl?
Answer: Use rglwidget() in combination with saveWidget() to save the 3D plot as an interactive web page.

Question: How do you create a 3D scatter plot with transparency in scatterplot3d?
Answer: The scatterplot3d package does not natively support transparency; consider using rgl for this feature.

Question: How do you create a 3D scatter plot with different point sizes in rgl?
Answer: Use plot3d(x, y, z, size = size_var) to create a 3D scatter plot with variable point sizes.

Question: How do you add a legend to a 3D plot in scatterplot3d?
Answer: Use the legend() function after creating the plot, specifying the colors or symbols used in scatterplot3d().

Question: How do you create a 3D pie chart in R?
Answer: Use the pie3D() function from the plotrix package to create a 3D pie chart.

Question: How do you create a 3D plot with custom axes limits in persp()?
Answer: Use the xlim, ylim, and zlim arguments in persp() to set custom limits for each axis.

Question: How do you create a 3D waterfall plot in R?
Answer: Use the waterfall3d() function from the plot3D package, where x, y, and z represent the data.

Question: How do you create a 3D heatmap in R?
Answer: Use heatmap3D() from the plot3D package or rgl::plot3d() with a color gradient to represent heatmap data in 3D.

Question: How do you create a 3D plot with categorical data in R?
Answer: Convert categorical data to numeric factors, then plot using scatterplot3d() or rgl with different colors or symbols for categories.

Question: How do you animate a 3D plot in R?
Answer: Use the rgl package with functions like play3d(spin3d()) to create animated 3D plots.

Question: How do you export a 3D plot as a GIF in R?
Answer: Use rgl to create an animation and save it as a GIF using rgl::movie3d() with the type = "gif" argument.

Question: How do you create a 3D ribbon plot in R?
Answer: Use the ribbon3d() function from the rgl package to create a 3D ribbon plot, representing data along a curved path.

Question: How do you create a 3D plot with error bars in rgl?
Answer: Use segments3d() in combination with plot3d() to add 3D error bars to your plot.

Question: How do you create a 3D plot with different shapes for points in rgl?
Answer: Use shapes3d() or specify the type parameter in plot3d() to customize point shapes.

Question: How do you create a 3D surface plot with custom colors in rgl?
Answer: Use plot3d() with the color parameter, or use rgl::rgl.material(color = "custom_color") to specify custom colors.

Question: How do you add text annotations to a 3D plot in rgl?
Answer: Use text3d(x, y, z, texts = labels) to add text annotations to specific points in the 3D plot.

Online Resources

Online Practice Paper Link: https://forms.gle/g88J43rv8rdwywmM9

QR Code :

YouTube Video Link:
https://www.youtube.com/playlist?list=PLzlh_31VWEFqrfOpw6HFn4RK2koTSY2mQ

QR Code:

Chapter 12: Data Interfaces

CSV File

Question: What function in R is used to read a CSV file?
Answer: The read.csv() function is used to read CSV files into a data frame.

Question: How can you specify which strings should be treated as NA when reading a CSV file?
Answer: Use the na.strings argument in read.csv().

Question: What is the default delimiter in the read.csv() function?
Answer: The default delimiter is a comma.

Question: How can you prevent R from converting strings to factors when reading a CSV?
Answer: Set stringsAsFactors = FALSE in the read.csv() function.

Question: How do you read a CSV file without headers in R?
Answer: Set the header argument to FALSE in read.csv().

Question: How can you skip the first 5 lines when reading a CSV file in R?
Answer: Use the skip = 5 argument in read.csv().

Question: What function would you use to read a large CSV file quickly in R?
Answer: Use the fread() function from the data.table package.

Question: How do you specify column classes when reading a CSV file?
Answer: Use the colClasses argument in read.csv().

Question: How can you read a CSV file from a URL in R?
Answer: Use read.csv() with the URL as the file path, e.g., read.csv("https://example.com/file.csv").

Question: How do you handle a CSV file with inconsistent row lengths in R?
Answer: Use fill = TRUE in the read.csv() function or fread().

Question: How do you write a data frame to a CSV file without row names in R?
Answer: Use write.csv(df, "file.csv", row.names = FALSE).

Question: How do you append data to an existing CSV file in R?
Answer: Use write.table() with append = TRUE and col.names = FALSE.

Question: How do you write a CSV file with a semicolon as a separator?
Answer: Use write.csv2() or specify sep = ";" in write.table().

Question: How do you read only the first 100 rows of a CSV file in R?
Answer: Use the nrows argument in read.csv(), e.g., read.csv("file.csv", nrows = 100).

Question: How do you save a data frame to a CSV file with a custom column separator?
Answer: Use write.table(df, "file.csv", sep = "|").

Question: How do you read a CSV file with a different encoding in R?
Answer: Use the fileEncoding argument in read.csv(), e.g., read.csv("file.csv", fileEncoding = "UTF-8").

Question: How do you handle CSV files with missing column names in R?
Answer: Set header = FALSE and manually assign column names after reading the file.

Question: How do you specify the number of decimal places when writing a CSV file?
Answer: Use write.table() with the digits argument, e.g., write.table(df, "file.csv", digits = 2).

Question: How can you change the default behavior of write.csv() to use a dot instead of a comma for decimal points?
Answer: Use write.csv2() for European decimal notation.

Question: How do you import multiple CSV files into a list in R?
Answer: Use lapply() to loop through a list of file names, applying read.csv() to each.

Question: How do you save a subset of a data frame to a CSV file?
Answer: Subset the data frame first, then use write.csv(), e.g., write.csv(df[1:10,], "subset.csv").

Question: How can you include the current date in the CSV file name?
Answer: Use Sys.Date() in the file name string, e.g., write.csv(df, paste0("file_", Sys.Date(), ".csv")).

Question: How do you read a CSV file with tab delimiters?
Answer: Use read.csv() with sep = "\t", or use read.delim().

Question: How do you ignore comments in a CSV file when reading it in R?
Answer: Use the comment.char argument in read.csv(), setting it to the comment character used in the file.

Question: How do you check the structure of a CSV file without loading it completely?
Answer: Use the head() function after loading the first few rows with nrows argument in read.csv().

Question: How do you load only specific columns from a CSV file?
Answer: Use the colClasses argument to set unnecessary columns to "NULL".

Question: How can you write a CSV file and automatically compress it in R?
Answer: Use write.csv() with the gzfile() function, e.g., write.csv(df, gzfile("file.csv.gz")).

Question: How do you read a large CSV file chunk by chunk?
Answer: Use read.table() with the nrows and skip arguments in a loop.

Question: How do you remove trailing whitespaces from all columns when reading a CSV?
Answer: Use the strip.white = TRUE argument in read.csv().

Question: How can you ensure numeric columns are read correctly from a CSV file?
Answer: Use colClasses to explicitly set column types, or check with is.numeric() after reading.

Question: How do you handle CSV files with leading or trailing spaces in headers?
Answer: Use trimws() to clean up the headers after reading the file.

Question: How do you include a custom string for missing values when writing a CSV?
Answer: Use na = "custom_string" in write.csv().

Question: How do you ensure special characters are correctly encoded when writing a CSV file?
Answer: Specify fileEncoding when using write.csv(), e.g., fileEncoding = "UTF-8".

Question: How do you verify that a CSV file was written correctly?
Answer: Use read.csv() to read back the file and check its structure and content.

Question: How do you control the behavior of R when it encounters an error while reading a CSV?
Answer: Use tryCatch() to handle errors in read.csv() and continue execution.

Question: How do you read a CSV file that uses different column separators, like pipes or semicolons?
Answer: Use read.csv() with the sep argument, e.g., read.csv("file.csv", sep = "|").

Question: How do you deal with duplicate column names when reading a CSV?
Answer: Use make.names() to create unique names after reading the file.

Question: How do you ensure date columns are read correctly from a CSV?
Answer: Use as.Date() or lubridate functions after reading the file to convert date columns.

Question: How do you ensure that a CSV file is written with a custom line terminator?
Answer: Use write.table() with eol = "\r\n" or other custom terminators.

Question: How do you write a CSV file from a list of data frames in R?
Answer: Use lapply() to loop over the list and write.csv() for each data frame.

Excel File

Question: What R package is commonly used to read Excel files?
Answer: The readxl package is commonly used to read Excel files in R.

Question: How do you read a specific sheet from an Excel file?
Answer: Use the sheet argument in read_excel() to specify the sheet name or number.

Question: How do you read only a specific range of cells from an Excel sheet?
Answer: Use the range argument in read_excel() to specify the cell range.

Question: How can you read an Excel file into R without converting strings to factors?
Answer: read_excel() does not convert strings to factors by default, so no extra argument is needed.

Question: How do you write a data frame to an Excel file in R?
Answer: Use the write_xlsx() function from the writexl package.

Question: How do you append data to an existing Excel sheet?
Answer: You must read the existing data, append the new data, and then write it back, as write_xlsx() does not directly support appending.

Question: How do you read an Excel file with multiple sheets in R?
Answer: Use excel_sheets() to list the sheets and then loop over them with read_excel().

Question: How do you specify column data types when reading an Excel file?
Answer: Use the col_types argument in read_excel().

Question: How do you read an Excel file from a URL?
Answer: Use read_excel() with the URL as the file path, assuming the URL directly points to the file.

Question: How do you handle missing data when reading an Excel file?
Answer: Use the na argument in read_excel() to specify strings that should be treated as NA.

Question: How do you write multiple data frames to different sheets of an Excel file?
Answer: Use the openxlsx package, where write.xlsx() can handle multiple sheets.

Question: How do you read an Excel file with merged cells in R?
Answer: Merged cells are often challenging, but they are generally read as repeated values in read_excel().

Question: How do you write data to an Excel file with custom formatting?
Answer: Use the openxlsx package, which allows you to add formatting options like font size and color.

Question: How do you read large Excel files efficiently in R?
Answer: Consider using readxl, which is memory efficient, or split the file into chunks before reading.

Question: How do you check the structure of an Excel file without fully loading it?
Answer: Use head() or specify a limited range or a small number of rows with read_excel().

Question: How do you read an Excel file with protected sheets?
Answer: Use the openxlsx package, which allows you to specify a password if the sheet is password-protected.

Question: How do you convert an Excel file to a CSV in R?
Answer: Use read_excel() to load the file and then write.csv() to save it as a CSV.

Question: How do you handle Excel files with different date formats?
Answer: Manually convert date columns after reading the file using as.Date() or lubridate.

Question: How do you read specific columns from an Excel file in R?
Answer: Use the col_names and range arguments in read_excel() to select specific columns.

Question: How do you read an Excel file with non-standard date formats?
Answer: Use read_excel() and convert date columns using as.Date() or custom date format strings.

Question: How do you handle Excel files with non-numeric characters in numeric columns?
Answer: Read the column as a character vector and clean the data before converting it to numeric.

Question: How do you handle errors while reading Excel files in R?
Answer: Use tryCatch() to handle potential errors in read_excel().

Question: How do you check for missing sheets in an Excel file before reading?
Answer: Use excel_sheets() to list the sheets and verify their presence.

Question: How do you add a sheet to an existing Excel file?
Answer: Use the openxlsx package, which allows adding sheets to an existing workbook.

Question: How do you handle Excel files with hidden sheets?
Answer: read_excel() ignores hidden sheets by default; you must explicitly specify the sheet to read it.

Question: How do you read a password-protected Excel file in R?
Answer: Use openxlsx::read.xlsx() with the password argument.

Question: How do you handle Excel files with formulas in cells?
Answer: read_excel() typically reads the evaluated result of formulas, not the formula itself.

Question: How do you create an Excel file with data validation or dropdowns?
Answer: Use the openxlsx package, which allows adding data validation and dropdowns.

Question: How do you read an Excel file with mixed data types in a single column?
Answer: Read the column as a character vector and manually process the data to handle mixed types.

Question: How do you handle multi-level headers in an Excel file?
Answer: Use read_excel() to read the headers into separate data frames and then combine them programmatically.

Question: How do you write an Excel file with custom column widths?
Answer: Use the openxlsx package to set column widths when writing the file.

Question: How do you read an Excel file with named ranges?
Answer: Use read_excel() with the range argument set to the named range.

Question: How do you read an Excel file with very large text fields?
Answer: Use read_excel() to load the file and specify col_types = "text" for large text fields.

Question: How do you save an Excel file with multiple data frames in different sheets?
Answer: Use openxlsx::write.xlsx() to save multiple data frames to different sheets.

Question: How do you read a specific cell value from an Excel file in R?
Answer: Use read_excel() with the range argument specifying the cell address, like "A1:A1".

Question: How do you handle Excel files with special characters in column names?
Answer: Use read_excel() to read the file and then rename the columns using make.names().

Question: How do you ensure that an Excel file is written with a specific date format?
Answer: Use openxlsx to set the cell styles, including date formats, when writing the file.

Question: How do you handle Excel files with varying column types?
Answer: Use the col_types argument in read_excel() to manually specify column types.

Question: How do you write data to an Excel file with protected cells?
Answer: Use openxlsx to create the file and protect specific cells or sheets.

Question: How do you automate the process of reading multiple Excel files and combining them into a single data frame?
Answer: Use lapply() to read each file and dplyr::bind_rows() to combine them.

Binary File

Question: How do you read binary data in R?
Answer: Use the readBin() function to read binary data into R.

Question: What is the purpose of the size argument in readBin()?
Answer: The size argument specifies the number of bytes to read per element.

Question: How do you write binary data to a file in R?
Answer: Use the writeBin() function to write binary data to a file.

Question: How do you determine the endianness of a system in R?
Answer: Use .Platform$endian to check the endianness of the system.

Question: How do you handle endianness when reading a binary file?
Answer: Use the endian argument in readBin() to specify "little" or "big" endian format.

Question: How do you read a binary file with mixed data types?
Answer: Use a combination of readBin() calls with appropriate size and what parameters.

Question: How do you skip to a specific byte position in a binary file?
Answer: Use the seek() function to move the file pointer before reading.

Question: How do you read a binary file as raw data in R?
Answer: Use readBin(file, what = "raw", n = file.size("file.bin")) to read it as raw data.

Question: How do you convert binary data to character in R?
Answer: Use rawToChar() to convert raw binary data to a character string.

Question: How do you read an integer from a binary file in R?
Answer: Use readBin(file, what = integer(), size = 4) to read an integer.

Question: How do you ensure data integrity when writing to a binary file?
Answer: Verify that the size and what parameters match the data type being written.

Question: How do you read a floating-point number from a binary file?
Answer: Use readBin(file, what = double(), size = 8) for double-precision floating-point numbers.

Question: How do you write a binary file with a specific endianness?
Answer: Use writeBin() with the endian argument set to "little" or "big".

Question: How do you read binary data in chunks?
Answer: Use readBin() in a loop with a specified chunk size to read data in segments.

Question: How do you handle missing or corrupt binary data?
Answer: Implement error-checking with tryCatch() and handle cases where readBin() returns unexpected results.

Question: How do you append data to a binary file in R?
Answer: Open the file in append mode using file("file.bin", "ab") and then use writeBin().

Question: How do you write text data as binary in R?
Answer: Convert text to raw with charToRaw() and then use writeBin() to write it as binary.

Question: How do you read a binary file that contains a mixture of text and numbers?
Answer: Read the file as raw data and then use conditional logic to convert segments to the appropriate types.

Question: How do you handle large binary files efficiently in R?
Answer: Use memory-efficient techniques like reading in chunks and processing the data incrementally.

Question: How do you ensure the correct byte order when writing binary data in R?
Answer: Explicitly specify the endian parameter in writeBin().

Question: How do you extract specific bytes from binary data in R?
Answer: Use the substr() function on raw data to extract specific byte sequences.

Question: How do you read and write binary data to and from a connection in R?
Answer: Use readBin() and writeBin() with a connection object, like a socket or file connection.

Question: How do you convert binary data to a numeric vector in R?
Answer: Use readBin() specifying what = numeric().

Question: How do you determine the length of a binary file?
Answer: Use file.info("file.bin")$size to get the file size in bytes.

Question: How do you interpret a binary file format in R?
Answer: Reference the file format specification and use appropriate readBin() calls to extract the data.

Question: How do you decode binary data encoded in base64?
Answer: Use the base64enc package to decode base64-encoded binary data.

Question: How do you read a binary file into a matrix in R?
Answer: Use readBin() to read data into a vector and then convert it to a matrix with matrix().

Question: How do you read binary data from a network socket in R?
Answer: Use readBin() with a socket connection created by socketConnection().

Question: How do you write a binary file that includes metadata in R?
Answer: Write the metadata first as binary data, followed by the main data using writeBin().

Question: How do you debug issues when reading binary files in R?
Answer: Verify size, what, and endian parameters and use tryCatch() for error handling.

Question: How do you convert binary data to hexadecimal format in R?
Answer: Use the as.hexmode() function on raw binary data.

Question: How do you handle padding in binary data?
Answer: Account for padding bytes manually and skip them with the seek() function.

Question: How do you work with binary data that includes a checksum?
Answer: Calculate the checksum in R after reading the data and compare it with the provided checksum.

Question: How do you serialize R objects to binary format?
Answer: Use the saveRDS() function to serialize R objects to a binary format.

Question: How do you handle binary files with a proprietary format in R?
Answer: Reference the proprietary format documentation and implement custom readBin() logic.

Question: How do you extract specific bits from a byte in R?
Answer: Use bitwise operations with the bitops package to manipulate and extract bits.

Question: How do you convert a binary file into a data frame in R?
Answer: Read the binary data into a vector and then convert it to a data frame using data.frame().

Question: How do you read binary files created on different platforms (Windows/Linux)?
Answer: Ensure correct handling of endianness with the endian argument in readBin().

Question: How do you write a binary file with a specific structure?
Answer: Define the structure using writeBin() with appropriate size and what parameters for each segment.

Question: How do you extract text data embedded in binary files?
Answer: Read the file as raw data, identify the text segment, and convert it using rawToChar().

JSON File

Question: What package is commonly used to handle JSON data in R?
Answer: The jsonlite package is widely used for working with JSON data in R.

Question: How do you read a JSON file into R?
Answer: Use the fromJSON() function from the jsonlite package.

Question: How do you write R data to a JSON file?
Answer: Use the toJSON() function from the jsonlite package.

Question: How do you handle nested JSON structures in R?
Answer: Nested JSON structures are automatically parsed into lists or data frames by fromJSON().

Question: How do you convert a data frame to JSON format?
Answer: Use toJSON(df) to convert a data frame to JSON format.

Question: How do you pretty-print JSON data in R?
Answer: Use the prettify() function in jsonlite to format JSON data for readability.

Question: How do you flatten a nested JSON structure in R?
Answer: Use the flatten() function from the jsonlite package to convert nested lists into a flat data frame.

Question: How do you read JSON data from a URL in R?
Answer: Use fromJSON(url) where url is the link to the JSON data.

Question: How do you parse a specific element in a JSON object in R?
Answer: Access elements in the parsed list or data frame using indexing, e.g., data$element.

Question: How do you handle JSON arrays with different lengths?
Answer: Parse them into lists and handle each element individually, or use rbind.fill() to combine into a data frame.

Question: How do you read a JSON file with encoding issues?
Answer: Use fromJSON("file.json", encoding = "UTF-8") to specify the correct encoding.

Question: How do you convert a JSON file to a CSV file in R?
Answer: Read the JSON with fromJSON() and then write it to CSV using write.csv().

Question: How do you extract key-value pairs from a JSON object in R?
Answer: Use names() to extract keys and index the list to extract corresponding values.

Question: How do you handle large JSON files in R?
Answer: Use streaming with stream_in() from jsonlite to handle large JSON files efficiently.

Question: How do you check if a string is valid JSON in R?
Answer: Use validate() from the jsonlite package to check JSON validity.

Question: How do you parse JSON data into a tibble in R?
Answer: Parse with fromJSON() and convert the result to a tibble with as_tibble().

Question: How do you handle missing values in JSON data in R?
Answer: fromJSON() treats missing values as NA by default, which can be handled using standard R techniques.

Question: How do you serialize R objects to JSON?
Answer: Use toJSON() to serialize R objects into a JSON string.

Question: How do you handle dates and times in JSON files in R?
Answer: Convert date-time strings to R Date or POSIXct objects after parsing the JSON.

Question: How do you read JSON data with dynamic field names?
Answer: Use list indexing with dynamic names, e.g., data[[dynamic_name]].

Question: How do you parse a JSON object into individual R variables?
Answer: Parse the JSON into a list and then assign list elements to variables.

Question: How do you merge multiple JSON files into one data frame?
Answer: Use lapply() to read each JSON file into a data frame and then use bind_rows() from dplyr to combine them.

Question: How do you handle deeply nested JSON objects?
Answer: Recursively parse the nested objects into lists or use flatten() if possible.

Question: How do you write a JSON file with pretty formatting?
Answer: Use toJSON(data, pretty = TRUE) to write the JSON with indentation for readability.

Question: How do you handle large JSON arrays in R?
Answer: Use stream_in() to process large arrays incrementally.

Question: How do you handle JSON data with missing or extra fields?
Answer: fromJSON() will create NA values for missing fields and ignore extra fields not specified in the R structure.

Question: How do you filter JSON data based on certain criteria?
Answer: Parse the JSON to a list or data frame, and then use dplyr or base R filtering functions.

Question: How do you convert a list of JSON objects into a data frame?
Answer: Use fromJSON() to parse each object and then bind_rows() to combine them.

Question: How do you handle JSON data with special characters?
Answer: Ensure proper encoding when reading and writing JSON, typically UTF-8.

Question: How do you validate and clean JSON data in R?
Answer: Use validate() to check for JSON structure and custom functions to clean the data after parsing.

Question: How do you handle JSON data that contains binary content?
Answer: Parse as a raw vector and then decode using appropriate methods like base64 decoding.

Question: How do you work with JSON data that changes structure over time?
Answer: Implement flexible parsing logic using conditionals and list indexing to adapt to structural changes.

Question: How do you include metadata in a JSON file in R?
Answer: Add metadata as additional key-value pairs in the JSON object before serializing with toJSON().

Question: How do you read a JSON file that contains multiple JSON objects in sequence?
Answer: Use stream_in() to read the sequence of JSON objects as they stream in.

Question: How do you parse JSON data with multiple root elements?
Answer: Ensure each root element is handled separately, either by splitting the file or reading as a list.

Question: How do you read a JSON file from a compressed archive?
Answer: Use unzip() to extract the file or gzfile() to read it directly, followed by fromJSON().

Question: How do you handle cyclical references in JSON data?
Answer: R does not directly support cyclical references; you'll need to manage them manually by parsing and reconstructing the structure.

Question: How do you parse JSON data from a database in R?
Answer: Retrieve the JSON string from the database and use fromJSON() to parse it into an R structure.

Question: How do you handle non-standard JSON formats?
Answer: Use custom parsing logic or preprocess the JSON string to standardize it before using fromJSON().

Question: How do you store JSON data in a relational database from R?
Answer: Serialize the JSON data with toJSON() and store it as a string in a text or JSON column.

XML File

Question: What package is commonly used to handle XML files in R?
Answer: The xml2 package is commonly used for working with XML files in R.

Question: How do you read an XML file into R?
Answer: Use the read_xml() function from the xml2 package.

Question: How do you parse specific nodes from an XML file in R?
Answer: Use xml_find_all() or xml_find_first() to query specific nodes using XPath.

Question: How do you extract attributes from an XML node in R?
Answer: Use xml_attr() to extract a specific attribute from an XML node.

Question: How do you convert an XML file to a data frame in R?
Answer: Parse the XML file and then use custom logic or a package like xml2::xml_df() to convert it to a data frame.

Question: How do you handle namespaces in an XML file when parsing in R?
Answer: Use xml_ns() to handle namespaces and include them in your XPath queries.

Question: How do you write data to an XML file in R?
Answer: Use the xml_add_child() and xml_save() functions from the xml2 package to create and save XML files.

Question: How do you read an XML file from a URL in R?
Answer: Use read_xml(url) where url is the link to the XML file.

Question: How do you handle large XML files efficiently in R?
Answer: Use xml2 for efficient parsing, as it works with streams rather than loading the entire file into memory.

Question: How do you validate an XML file against an XSD schema in R?
Answer: While R doesn't have built-in XML validation, external tools like xmllint or scripting languages like Python can be integrated for validation.

Question: How do you add a new node to an existing XML file?
Answer: Use xml_add_child() to add a new node to an existing XML document in R.

Question: How do you extract text content from an XML node in R?
Answer: Use xml_text() to extract the text content from an XML node.

Question: How do you handle CDATA sections in XML files?
Answer: CDATA sections are treated as text nodes, and you can extract them using xml_text().

Question: How do you read an XML file with deeply nested structures?
Answer: Use recursive parsing techniques, accessing children nodes with xml_children().

Question: How do you read and parse an XML file with multiple root elements?
Answer: XML should have a single root element, but if you encounter multiple roots, parse them separately or restructure the file.

Question: How do you work with XML attributes and child nodes together in R?
Answer: Extract attributes with xml_attr() and child nodes with xml_find_all() or xml_children().

Question: How do you flatten an XML structure to a data frame in R?
Answer: Write custom logic to extract and flatten elements or use specialized XML flattening functions

Question: How do you remove specific nodes from an XML document?
Answer: Use xml_remove() to delete specific nodes from an XML document in R.

Question: How do you handle XML files with missing or optional elements?
Answer: Use conditional checks to handle missing elements during parsing.

Question: How do you convert an XML document to JSON in R?
Answer: Parse the XML with xml2, convert it to a list or data frame, and then serialize it to JSON using jsonlite::toJSON().

Question: How do you extract specific elements from an XML file based on their attributes?
Answer: Use XPath queries with attribute filters in xml_find_all() or xml_find_first().

Question: How do you handle XML files with unknown or dynamic structure?
Answer: Implement flexible parsing logic using recursive functions and conditionals to adapt to different structures.

Question: How do you save an XML file with pretty formatting in R?
Answer: Use xml2::write_xml() with formatting options for better readability.

Question: How do you extract a subset of an XML document in R?
Answer: Use xml_find_all() with appropriate XPath queries to extract the desired subset.

Question: How do you work with XML files that include embedded HTML?
Answer: Parse the XML normally, but use HTML-specific functions like xml2::read_html() for embedded HTML content.

Question: How do you handle encoding issues when reading XML files?
Answer: Specify the correct encoding in read_xml(), or use iconv() to convert the encoding after reading.

Question: How do you parse an XML file that is embedded within another file, like a PDF?
Answer: Extract the XML portion first, then parse it using xml2.

Question: How do you handle XML files with invalid structures in R?
Answer: Use external tools to correct the structure before parsing, or implement custom logic to bypass or fix issues during parsing.

Question: How do you merge multiple XML files into one in R?
Answer: Parse each XML file separately, combine the nodes, and then save the merged document using xml2.

Question: How do you query an XML document using XPath in R?
Answer: Use xml_find_all() or xml_find_first() with an appropriate XPath query string.

Question: How do you extract the root element of an XML document?
Answer: Use xml_root() to get the root element of an XML document.

Question: How do you save changes made to an XML document in R?
Answer: Use xml_save() to write the modified XML document back to a file.

Question: How do you handle whitespace and indentation in XML nodes?
Answer: XML typically preserves whitespace in text nodes; use trimws() in R to clean up unwanted spaces.

Question: How do you read an XML file that includes DTD or schema references?
Answer: XML files with DTDs are parsed normally, but schema validation requires external tools or languages like Python or Java.

Question: How do you parse an XML file from a compressed archive in R?
Answer: Use unzip() to extract the file or gzfile() to read it directly, followed by read_xml().

Question: How do you extract a list of all unique tags from an XML document?
Answer: Use xml_name() in combination with xml_find_all() to extract and then unique() to find unique tags.

Question: How do you create a new XML document from scratch in R?
Answer: Use xml_new_document() and xml_add_child() to construct the XML tree.

Question: How do you extract multiple elements from different levels in an XML file?
Answer: Use multiple xml_find_all() calls with specific XPath queries targeting different levels.

Question: How do you handle XML files with special characters in element names?
Answer: Special characters are generally not allowed in XML element names; if they exist, they need to be sanitized before parsing.

Question: How do you read and convert an XML file to a relational database table in R?
Answer: Parse the XML with xml2, convert it to a data frame, and use dbWriteTable() to save it to a database.

Database

Question: How do you connect R to a database?
Answer: Use the DBI package along with a specific driver (e.g., RMySQL, RSQLite) to establish a connection using dbConnect().

Question: How do you execute a SQL query in R?
Answer: Use dbGetQuery(con, "SQL_QUERY") to execute a SQL query and retrieve the results as a data frame.

Question: How do you write data from R to a database?
Answer: Use dbWriteTable(con, "table_name", data_frame) to write a data frame to a database table.

Question: How do you handle large datasets when querying from a database in R?
Answer: Use dbSendQuery() and dbFetch() to fetch data in chunks, rather than loading the entire dataset into memory at once.

Question: How do you disconnect from a database in R?
Answer: Use dbDisconnect(con) to safely close the database connection.

Question: How do you list all tables in a connected database in R?
Answer: Use dbListTables(con) to retrieve a list of all tables in the connected database.

Question: How do you retrieve the structure of a database table in R?
Answer: Use dbListFields(con, "table_name") or execute a DESCRIBE SQL command with dbGetQuery().

Question: How do you perform a join operation on database tables from R?
Answer: Use SQL join queries in dbGetQuery() or pull the data into R and use dplyr's inner_join() or left_join() functions.

Question: How do you optimize a database query in R?
Answer: Optimize by filtering and aggregating within the SQL query itself, reducing the amount of data transferred to R.

Question: How do you manage database transactions in R?
Answer: Use dbBegin(con), dbCommit(con), and dbRollback(con) to manage transactions within your database operations.

Question: How do you write a data frame to a database without overwriting the existing table?
Answer: Use dbWriteTable() with append = TRUE to add rows to an existing table without overwriting it.

Question: How do you handle database connections in a Shiny application?
Answer: Maintain a persistent database connection in the global environment or establish a connection within the server function, ensuring to close connections properly using dbDisconnect().

Question: How do you secure database credentials in R?
Answer: Store credentials in environment variables or use secure packages like keyring or config to manage sensitive information.

Question: How do you query only a specific number of rows from a database table?
Answer: Use LIMIT in your SQL query or specify the nrows argument in dbFetch().

Question: How do you execute a parameterized SQL query in R?
Answer: Use dbSendQuery() with dbBind() to execute parameterized queries.

Question: How do you handle SQL injection risks in R?
Answer: Avoid direct user input in SQL queries. Use parameterized queries with dbBind() to mitigate SQL injection risks.

Question: How do you check if a table exists in a database from R?
Answer: Use dbExistsTable(con, "table_name") to check if a table exists in the database.

Question: How do you read data from a database into a tibble in R?
Answer: Use dbGetQuery() and convert the result to a tibble with as_tibble().

Question: How do you handle database connections in a parallelized R environment?
Answer: Ensure each parallel worker has its own database connection, or use connection pooling techniques with packages like pool.

Question: How do you execute a stored procedure in a database from R?
Answer: Use dbExecute(con, "CALL stored_procedure_name()") or dbSendQuery() if the stored procedure returns a result set.

Question: How do you update records in a database table using R?
Answer: Use dbExecute(con, "UPDATE table_name SET column_name = value WHERE condition") to update records.

Question: How do you delete records from a database table in R?
Answer: Use dbExecute(con, "DELETE FROM table_name WHERE condition") to delete records from a table.

Question: How do you import a CSV file into a database table using R?
Answer: Read the CSV file into a data frame using read.csv() and then use dbWriteTable() to write it to the database.

Question: How do you create a new database table from R?
Answer: Use dbCreateTable() or execute a SQL CREATE TABLE statement with dbExecute().

Question: How do you remove a table from a database in R?
Answer: Use dbRemoveTable(con, "table_name") to delete a table from the database.

Question: How do you handle errors during database queries in R?
Answer: Use tryCatch() to handle and debug errors during database queries.

Question: How do you retrieve metadata about the columns of a table in R?
Answer: Use dbGetQuery(con, "PRAGMA table_info('table_name')") for SQLite, or the equivalent SQL query for other databases.

Question: How do you manage multiple database connections in R?
Answer: Use connection pooling packages like pool to manage multiple connections efficiently.

Question: How do you export data from a database to an Excel file in R?
Answer: Use dbGetQuery() to retrieve the data and then use writexl::write_xlsx() to save it as an Excel file.

Question: How do you perform a bulk insert into a database table from R?
Answer: Prepare the data in a data frame and use dbWriteTable() with append = TRUE for bulk inserts.

Question: How do you retrieve the SQL query plan for optimization in R?
Answer: Use dbGetQuery(con, "EXPLAIN QUERY PLAN SQL_QUERY") to retrieve the query execution plan.

Question: How do you handle database connection timeouts in R?
Answer: Use the timeout parameter when connecting to the database and implement retry logic if needed.

Question: How do you execute a SQL query asynchronously in R?
Answer: Use future or parallel packages to execute SQL queries asynchronously, especially when dealing with long-running queries.

Question: How do you merge data from multiple database tables into one data frame in R?
Answer: Use SQL join queries in dbGetQuery() or pull the data into R and merge them using dplyr functions like inner_join().

Question: How do you ensure transactional integrity when working with databases in R?
Answer: Use dbBegin(), dbCommit(), and dbRollback() to manage transactions, ensuring that operations either fully complete or fail without partial changes.

Question: How do you handle large query results without exhausting memory in R?
Answer: Use dbSendQuery() followed by dbFetch() in chunks to handle large query results efficiently.

Question: How do you log database query performance metrics in R?
Answer: Use system.time() to measure query execution time and log it along with the query text for performance analysis.

Question: How do you generate dynamic SQL queries in R?
Answer: Use paste() or glue() to concatenate strings and variables, creating dynamic SQL queries.

Question: How do you work with database views in R?
Answer: Treat views like regular tables in SQL queries using dbGetQuery() to retrieve data.

Question: How do you handle database migrations in R?
Answer: Use SQL scripts managed within R or an external tool for database migrations, ensuring consistency across environments.

Online Resources

Online Practice Paper Link : https://forms.gle/wReq7m78gJPDcLyDA

QR Code :

YouTube Video Link :
https://www.youtube.com/playlist?list=PLzlh_31VWEFqrfOpw6HFn4RK2koTSY2mQ

QR Code :

ADDITIONAL RESOURCES

R Programming Insights Interview Questions & Answers Videos Playlist-

Link: https://www.youtube.com/playlist?list=PLzlh_31VWEFr32KxhXLdNP0LnsVyJm2IO

QR Code:

YouTube Videos Playlists for all Chapters

CHAPTER 1 Link: https://www.youtube.com/playlist?list=PLzlh_31VWEFrbD40dOF1n0fUG9hgq3NyY

QR Code :

CHAPTER 2 Link: https://www.youtube.com/playlist?list=PLzlh_31VWEFpv-ZOWtwcktU04Swa9YUCI

QR Code:

CHAPTER 3 Link: https://www.youtube.com/playlist?list=PLzlh_31VWEFq981M6tjkByIlEi13qlb84

QR Code :

CHAPTER 4 Link: https://www.youtube.com/playlist?list=PLzlh_31VWEFp6_N-rIl5LQXyCEG6dr3V4

QR Code:

CHAPTER 5 Link: https://www.youtube.com/playlist?list=PLzlh_31VWEFqlE97qh1xOzVC3jSSiuyod

QR Code:

CHAPTER 6 Link: https://www.youtube.com/playlist?list=PLzlh_31VWEFqVDlvibcx_BcYaQMRUnpIg

QR Code:

CHAPTER 7 Link: https://www.youtube.com/playlist?list=PLzlh_31VWEFo2g7iaeY2-j-FF3BcUlMZ2

QR Code :

CHAPTER 8 Link: https://www.youtube.com/playlist?list=PLzlh_31VWEFpDkrVHJ7xOa5vo-cLgi6nO

QR Code :

CHAPTER 9 Link: https://www.youtube.com/playlist?list=PLzlh_31VWEFosbvQhW4P3GQJzVKdSskgX

QR Code :

CHAPTER 10 Link: https://www.youtube.com/playlist?list=PLzlh_31VWEFqLuHlOTONvuYlGX1u9uffb

QR Code:

CHAPTER 11 Link: https://www.youtube.com/playlist?list=PLzlh_31VWEFpw7QdBuCALFmICm3fojMeP

QR Code :

CHAPTER 12 Link: https://www.youtube.com/playlist?list=PLzlh_31VWEFqrfOpw6HFn4RK2koTSY2mQ

QR Code :